Praise for *The Entrepreneurial Attitude*

The Entrepreneurial Attitude contains insightful advice from successful Junior Achievement alumni around the world. Larry Farrell's new book delivers inspiring and practical advice for young aspiring entrepreneurs everywhere.

—Steve Case, Chairman & CEO, Revolution
and Founder, America Online

Larry Farrell captures the spirit of Junior Achievement, which shaped the careers of an extraordinary diverse group of leaders. I loved my four years in JA, which instilled in me a deep respect for the business community and lifelong passion for creating jobs.

—Donna Shalala, Trustee Professor, University of Miami, formerly:
President, Clinton Foundation, President, University of Miami,
and U.S. Secretary of Health and Human Services

Junior Achievement provides a transformational, progressive, and inclusive environment for young people of the world to build capacities in work readiness, entrepreneurship, and financial literacy. This honorable organization builds character and integrity, triggers vision, and remains a platform for effective and solution-oriented leadership. As a JA alumnus myself, I applaud Mr. Farrell's efforts to chronicle the story of Junior Achievement's impact globally. The world needs to continue to develop "the entrepreneurial attitude."

—Anthony Carmona, President, Republic of Trinidad and Tobago

The Entrepreneurial Attitude is a handy master class focusing on what it takes to be a successful entrepreneur and change-maker. Larry Farrell's documentation of JA alumni success stories is a testament to the lifelong impact a youth movement can have. Junior Achievement's model of providing global entrepreneurial education to young people has proven to be an investment that stands the test of time!

—Adedayo Fashanu, Journalist and Author (Nigeria)

The JA organization is overflowing with success stories waiting to be told, and Larry does an incredible job of putting together the lessons and values JA alumni have to share. If you're looking for the means and the encouragement to help you take your first steps into entrepreneurship, *The Entrepreneurial Attitude* is exactly what you need to get started.

—Edward K. Lee, Founder and Chairman,
COL Financial Group Inc. (Philippines)

I found *The Entrepreneurial Attitude* very inspiring. It shared a valuable and deep message about entrepreneurship. I loved the way it captured the passion and lifelong lessons of so many inspiring JA alumni leaders.

—HH Shaikha Hessa Al Khalifa, Founder and
Executive Director, INJAZ Bahrain

The innovation, enterprise, and camaraderie that I got from Junior Achievement was immense—and I have no doubt today that I am able to stand up and hold my own in the U.K. houses of parliament because of those experiences when I was a teenager. Somewhere out there is a young man or woman who needs the inspiration, self-belief, and courage to take that next step. In *The Entrepreneurial Attitude*, they'll find many and varied examples of so many JA alumni that can help them on their way. Even at my stage and career as an MP in the United Kingdom, I still found the stories in Larry's book awe inspiring.

—David Lammy, Member of Parliament, United Kingdom

the

ENTREPRENEURIAL
ATTITUDE

Lessons from
Junior Achievement's
100 Years of Developing
Young Entrepreneurs

LARRY C. FARRELL

Foreword by Asheesh Advani, CEO,
JA Worldwide

Mc
Graw
Hill
Education

New York Chicago San Francisco Athens London Madrid
Mexico City Milan New Delhi Singapore Sydney Toronto

1 2 3 4 5 6 7 8 9   LCR   23 22 21 20 19 18

ISBN   978-1-260-02670-2
MHID   1-260-02670-1

e-ISBN   978-1-260-02671-9
e-MHID   1-260-02671-X

Library of Congress Cataloging-in-Publication Data

Names: Farrell, Larry C., author.
Title: The entrepreneurial attitude : lessons from Junior Achievement's 100 years of
    developing young entrepreneurs / Larry Farrell.
Description: New York : McGraw-Hill, [2018]
Identifiers: LCCN 2017054998| ISBN 9781260026702 (alk. paper) | ISBN 1260026701
Subjects: LCSH: Junior Achievement. | Young businesspeople—United States. |
    Businesspeople—United States. | Entrepreneurship—United States. | Success in
    business.
Classification: LCC HC102.5.A2 F246 2018 | DDC 658.4/09—dc23 LC record
    available at https://lccn.loc.gov/2017054998

All photos in the book have been reprinted with permission of the person being interviewed except: Steve Case's photo is reprinted with permission from Revolution; Jack Kosakowski's photo is reprinted with permission from Junior Achievement USA; Monica Rivera's photo is reprinted with permission from JA Colombia; Jerome Cowans's photo is reprinted with permission from JA Worldwide; Max Tang's photo is reprinted with permission from JA Worldwide.

Contents

PART 1

The Four Fundamental Practices of the World's Great Entrepreneurs

PART 2

JA's Seven Competencies:
The Entrepreneurial Attitude in Action

APPLICATIONS
My Entrepreneurial Start-Up Action Plan

Foreword

When Junior Achievement launched a century ago, we were among the first organizations to recognize that entrepreneurship and other employability skills were missing from the educational system. Back then, a small group of students met after school to learn how to run a business. Today, JA Worldwide is a global NGO powered by over 470,000 volunteers and mentors who serve more than 10 million young people, in more than 100 countries, every year.

Whether in a small village in Peru or a high-rise in Hong Kong, today's JA activates young people for the jobs and the economies of the future. JA students participate in programs designed to teach financial literacy, work readiness, and entrepreneurship. While in school, one of our flagship programs enables students to create real companies with real products, working as a team on product development, marketing, operations, and finance. Along the way, they master seven critical skill sets: goal orientation and initiative; leadership and responsibility; creativity; teamwork; perseverance; resourcefulness; and, above all, self-efficacy—that critical ability to stay on course, regardless of setbacks, without any doubt of eventually achieving success.

As an alumnus of JA myself, I remember the active learning and self-belief that comes from building a business as a teenager—with a real product, real customers, and real profit. I recall how having a title like chief executive officer or chief financial officer of a small business in high school has the capacity to raise ambitions and change life's trajectory. In my case, I ended up pursuing a business degree and launching entrepreneurial ventures in my twenties. My first successful venture was acquired by Richard Branson's Virgin Group when I was in my thirties. And today, Virgin is an active supporter of the JA network in the United Kingdom, and Richard Branson has praised JA as, "a wonderful model, which through providing a project-based, highly engaging, and relevant education is helping students find their passions, grow their purpose, and realize their dreams." My life has come full circle, bringing me back to JA in a leadership role. Attending student programs in which I meet future entrepreneurs and job creators who are gaining the self-confidence to own their economic success is as empowering for me as it is for them.

One of JA's achievements of which I am most proud is the number of young women across the globe who start businesses as a result of JA. Whereas early generations of JA students were primarily male, we now see roughly equal numbers of young men and women participating in our programs all over the world. Last year, at the INJAZ Young Entrepreneurs Competition (JA's Company of the Year in the Middle East and North Africa), over 50 percent of competitors were female!

As I look to the future, I view JA alumni—which now number over 100 million—as a global force for good, with ambitions beyond their own financial reward. Many start businesses that serve a social need, solve a vexing problem, or otherwise improve the world around them. Others donate time and money to their communities. Still others give back to the next generation of young people by volunteering and mentoring. You'll see an inspiring selection in the following pages.

Larry Farrell approached JA with the idea to write a book about our alumni. Over the years, he has been a consultant and thought partner in helping JA develop entrepreneurship training programs. It's not surprising, therefore, that this project has been a labor of love for Larry as he has witnessed the legacy of his work by meeting some of the people who JA's programs have impacted. In reading through the alumni stories in this book, I'll be looking for Larry's writing to provide lessons for future entrepreneurs. I'll be looking for this book to provide the essence of the entrepreneurial attitude that I have seen in JA students and alumni all over the world.

As JA celebrates 100 years of educating and advocating for young people in every part of the globe, we recognize the opportunity ahead. Today's youth will have over 20 jobs, on average, over the course of their careers, some involving multiple career changes, as technology and automation increase. An entrepreneurial attitude is no longer just for entrepreneurs. Changing jobs and changing careers—whether from mining to coding or from accounting to robotics—requires adaptability, resilience, and a willingness to believe in one's own abilities.

That's what JA teaches. Find out more at jaworldwide.org.

—Asheesh Advani, CEO, JA Worldwide

Acknowledgments

The *Entrepreneurial Attitude* is my fifth book on the entrepreneurial spirit. One thing I've learned about writing books is that it can be a lonely job. At the same time, rather paradoxically, succeeding at this lonely endeavor requires a large network of active supporters and allies.

For me, the first level of support has come from Sylvia, my beautiful and supportive wife. She was herself a youthful entrepreneur, the first Hispanic single woman in the state of Arizona to get a Small Business Administration loan—to expand her already existing business. After fashion design school, she opened her first store at age 24—ultimately designing and manufacturing her own line of women's clothing, sold through her chain of 12 Sylvia Ann's stores around the state. Indeed, Sylvia knows the message of the book firsthand.

This book would not be possible without the wonderful cooperation and support of JA Worldwide. It is in fact written in honor of that great organization's centennial celebration. CEO Asheesh Advani has been the number one champion of this book project. And thanks to JA's staff around the world, I was able to interview and include in the book the entrepreneurial success stories of 70 JA alumni from every corner of the globe. JA currently teaches work readiness, financial literacy, and entrepreneurial skills to over 10 million young people a year, more students than all the business schools in the world combined. I am forever indebted to them for partnering with me on *The Entrepreneurial Attitude*.

Next, of course, are the publishing pros who make it all happen. Once again, I'm thankful to my literary agent, Bob Diforio, who first inspired me to write and has been there for all five of my books. Bob has been a friend since our days together at Harvard Business School and literally changed my professional life when he encouraged me to write my first book. I must also thank Donya Dickerson, the super-smart and super-supportive editorial director at McGraw-Hill Professional in New York City. Her advice and enthusiasm for the book have been all any author could ask for. We are all very thankful and proud to have a world-class organization like McGraw-Hill as the publisher of this book.

Finally, I want to acknowledge, and thank in advance, all the future readers of the book. *The Entrepreneurial Attitude* has been written for them, and I wish them all great success as they pursue their own entrepreneurial dreams.

Larry C. Farrell
Arizona and Virginia
January 2018

Introduction: Getting the Entrepreneurial Attitude

Why It's so Important for Young People in Today's Global Economy

If a kid has any interest in starting or running a business, JA is unquestionably the place to start. Not to be the next Mark Cuban, but to become the person they dream of being.

MARK CUBAN, Entrepreneur/Investor, *Shark Tank* Judge, Owner Dallas Mavericks, JA Alumnus, Pennsylvania, USA

Move over Harvard Business School, INSEAD, and Tsinghua School of Management—it turns out the number one educational institution in the world for developing successful entrepreneurs, CEOs, and professional leaders is JA Worldwide. From Mark Cuban and Steve Case in business, to Donna Shalala and MP David Lammy in government, to Sanjay Gupta in medicine and to Christina Aguilera in the world of entertainment, you won't find any other organization, anywhere in the world, that has produced so many entrepreneurial leaders.

Founded in 1918 by the chairman of AT&T and a few of his peers, JA has become one of the world's largest nongovernmental educational organizations in the world with more than 100 million alumni alive today and untold millions more since its founding. Reaching over

10 million young people a year, across 100 plus countries, JA teaches more students each year about business and career development than any other private educational organization in the world. Perhaps even more amazing, JA doesn't teach the three R's (reading, 'riting, and 'rithmatic) that the world's schools should and do always teach—instead JA teaches middle and high school kids in three areas that our schools have never taught: entrepreneurship, work readiness, and financial literacy.

JUNIOR ACHIEVEMENT: AN IDEA TOO GOOD TO FAIL

Junior Achievement, or JA as we have shorthanded it throughout the book, came along in the early days of the twentieth century as one of those ideas too good to fail. The founders' concept was since our schools don't teach kids anything about economics, or business, or financial skills, why don't we provide those things as specialized education programs in the country's public and private schools, along with knowledgeable people to teach the programs, all as a gift from the world of business. After all, the founders reasoned, since our economic survival and prosperity depends on our free enterprise economic system, why shouldn't we teach a bit about that to all our children? It even appeared to some of the early supporters as an educational necessity— to sustain the national economy, create a lot of jobs, and ensure the students' personal and family prosperity. The schools bought in, providing the students and classrooms; companies bought in, with money for the teaching materials and volunteer instructors to teach; and even the government did its part by treating it all as a tax-deductible educational contribution for private and corporate donors. Bingo—the world's largest nongovernmental educational institution was born. As I said—an idea too good to fail.

This book, as the title indicates, focuses on entrepreneurship, the first pillar of JA's curriculum. It's written with two closely connected themes in mind. First, it's a "how-to handbook" for aspiring entrepreneurs everywhere, complete with Application planning exercises, all based on the lessons of the world's greatest entrepreneurs. I should add that these lessons and applications are compatible with JA's two entrepreneurship programs, JA It's My Business for middle schoolers, and JA Be Entrepreneurial for high school students—which my company had the privilege of developing with JA's editorial staff some years ago. Second, the book is also being written and published as part of JA Worldwide's centennial celebration—particularly through interviews with many of JA's most successful entrepreneurial alumni all around the world. I've personally conducted every one of the interviews with this most amazing and enterprising collection of alumni, and I promise—you will not be disappointed.

The reader will learn the proven lessons of the world's great entrepreneurs on how to start up their own entrepreneurial venture—and these lessons will be enriched and brought to life by very current examples and personal advice from JA's successful entrepreneurial alumni from every continent of the world. This double-barreled, global approach should give you everything you need to know to begin pursuing your entrepreneurial dreams. So enjoy the book as you develop your very own *entrepreneurial attitude.*

DRIVING THE ENTREPRENEURIAL BOOM

The growing popularity of global entrepreneurship, propelled by the folk-hero status of the likes of Steve Jobs, Richard Branson, and Oprah Winfrey, and more recently Mark Cuban, Jack Ma, and Elon Musk, has captured the imagination of people everywhere, especially the young. Look around you. Seventy out of the next 100 young people you see have dreamed about becoming an entrepreneur. Fifteen of the 100 will actually give it a go in the next couple of years. Five will be successful on their first try. All of them, the dreamers, the doers, and the dazzling few, are part of the greatest explosion of entrepreneurship the world has ever seen. They all know the rules of survival have changed in our downsized and uncertain world. And more and more they believe the best weapon for creating their own economic prosperity in the twenty-first century will be themselves—their labor, their knowledge, and their own entrepreneurial spirit. Of course they're right. Whether you're a student pondering your future, or already working for a company, a nonprofit, or even the government, getting an entrepreneurial attitude is the new name of the game. Like it or not, we're all working and living in the entrepreneurial age.

Some 100 million new entrepreneurs come on the scene each year, from every corner of the globe. We've never seen anything like it in history. So what's really causing this? Here are the key factors driving the unprecedented entrepreneurial boom around the world:

- **The Engine of Prosperity.** Every economist in the world today agrees that the engine of prosperity for every country in the world is entrepreneurial small business. Entrepreneurs create most of the growth, most of the jobs, and virtually all of the world's new products and services. These are simply economic facts. It's clear that the world has moved from the industrial age, through the managerial age, to the current entrepreneurial age. Today, economists, politicians, business thinkers, and even the press all agree that entrepreneurship is the best economic tool ever invented to create individual, family, and national prosperity.

- **80 Percent of All New Jobs.** As the fundamental measure of success for all economies is its ability to create jobs, and we know that 80 percent of all new jobs are created by entrepreneurs, most governments today are funding programs and providing incentives to grow their entrepreneurial sectors. From China, to Northern Ireland, to Brazil, to New York City, government and political leaders are rethinking the economic development theories of the past century, and are putting most of their eggs in the entrepreneur development basket. All this is further driving the entrepreneurial boom.

- **The Global Marketplace.** Fortunately for the entrepreneur, we really do live in a global marketplace. Today if someone in your town comes up with a good product—they can sell that product tomorrow in Germany, Brazil, the USA, even China. They can sell it anywhere in the world. If your grandparents started a small business 60 years ago and came up with a good product, their market would be limited to their town or maybe their county. They didn't even think about selling it internationally. Today you can be "in business" anywhere in the world for pennies on the dollar of what it used to cost. It's so easy, and cheap, because we live in a truly global economy, which benefits the entrepreneur greatly.

- **Huge Niche Markets.** Entrepreneurs are also fortunate today because there are great niche markets across the global economy—and our big companies are too big to even think about them. Imagine a giant pharmaceutical firm like Glaxo or Merck. They can't even think about researching a product that only has a $25 or even $50 million market. It's too small for them. The research is too expensive, so they don't do it. They can only research products for big diseases. But this provides an enormous opportunity for the small, entrepreneurial medical firm. And this is why there are hundreds of them around the world right now, working in this niche marketplace—living off of these $25 million markets. Of course this would be a great business for most of us—a $25 million market with no competition from the big players.

- **Start-Up Capital Available.** The world is simply awash in entrepreneurial capital. With the average cost of starting a business in the USA only $15,000, start-up money isn't actually a problem for most entrepreneurs. Between personal savings (still the number one source of start-up funds), the $300 billion available from VC firms and angel investors, government "enterprise funds" around the world with billions more to loan, money just isn't a big problem for most new entrepreneurs. And of course there is always the smart idea of lining up your first customers to help finance your start-up. So money is readily available for entrepreneurs with good product/service ideas—which continues to fuel the boom.

- **The Biggest Risk of All.** Most entrepreneurs say the big risk today is working for a big business. The facts are on their side. Over the past 30 years, big corporations around the globe have downsized and shipped millions of high-paying jobs to lower cost countries. So not having the confidence and knowledge to fend for yourself and your family's economic well-being—and hoping your future employers will provide lifetime employment, big benefits, and a hefty pension—may indeed be the biggest risk of all.

- **The Ultimate Meritocracy.** The last and most important point is that entrepreneurship is the ultimate meritocracy. It doesn't matter what gender you are, the color of your skin, what country you're from, who your parents are, or where you went to school. If you come up with a good product/service idea in today's world, you cannot be stopped! This is why entrepreneurship is more important for poor people than rich people. Rich, and even middle-class people, have options in life. Their children have options. But poor people, and poor kids, don't have options. Entrepreneurship can offer those options to the poorest level of society. It's the surest way out of poverty for people. Come up with a good idea, be willing to work at it, and you cannot be stopped.

Of course the question that may still be on your mind is: "What exactly would I do as an entrepreneur? And how would I go about it? What should I do to prepare, and what should I concentrate on once I'm started?" Well, read on. We've got the answers for you. Learning all this may not turn you into the next Warren Buffett or Oprah Winfrey or Richard Branson or Jack Ma, but in these pages you will find the guaranteed first steps toward making sure you are getting the entrepreneurial attitude!

GREAT MYTHS AND SIMPLE TRUTHS

Risk? What risk? I started Microsoft for just $700.

BILL GATES, Cofounder, Microsoft

It might be useful, at this point, to dispel once and for all yesterday's lingering myths about entrepreneurs, and replace them with today's simple truths. The reality is millions of new businesses are fueling economies all around the world each year. The people behind these start-ups come from every walk of life. All the statistics show they're a pretty average lot. Most never planned to be an entrepreneur. It usually happens because of circumstance—like being dirt poor, or full of frustration, or getting fired—the number one reason today for people becoming self-employed entrepreneurs. And yes, it can also happen when an unexpected opportunity comes your way and you just go for it. Even so, these are almost always ordinary people who simply find themselves in an extraordinary situation.

All this is important to keep in mind while the business and popular media bombard us with entrepreneurial myths. It's absolutely essential to keep in mind if you're seriously thinking about becoming an entrepreneur yourself. Here are some of the more damaging myths about those people who create and build businesses.

Myth Number 1

Entrepreneurs are born, not made. It's in their genes. This is the most common myth of entrepreneurship.

THE TRUTH

If you really believe it's genetic, you never visited communist East Germany. Listen to Claus Schroeder, the founder of a container shipping business in Hamburg, describe what 45 years of numbing communism gets you. Claus recalled that Germany's big gift from the end of the cold war was getting 20 million East Germans who wouldn't know a hard day's work if it were injected into their socialist veins. In the early nineties he eagerly expanded his business to the former communist region. Motivated by both patriotism and business possibilities, his decision turned into a nightmare: "It's just unbelievable. I can't believe they're Germans. They have no concept of work. If the container ship isn't sitting at the dock when they arrive in the morning, they just go home for the day. The ship docks 30 minutes later for unloading, and there it sits until tomorrow. Nobody thinks, nobody acts, and nobody cares. I'm afraid the whole generation is lost. Maybe their children and grandchildren will be different." Western Germany had hardworking, self-motivated people who transformed their land from total ruin to the world's third richest economy. In eastern Germany, you had uninspired and unproductive workers, looking for a government handout—and they all came from the same grandparents! I rest my case.

Myth Number 2

They're high risk takers. Real dart throwers.

THE TRUTH

Ask Bill Gates, who risked $700 to start Microsoft. Or Steve Jobs, who risked $1,350 to start Apple. Or Richard Branson, who risked £4 (yes, that's £4!) to start Virgin. The fact is, every entrepreneur I've ever met believes the greatest risk today is to leave your future in the hands of a series of corporate bosses, all of whom have their own agenda to push. And once they get started, a lot of entrepreneurs turn downright frugal. Remember, it's their own money they're risking. The reality is big company executives regularly take greater risks with shareholders' money than entrepreneurs ever take with their own.

Myth Number 3

They all invented something in a garage when they were 15, wear strange clothes to work, and speak in technobabble. We may have the same grandparents, but they are kind of weird and just different from you and me. This is the "nerd theory" of entrepreneurship.

THE TRUTH

The mundane facts are, the average entrepreneur is 35 to 45 years old, has 10 years plus experience in a large company, has an average education and IQ, and contrary to popular myth, has a surprisingly normal psychological profile. They dress, talk, and look a lot like you and me—a fairly average bunch.

Myth Number 4

The overriding goal is to be a millionaire. They do it for the money pure and simple.

THE TRUTH

Every shred of research denies this myth. In fact few entrepreneurs ever earn the kind of bucks paid to corporate CEOs these days. Their real obsession is to pursue their own, personal sense of mission. Money is the necessary fuel to do this. Venture capitalists, shrewd evaluators of the entrepreneurial quotient in people, can spot the get-rich-quick types in a minute and avoid them like the plague. As Ed Penhoet, the great biotech entrepreneur, once told me: "People who just want to start a company to become wealthy—well, that's a certain recipe for disaster."

Myth Number 5

Entrepreneurs are unscrupulous characters, ready to take legal short-cuts, and are generally on the prowl for suckers to cheat. Reading between the lines, this myth really says that big, well-known corporations and their buttoned-down executives are more trustworthy than entrepreneurs.

THE TRUTH

This nasty myth gets harder to believe every time another blue-chip corporate executive marches off to jail. And compared to some well-known CEOs, raking in their $10 million-a-year salaries even as their employees and shareholders are bleeding, entrepreneurs don't seem so greedy after all. With the Volkswagen, Toshiba, and Wells Fargo corporate scandals etched in our brains, the Hondas, Bransons, and Waltons of the world look more and more like saintly protectors of old-fashioned virtue.

Myth Number 6

Getting an MBA is the way to go. Business schools will teach you how to be an entrepreneur.

THE TRUTH

Save your $100,000 and go do something useful like learning how to create a product or service the world needs—just as 99 percent of the world's entrepreneurs still do. The MBA factories around the world are promising to turn you into the next Steve Jobs, but they forget to mention how Steve Jobs himself described the MBA style managers he hired at Apple: "So we hired a bunch of MBA type managers—sure, they knew how to *manage*—but they couldn't *do* anything." The moral? Until you learn how to *do* something, like inventing a great product or designing a great service, don't waste your time and money getting an MBA.

So, despite all the myths, the truth is the new entrepreneurs are us, and other "normal folks" like us. And the things they, and you, will have to do as new entrepreneurs are not so strange or complicated after all. In fact, creating and building a company might be sounding more and more like—a lot of common sense.

THE LIFE CYCLE OF ALL ORGANIZATIONS

Bigger is better turned out to be another twentieth-century myth. Larry Farrell has just described why.

PETER DRUCKER, The Twentieth Century's Greatest Management Thinker, (*Business Week* CEO Conference, Taiwan)

It's not every day one gets to present a critique before the world's greatest management thinker. And it's even rarer that the world expert agrees with your contrarian conclusions. But that's what happened the first time I met the great Dr. Peter Drucker, "the father of modern management." We were both speaking at a *Business Week* conference in Taiwan, when he followed me to the podium and delivered the grandest endorsement my work has ever received! He was speaking about our research on the *Life Cycle of All Organizations*, which describes how companies move through four phases over time: Start-up, High Growth, Decline, and finally Survival. Suffice to say, Peter Drucker knew the past and saw the future. He "blessed" the entrepreneurial spirit as the driving force behind all economic growth and prosperity—and "endorsed" my own humble research conclusion that big business inevitably gets too big, becomes a hopeless bureaucracy, then over time loses the very entrepreneurial spirit that got it going in the first place, and ultimately withers away. All young entrepreneurs need to understand it; the future life cycle of their start-up venture—to prevent it, or at least delay it from happening. Figure I.1 is the graphic of our organization life cycle, to which Dr. Drucker referred:

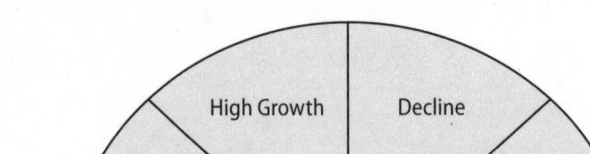

Figure I.1 | **The Life Cycle of All Organizations**

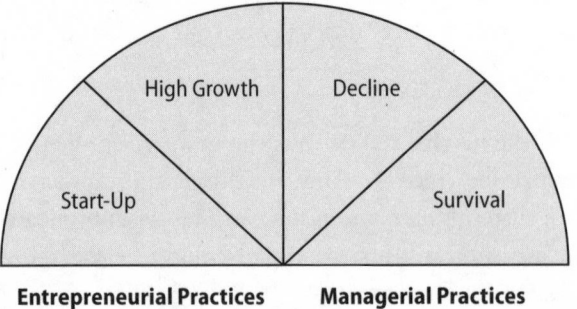

All companies begin with an abundance of the entrepreneurial spirit, inspiring the owner as well as the workers. Basic entrepreneurial practices fuel the start-up and drive the company well into a phase of high growth. During the start-up and high growth eras, everyone is fixated on a few fundamental notions such as making great products that customers will buy because it's the only way to get paid. The resultant high growth gets you size. And the passage of time gets you new leaders. The new leaders are almost always professional managers. These subtle shifts in size and leadership produce a new set of objectives. Presto! Planning, streamlining, and controlling the enterprise become the new order. Managing this and that become more important than making this and selling that. The highest paid jobs become managing other managers. Meetings, reports, and bureaucracy erupt on every front. And slowly but surely, lost in the shuffle are the simple, basic entrepreneurial thrusts that got you going in the first place.

The evidence supporting the life cycle idea is clear. From the first *Fortune 500* list of companies in 1955, 75 percent have already fallen completely off the radar. So it's also clear that beating the life cycle is tough indeed. The question for future entrepreneurs is, What creates entrepreneurial high growth in the beginning, and why do all companies lose it and shift from growth to decline?

THE ENTREPRENEURIAL ATTITUDE—WHAT IT IS

> *The conduct of successful business merely consists in doing things in a very simple way, doing them regularly and never neglecting to do them.*
>
> **WILLIAM HESKETH LEVER,** Founder, Lever Brothers (Unilever)

What are those *things* we must do simply, regularly, and never forget to do? You won't find them on the managerial side of the cycle. They're not the things that business schools teach or management consultants preach. If you want to find the bedrock fundamentals of enterprise, those simple things practiced obsessively, you've got to look at the entrepreneurial phase of business. There you will find the lessons of the world's greatest enterprisers, from past masters such as Lever, Matsushita, Watson, and Disney, to more recent icons like Honda, Walton,

Jobs, and Branson, right up to today's entrepreneurial wizards Elon Musk, Lito Rodriguez, Jack Ma, and Oprah Winfrey. And, you've come to the right place for doing just that. The following chapters describe, in detail, the fundamental practices of the world's great entrepreneurs— all brought to life with current examples from successful JA alumni around the world. So read on.

Do Application 1 now, in the Application section at the end of this book. All the Applications are designed to give you a chapter-by-chapter road map for future action. Upon completion, you will have your own personal start-up action plan—for becoming an entrepreneur. I think you may discover that the Applications will become the most valuable and practical part of the entire book as you embark on your future enterprise. Enjoy!

Application 1: YOU'RE AN ENTREPRENEUR! WHAT NEXT?

JA ALUMNI INTERVIEW

Brian Sidorsky

Serial Entrepreneur (retail furniture, real estate, land development), JA Alumnus, Canada

I am JA!

My JA Experience:

"I'm excited to talk about JA because—*I am JA!* But more importantly, JA allowed me to accomplish things that I would have never even been aware of. The "learn by doing" concept, the creation of a business, the building of relationships, the sales process, have all been essential to my success. Through JA, I became part of a team and then learned how to lead the team. JA literally changed my life as a young 15-year-old with very low self-esteem. I came to realize my potential through JA and learned that almost anything is possible.

"I was 15 when I got involved with JA. I was in grade 10. I was a terrible student. I had already failed grade 6. I came from a very impoverished family. My father was an addicted gambler, never made a lot of money, never paid the rent on time, and we moved around a lot. So I was lucky when I heard about JA. It was an after-school program with 15 or 20 teenage kids, and we got a few dollars from raising shares in our JA company. With that working capital we opened the company and made our first products, which were cookie sheets. We packaged them, put labels on them, and went door-to-door to sell them.

"Meanwhile, my father had been fired from his job, and he opened a small secondhand store to buy and sell used furniture. He ran the store, and I would work in the back repairing kitchen chairs and putting stuff together. We didn't really understand anything about buying and selling. One day I was in the store when a young couple came in and I asked my dad if I could look after them. He said OK. So I started asking them some of the sales questions I learned in JA; finding out their needs, overcoming objections, and so on—and I sold this couple an entire house full of furniture using the JA sales process. It really worked!

"The second year of the JA program I was vice president. The third year I became president. I also did a fourth year. And after I finished school I even came back for a fifth year as an advisor. Now it's time to give back with compound interest. I'm currently working with JA Worldwide on what we're calling JA University. I've joined as a chancellor, along with others, and we're starting to compile a curriculum. We hope to bring this plan into reality. This is what I've been working on recently with JA."

My Career / Business:

"I went from JA right into my own business and after a few years of hard work and struggle created the largest retail furniture and appliance business in southern Alberta. I went on into real estate and land development and have created a very large development company that I could have never dreamed possible. The application of what I learned at JA has given me the power and the tools to reach all the goals I set.

"I could be the poster boy for JA. I worked all my life, 18 hours a day, seven days a week. I lived in the back of my first furniture store. I started with no money but sold my first furniture company at 35 years old for $5 million. After that I went back into business, land development, subdivisions, shopping centers, a lot of different things in Western Canada. Since 1981 I've taken that $5 million and turned it into $700 million. Today I remain involved with all my companies on a day-to-day basis, and last year we had our best year in history. Really, all my companies have been extensions of my JA experience. The fundamental principles are the same as I learned in JA."

My Advice to Young People:

- "First, you can never learn enough. You have to be a lifetime student. You have to learn and learn and learn some more. You'll find the more you know, the more you don't know, but also the more you learn, the more you earn. So it's a cycle of learning and earning. Like I said, you've got to be a lifelong learner.

- "Second, always go the extra mile in life. Do more than you're paid to do. Whether it's your own business or you're working for someone else, always go the extra mile. It always pays off.

- "Third and maybe the most important thing is knowing and doing what you want. If you do that you at least have a chance to be successful. For example, I wanted the largest retail furniture store in Calgary. I didn't know how to do it, but I knew what I wanted. To be successful, young people have to know *what* they want first, be able to describe and visualize it, and they can figure out *how* to do it later.

- "Finally, to young people everywhere—if you join JA, you will have the opportunity of a lifetime to learn the basics. In JA you learn by doing: communicating with others, actually making a product, knocking on doors to sell it, risking a lot of rejection, overcoming objections, and finally asking for the order. The single most important thing to learn in life is—always ask for the order!"

JA ALUMNI INTERVIEW

Shaikha Hessa Al Khalifa

Founder and Executive Director, INJAZ Bahrain, JA Alumna,
United Kingdom

> *So yes, INJAZ Bahrain is my baby and I can't abandon it. I'm very passionate about it because I really believe we can change people's lives!*

My JA Experience:

"I first encountered Junior Achievement (we called it Young Enterprise in the UK) while I was studying at a boarding school—Cheltenham Ladies College in Gloucestershire. I had the intention of going to medical school. Part of my education at the boarding school was to take extracurricular activities and we were introduced to Young Enterprise. To be honest I didn't really want to do it because I was into the sciences and I wanted to be a doctor, and this was about running a business. But I said OK, it's important in life to not say no to new opportunities—and it will be a time to socialize with my friends and learn another way of thinking apart from my science studies.

"So I joined the JA Company Program at 16. A JA volunteer came in once a week and talked to us about how to form a company. My company had six girls, and I was the accountant because I loved math. We started a company that printed stationery and business cards for the other competing companies in the program. It was all new to us, putting strategy into place, where to produce these things, learning about production and marketing, working together as a team, and we really enjoyed it. I looked forward to the volunteer coming in each week and listening to what he had to say, because it was something completely different from school. When the program finished, we had a competition, and while our company didn't win—we learned so much! I personally learned from the JA Company Program that I could be entrepreneurial and creative—something I could not be in my other academic studies.

"After my stint as an accountant in the JA program, I realized there was more to life than studying mathematics and science—there were other careers out there. I wanted something more practical, more hands-on. I began feeling I didn't have the calling to be a doctor after all. I applied to the London School of Economics where I received my bachelor's degree in management in 1998 and my master's degree in social policy in 2002. Basically, you could say that doing that JA program at 16 was an eye-opener for me—it gave me an opportunity to consider other disciplines. I really think if I had not had that opportunity I would have stayed on the science path. It changed my thinking about the way forward."

My Career / Business:

"I went home and started working in the Supreme Council for Women, which King Hamad bin Isa Al Khalifa had set up in 2001 as an advisory board on gender issues in the Kingdom of Bahrain. He is also the king who set up the first parliament in Bahrain, so it was a very dynamic time with lots of legislative changes designed to improve Bahrainis' lives. It was a very good time for me—being young and working with new ideas—to be starting my career in Bahrain.

"I must say, my family always expected me to work. My grandfather, who was the ruler before our current king, was very proud of me as a girl who was a high achiever academically. He always said you can do as well as any boy. He and my grandmother never gave me the attitude that I couldn't work and achieve things. Also my mother owned her own business—so my family always encouraged me to think: 'Yes, I can work. I can do something with my life.'

"Then in 2004 I had a personal experience that really motivated me to take action. I was with HRH Princess Sabeeka (wife of the current king) visiting the University of Bahrain where she gave a talk on how the labor market reforms were encouraging young people to join the labor force, especially the young graduate girls. As we were leaving, some of the girls were saying: 'We're going to be university graduates, but there aren't enough governmental positions to fill.' I turned around and said to them: 'Well, why don't you start your own company, instead of just sitting at home waiting?' They all replied:

'We don't know how to do that.' And I said: 'What do you mean? You don't know how to start your own company? Just do it! Anyone can start a company. It's so easy.' That was the moment when I began to understand the difference; I believed I knew how to start a company, but they didn't. They couldn't imagine it, so they were just going to wait for a job.

"I realized that I had confidence about starting a company because I had already done it in the JA Company Program. I also understood that I had received a really good education in my life and many of my country sisters had not. And of course, I'm from the royal family, which obviously provided advantages they didn't have. So I began thinking how lucky I was and that I really had to find a way to give back to others, at least some of what I had experienced. This may sound strange but it's true—because I'm from the royal family, I do have a sense of patriotism that we should always give back to our people. Giving money is one way, having good government policies is another, but I wanted to give back something special to young people who didn't have the educational opportunities I had—and the Young Enterprise program just clicked into my mind.

"I looked it up online and realized for the first time it was part of a worldwide organization called JA. I discovered the only country in the Middle East that had it was Jordan. So I called up their office in Amman. I told them out of the blue, 'I'm calling from Bahrain and I'm a Young Enterprise graduate and I think you should set up Young Enterprise or JA here.' At first they thanked me for the call but told me that Bahrain is a small country, it wasn't a priority for them, and so on. But I persisted and told them, 'Look, I will do everything here in Bahrain. Just tell me what to do and I'll do it.' Well, they saw I was really interested and insistent, and they finally said OK. 'If you can set up a meeting with the Minister of Education, we will come to Bahrain to discuss it.' I did, and they did, and by 2005, INJAZ Bahrain was a reality—and we've never looked back.

"So yes, INJAZ Bahrain is my baby and I can't abandon it. I'm very passionate about it because I really believe we can change people's lives! We're here to inspire and prepare students to succeed in the global economy. That's our mission, and this is what we live by every day."

My Goals for INJAZ Bahrain:

"Today we have 20,000 students a year in JA programs in our small country. It's amazing—in 10 years we've done 120,000 young people, and we have 20,000 new alumni every year to be spokespeople for JA in Bahrain. We have one of the highest rates of penetration of student population of any JA country in the world, and now we want to go global. We want our students to feel that JA is an international organization. We want the Company Program students to visit other regions like Europe and Asia and the Americas. We want some sort of media platform where students can meet each other, talk about entrepreneurship, and really get connected. This is how I want to see us move forward."

JA ALUMNI INTERVIEW

Michel De Wolf

Dean, Louvain School of Management / JA Worldwide Board of Directors, JA Alumnus, Belgium

The main opportunity I see is to use JA's fantastic tools for developing business skills, financial literacy, and entrepreneurship in those parts of the world where JA could be the way out of poverty for so many young people.

My JA Experience:

"1978 was just JA's second year in Belgium. That's when I read an article in the press saying it was possible to simulate an enterprise: Make a product, sell it, keep financial records, and so on. The article said if you want to participate in the program, write to this person, so I did. I became an Achiever with the program, a mini-entrepreneur. We were a team of 15 young people, 17 to 18 years old, who didn't know each other.

"We first had a brainstorming session about what our product should be. We decided our product would be a baby carriage, a baby buggy. We thought most baby buggies were too low for adults, so we built it to be higher so most people could avoid bending over so much. That was our product, but it was not actually a very good idea. Also we could not really produce it so well as we tried to make it in plastic and it was too soft and broke. So we switched to aluminum, but we did it too late. The JA Company Program was only one school year. So our company was not really a financial success—but even so, we learned a lot.

"First we learned a lot about teamwork. We learned that having the critique of others is the best way to get new ideas and work together. This was the main thing I learned from my initial JA experience. And at that time, the rule in JA Belgium was that former Junior Achievers would become Junior Advisors for the next generation of students. So I next became a JA Junior Advisor for the new groups in the following school year. In summary, I was a very early member of JA in Belgium and have been involved with JA in many capacities over the years: I was a student, a Junior Advisor, a JA volunteer, JA Board Chair for French-speaking Belgium, member of the JA Europe Board, and now I'm on the JA Worldwide Board. This covers about 40 years!"

My Career / Business:

Editor's note: For this brief interview, we've concentrated on Michel's lifelong role with JA.

My Goals for JA Worldwide:

"Now that I am on the JA Worldwide Board of Directors, the main opportunity I see is to use JA's fantastic tools for developing business skills, financial literacy, and entrepreneurship in those parts of the world where JA could be the way out of poverty for so many young people. By this I primarily mean Asia-Pacific, Africa, and Latin America—those continents where huge numbers of young people need to develop their own entrepreneurial spirit."

The Four Fundamental Practices of the World's Great Entrepreneurs

*The inclination of my life has been to do things and make
things which will give pleasure to people in new and
amazing ways. By doing that I please and satisfy myself.*

WALT DISNEY, Founder, The Walt Disney Company

Part 1 of the book describes the four fundamental practices of the world's great entrepreneurs and how they can be applied by anyone, in any organization, in any field. The four entrepreneurial basics are further illustrated through interviews with successful JA alumni around the world, who provide current and lively examples of each of the four practices.

Walt Disney provides a wonderful description above of those four entrepreneurial practices. To fully examine each one, how they are applied, and how you can use them to further your own entrepreneurial dreams, read on!

CHAPTER 1

Sense of Mission

Creating an Entrepreneurial Strategy and Culture

> *From my very first day as an entrepreneur, I've felt the only mission worth pursuing in business is to make people's lives better.... Above all, you want to create something you are proud of.*
>
> **RICHARD BRANSON,** Founder, Virgin Group

You say Richard Branson's quote is a bit high-minded? You bet it is. The fact is entrepreneurs truly believe they are doing something important in the world. They believe they're creating value for customers, employees, and of course themselves. We call it having a "sense of mission" about their work. Such high purpose, however, gets quickly translated into two very practical questions: *What* is our business strategy (essentially what products, for what customers) and *how* must we operate (essentially which operating factors, or values, must we focus on) to achieve the strategy? To legendary entrepreneurs like Matsushita and Watson and current masters like Richard Branson, these simple words represent the two most important questions in business. The entrepreneur's "what" and "how" is the no-frills version of what the MBA crowd calls Corporate Strategy and Corporate Culture.

The entrepreneur lives and dies on his answers to *what* and *how*—and they're inextricably connected. When your operating values directly support your product/market strategy, watch out! It's the most powerful way ever invented to energize a group of individuals to achieve a common purpose. That's why having a powerful sense of mission is the first entrepreneurial practice of the world's great entrepreneurs.

THE "WHAT" AND THE "HOW" OF THE MISSION

If you ask entrepreneurs, "What's your sense of mission?" they may look at you like you're crazy—or at least suspect you're a management consultant. Entrepreneurs aren't typically up on such business school jargon. But what they are up on, and can articulate with unbelievable clarity, is *what* they're doing and *how* they go about doing it. When you think about it, to succeed at any mission, whether it's a business mission, a military mission, a political mission, or whatever, you absolutely have to know these two things: *what* the mission is, and *how* you're going to accomplish it. We've labeled these two critical aspects of Sense of Mission: the strategy (the what) of the business, and the culture (the how) of the business. If the words "strategy" and "culture" sound a bit grandiose to describe your first-time entrepreneurial start-up, just call them your "business plan" and your "business values." Whatever we call them, being very good at both—setting a smart strategy and creating a strong, supportive culture—is a characteristic all great entrepreneurs share.

Of course, the business plan of any business can be smart or dumb. And the values can be strong or weak in support of that plan. The graph in Figure 1.1, using a 1 to 10 scale, illustrates the four possible positions you can find yourself in:

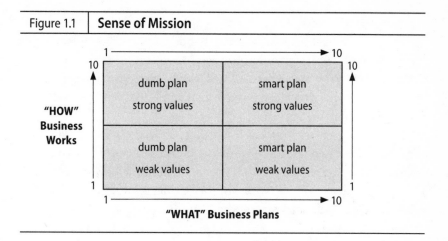

Figure 1.1 | Sense of Mission

- **Smart Plan/Strong Values (10-10).** This is Matsushita and Watson (IBM) territory—you know exactly what to do and exactly how to do it. You've got the right products and markets, all strongly supported by the right operating values. This is exactly where you want the business to be.
- **Smart Plan/Weak Values (1-10).** You know what to do, but you don't know how or you're not so good at doing it. You've picked the right products and the right markets, but your operating values are too weak to achieve your plan. You need to start focusing on the right things operationally to improve and grow the business.
- **Dumb Plan/Weak Values (1-1).** You don't know what to do, and you don't know how to do it. A really bad place to be—bankruptcy is just around the corner if you can't improve both the "what" and the "how" of the business. Avoid this position like the plague!
- **Dumb Plan/Strong Values (10-1).** You don't know what to do, but you know how to do it. In other words you're very good, operationally, at doing the wrong things. If you find yourself in this position, you need to start making the right products for the right markets—pronto!

The bottom line is, entrepreneurs are highly focused on both "what" they are doing (the strategy or plan) and "how" they go about doing it (the culture or values). Whether you're General Electric or a one-person start-up, the challenge is to be great at both. It's not good enough to have a smart business plan, but a weak, disconnected set of operating values. Conversely, strong values will never overcome a stupid plan. And of course you won't be around long if you know neither what to do nor how to do it.

New entrepreneurs quickly learn that while both the "what" and the "how" are essential, the plan of the business comes first. You have to know what you're doing before you can determine how to do it. The reality is, until you set the "what" of the business—what markets, what products, etc., you have no idea what kind of operating values and priorities you will need. For example, if you're starting a commuter airline, safety had better be at the top of your values list. There's no faster way to bankrupt an airline than having a few headline-grabbing crashes. On the other hand, if your entrepreneurial start-up is in the software business, where product life cycles are less than six months, product innovation and speed are probably the values you will need to focus on. Indeed the only purpose of developing a set of company values is to get absolutely focused and operationally superb on those few things that will ensure that you achieve your business plan.

Perhaps the twentieth-century master for developing smart, simple, and successful business plans was the great founder of Matsushita Electric in Japan. Here is how Konosuke Matsushita did it starting back in 1918.

CREATING ENTREPRENEURIAL BUSINESS PLANS À LA MATSUSHITA

> *Our duty as industrialists is to provide conveniences for the public, and to enrich and make happier all those who use them.*
>
> **KONOSUKE MATSUSHITA,** Founder, Matsushita Electric
> (founded in 1918, just one year before JA)

There is no more overhyped and overused activity of business than corporate strategy and planning. For some never explained reason, this rather passive aspect of enterprise has generated more books, techniques, diagrams, and consultant engagements than anything else.

And almost without exception, would-be entrepreneurs at business schools are advised that the most important step in starting up a company is to write a great business plan. Of course, no one bothers to remind the MBA students or, for that matter, the millions of other young entrepreneur wannabes dreaming about striking out on their own, that no great enterpriser from Konosuke Matsushita and Thomas Watson to Bill Gates and Richard Branson ever started a business this way.

Fortunately, there is a simpler way to do a business plan. It's the old-fashioned entrepreneurial way. If you want to try this way first, read on. Let's start with Japan's most revered entrepreneur of all time, Konosuke Matsushita, the founder of Matsushita Electric and its world-class Panasonic and National products. (The company was renamed Panasonic Corporation in 2008.)

Konosuke Matsushita was a young salesman in Osaka. In 1918, he invested his life savings of 100 yen (about $50) in imported electric sockets from Great Britain. He was excited and very focused on getting the first batch sold and ordering more. He was certain this type of product would sell very well in the new, miracle age of electricity. He was wrong. None of the shops he called on were interested in stocking his electric socket. It was so bad, in fact, he went bankrupt. So the great Matsushita's first entrepreneurial venture was a bust. And in Japan, at that time, failing in business was about as shameful an act as one could commit. Then he did something that few salesmen ever do—and changed his life forever.

He went back to all the shopkeepers who wouldn't buy his product and asked them: "Is there anything I could do to change this socket so that you would want to buy a few for your shop?" Many of the shopkeepers gave him suggestions like "make it bigger, make it smaller, change the color, do this or do that." He took all their suggestions and began tinkering with his sockets at home. He even fashioned a few prototypes of his own from scratch. He went back to the market with the customized versions and tried again. And again. And again. He kept repeating his routine of asking the potential customers how he could change the product so they would want to buy it. It was this process of back and forth customer/product strategizing that produced Konosuke Matsushita's marvelous invention; the world's first two-way electric socket. With it he began winning customers, and the fledgling Matsushita Electric played a critical role in exploding the electrical appliance industry in Japan. Now, a single electric line to a house could connect two appliances at once—an electric fan and a radio, or a cooker, etc. And as we know today, it gave birth to the world's largest producer of electric and electronic products. It also was a lesson in corporate strategy that Matsushita Electric never forgot.

In 1932, some 14 years after start-up, Konosuke Matsushita again did something that most salesmen (and great entrepreneurs) never do. He started thinking about and putting on paper the principles of enterprise as he had lived them. It took him five years to get it down. The result was a very thin, 23-page booklet titled *Matsushita Management Philosophy*. These 23 pages contain as much wisdom about enterprise as some entire business school libraries. They provide a philosophical and strategic framework for any company, which, not surprisingly, all boils down to making products that markets actually need. It should be required reading at every MBA program in the world.

For 100 years, the "what" of the business at Matsushita has been driven by knowing, very specifically, *what customers* want *what products*. Doing this better and more consistently than its competitors has always been the ultimate competitive advantage of Matsushita Electric, and its famous brands like Panasonic and National. In so doing, Konosuke Matsushita raised customer/product planning from black magic to near certainty, and it all comes from those unsold electric sockets way back in 1918.

WHAT'S IN THE "WHAT" OF THE BUSINESS

Your strategy or business plan is supposed to tell you what you are doing, so you need to be crystal clear on what's included in the "what." Right out of the Matsushita playbook, listed below are the five most important questions every aspiring entrepreneur has to answer. These are the "what" questions that matter most. If you can answer every one of these questions, with confidence, you're on top of your future business and your odds of success are good. If you can't answer these basic questions, you not only don't have a useful plan, you won't have a business to worry about in the future.

- **What Do I Really Like to Do?** What products or services do I have a passion for? What's the scope of products and services I am interested in making and selling?
- **What Am I Really Good at Doing?** What product/services could I make or deliver? What additional knowledge will I need? Will those products and services be better and/or cheaper than my competitors?
- **What Unmet Market Needs Do I See?** What unmet, or poorly met, needs do I see in the market—which require products or services I might like to do or might be good at doing?
- **What Capabilities Must I Have?** What operating capabilities and resources are required to make, sell, and service our products and customers?
- **What Cash Flow Will I Need?** Can I pay for all this? Where will the cash come from, and where will it go? Remember, your early customers can be a critical part of your start-up cash flow.

That's right: the questions are mostly about products and customers. They are the straightforward questions intended to keep your feet on the ground. There may be other things to examine, but I guarantee you this: these questions have to be answered by every successful entrepreneur. If you can't answer them now, do yourself, and your family, a huge favor and don't quit your day job just yet!

PICKING PRODUCT/MARKET WINNERS

Whether your planning process is formal or informal, six months out or 10 years, uses discounted cash flows or numbers on a napkin—the part you have to get right is "what products" and "what customers." So how exactly do you do this? First of all, where do you even come up with market and product ideas? Then how do you choose among them? What criteria should be guiding your choices? Are there any rules to follow in picking customers/markets and products/services? You are now face-to-face with the number one question in enterprise: What products and services will you offer, and to whom will you offer them? You can read a ton of research and hire a thousand consultants to help you figure this out, but at the end of the day, there are just three things you absolutely, positively, have to do. Here they are:

- **Stay Focused on Products.** What are the things you like to do? What are the things you are good at doing? Answering these two questions happens to be the number one way successful entrepreneurs identify the kind of business they start. So if you don't want to miss the greatest source of entrepreneurial ideas you'll ever have, you had better stay focused on possible products and services—those that you are passionate about and those that you are knowledgeable about.
- **Stay Focused on Customers.** Think of every market segment you know anything about, either as a customer or just an observer. What needs do you see that are going unmet, or are not being met satisfactorily? Carefully thinking this through can be a rich source of business ideas for entrepreneurs. And do some simple research: Are the markets you're looking at growing, declining, loaded with tough competitors, or ripe for better and cheaper products/services?
- **Know the Criteria That Count.** There are only two make-or-break criteria in choosing markets and products. They are *Market Need* and *Competitive Position.* The information entrepreneurs want and need most is intimate knowledge about the market need and a factual appraisal of their likely competitive position against the best competitors in the field. These are the two criteria that always count most!

So in evaluating products and markets for your start-up venture, you really have to know the answers to these simple questions: "How good is my market and how good is my product?" The Market Need may range from great in every way to downright lousy. And the Competitive Position of your product can be anywhere from best in the world to absolutely awful. To keep it simple, we'll just use *big* and *small* to rate Market Need and *high* and *low* for Competitive Position.

The best story to illustrate the power of these two criteria occurred, believe it or not, on one of those dreaded long flights sitting next to an entrepreneur. Entrepreneurs are famous for talking on and on about their company—especially when they have you captive on a long flight—but once in a while you hit gold and learn something really valuable. This was one of those times. It was the Stockholm to New York run, and the Swedish scientist in the next seat was already giving me his life story: "So I now live in Florida. . . . I used to be an R&D director for Squibb Pharmaceutical. . . . I worked at their headquarters in Lawrenceville, New Jersey . . . after years of seeing Squibb reject so many good products because the market need was not big enough for them, I left to start my own small medical products business." Whoa! This was getting more interesting. He went on to illustrate a terrific entrepreneurial application of the Market Need/Competitive Position idea.

As he told it, everyone in the healthcare industry knows there are hundreds of small, unmet needs in the medical and pharmaceutical markets. Giant companies, like his former employer, can't afford to even think about them. A tiny $25 million market doesn't get a second look from Squibb, Merck, Glaxo, or Sanofi. As my seatmate told it, his first product, diapers for elderly people, was a no-brainer. There was a small but real need in the market, and no one was producing diapers specially made for aging adults. He leased time at one of the numerous medical research facilities available today, perfected his design, contracted for production and distribution, and had his first successful product. He agreed that it fits squarely in the upper left-hand corner of the Market Need/Competitive Position matrix shown in Figure 1.2: small market need/high competitive position.

This led to a full discussion of his broad perspective on inventing products for different types of markets, first as a small cog in a giant wheel at Squibb, and now as the "big wheel" in his own little business. As he described the rich array of market and product possibilities in the pharmaceutical industry, he verbally categorized each one. So we can, courtesy of my Swedish seatmate, complete the explanation of the Market Need/Competitive Position matrix with examples from the world of medicine. Figure 1.2 shows the Picking Winners graph with full explanations that follow:

Figure 1.2	**Picking Winners**

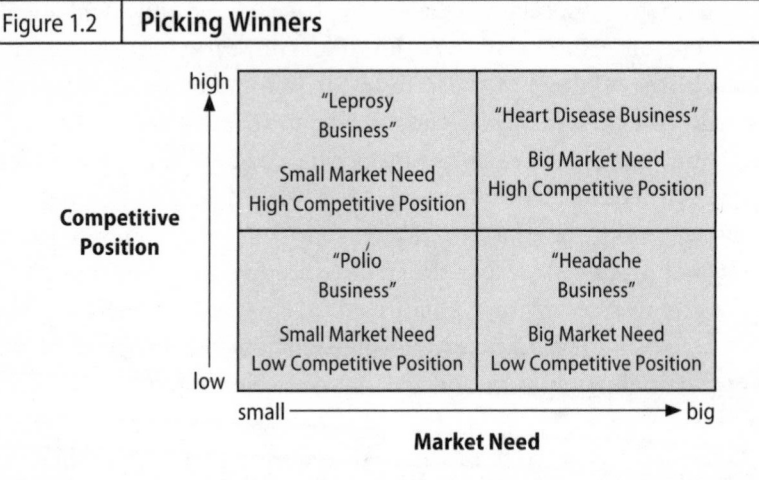

- **The "Leprosy Business."** For starters, as our Swedish entrepreneur explained, there are plenty of limited medical needs in the world for which there are no products, or only inferior products. Take leprosy for example. It's a horrible disease with a relatively small number of cases—and no cure. And why is there no cure? Because it's a small market, found mostly in poor countries, and the Mercks and Glaxos of the world aren't working on it. But suppose you and your team have a research breakthrough and discover the cure. You would have a classic example of a small market need/high competitive position product. The "leprosy business" category is a common place for entrepreneurs. They can do extremely well in these niche type businesses. (There's probably a lesson here for consumers, too. If you're going to get a bad disease, hope and pray it's something popular—so maybe there'll be a cure!)
- **The "Headache Business."** How about the flip side of the "leprosy business"? Think of the biggest display section of every drugstore in the world. That's right, it's the painkiller section. It seems that the whole world is suffering from headaches, the flu, and various aches and pains. There are dozens of brands, and hundreds of variations. They all make the same claims and have similar sounding ingredients—resulting in important medical "innovations" like "regular aspirin, extra-strength aspirin, aspirin

PM, coated aspirin, nonaspirin aspirin"—well, you get the point. I recently noticed in fact that the ingredients are exactly the same for two separate products from the same company. Check it out. Extra Strength Excedrin and Migraine Excedrin are identical, right down to the 65 milligrams of caffeine in each. Why all this marketing madness? Because the market is so damn big. It's the humongous "headache business," and it perfectly fits the big market need/low competitive position quadrant of the matrix. Entrepreneurs can prosper here also, if they're ready to compete on price at the low end of the market.

■ **The "Polio Business."** The place no entrepreneur wants to be is in the small market need/low competitive position quadrant. There are plenty of recognizable medical needs here—mostly diseases that have been virtually wiped out years ago like polio, smallpox, and scarlet fever. These are markets that are dead or dying, and even if they weren't, the old product patents have expired and everyone could be in the market tomorrow with a me-too, low-cost cure. The "polio business" arena is no place for fast-moving, entrepreneurial start-ups. There's little money to be made here by entrepreneurs, pure and simple. If you ever find yourself in this quadrant, your best move will probably be to take your losses and kill the business. There's little upside in this product/market arena.

■ **The "Heart Disease Business."** And finally we come to the place most entrepreneurs and big companies dream about—the big market need/high competitive position quadrant. Think about this. The number one killer in the world, for both men and women, is still heart disease. There have been advances in treating all manner of heart problems, but there's still no cure in sight. What if—and here comes the dream—you and your band of entrepreneur/scientists come up with the absolutely perfect, rejection-free artificial heart? You could give a lifetime guarantee for your perfect heart to your customers. That's a better deal than they get when they're born! So your "heart disease business" would rank right up there with the wheel, electricity, cars, computers, and penicillin, as one of history's true blockbuster products. Can entrepreneurs be successful here? Absolutely. Success is virtually guaranteed—with one caveat. You may become too successful. Getting too successful here will ultimately guarantee hordes of envious competitors. So go for it by all means—and get ready to take the heat of intense competition.

Beyond helping you pick product/market winners and getting your entrepreneurial venture off the ground, the two criteria—Market Need and Competitive Position—will continue to be important as you grow. They will always tell you what kind of actions you need to take to improve each of your product/market businesses. For example, if you're in the small market need/high competitive position quadrant, you need to find more customers for your great product. So focus on marketing, distribution, exporting, etc., would be essential to growing your business. Conversely, if you're in the big market need/low competitive position quadrant, you need to raise the competitiveness of your product. This means that raising your product's quality, lowering the costs, and innovating new ways to deliver the product to customers could all be key to generating more growth. The bottom line is, these criteria will help you grow your business—which is exactly what entrepreneurs do best.

So now you should have a clear plan for what products and what markets. The only thing standing between you and success is how well you can do it. This is where corporate culture, and the power of the values that drive it, must get plugged into your business mission. To really understand corporate culture, where the original idea came from, and how it can make a company great, there is only one person to ask. That would be Thomas J. Watson, the great American entrepreneur who founded the twentieth century's greatest company. Of course that would be IBM.

CREATING ENTREPRENEURIAL BUSINESS VALUES À LA WATSON

The beliefs that mold great organizations frequently grow out of the character, the experiences, and the convictions of a single person. More than most companies, IBM is the reflection of one individual—my father, T. J. Watson.

THOMAS J. WATSON, JR., Chairman, IBM, (founded in 1914, just five years before JA)

If planning is the most overused management practice in business, defining and maintaining a company's culture or values is surely the most misused. Several decades ago the subject of corporate culture burst onto the scene. Every company worth its salt had to have a written mission statement and posters everywhere proclaiming the company's values. A lot of otherwise good managers actually believed that business values were things you dreamed up in a staff meeting, plastered on every wall, and then went back to your real job where you never thought about them again. Of course all this was, and is, downright ridiculous.

The entrepreneurial version of this story actually begins with Thomas J. Watson Sr., the great founder of IBM, who is broadly credited with originating the idea that organizations have cultures and they are defined by a set of values, or as he called them—beliefs. Of course, Watson wouldn't recognize what his simple idea was turned into by modern management gurus. For starters, he never uttered the words *corporate culture*. He also never wrote a mission statement for IBM. He certainly didn't plaster the walls of IBM with posters listing the company's values. And most telling of all, he never wrote down his business philosophy anywhere. The only reason we know he even had a "business philosophy" is because his son gave a speech at Colombia University in 1963 to honor his father's life, which was printed up as a handout for students. That speech and handout, written down half a century after IBM's founding, is our only record of Watson's great treatise on "the beliefs that mold great organizations."*

What Thomas Watson did do, however, was profound. He figured out that if IBM identified and got very good at those few specific operating factors most critical to the accomplishment of its strategy or business plan, it could beat the plan year after year—through good times and bad. The critical operating factors he identified are known today as the IBM Beliefs. When Watson founded IBM in 1914, he immediately went about instilling in all IBMers that now-famous set of beliefs: outstanding customer service, respect for every employee, and superior performance in even the smallest of tasks. History shows these

---

* As a point of history, McGraw-Hill Book Company (the publisher of this book) obtained that speech and published a marvelous 33-page booklet titled *A Business and Its Beliefs: The Ideas That Helped Build IBM*. The booklet on IBM makes a great companion piece to Matsushita's 23-page booklet mentioned earlier in the chapter. I'm fortunate to possess copies of both of these out-of-print masterpieces.

beliefs—or values—have served IBM well for over 100 years. They certainly made IBM the most profitable company in the world over the entire twentieth century!

Beyond not writing down your values for 50 years, there are two major lessons in Watson's story. First, the only reason to come up with core values for your operations, or the "how" of the business, is to ensure you accomplish the strategy, or the "what" of the business. Second, crafting beautifully written mission statements and putting your values on wall plaques, so easily forgotten back on the job, is no substitute for actually living them day in and day out. Watson's full legacy is clear: If you have to pick a single factor at the core of IBM's long run at greatness, it was that it was the best in the world at doing those few critical things that were absolutely essential to the achievement of its business strategy.

Finally, the unique values you choose for your own business must be tested against no-nonsense criteria. The two most important are Competitive Advantage and Personal Commitment. These are the only musts on the list. In defining the core values that will most powerfully support your business strategy and plan, consider the following:

- **How Can I Raise My Competitive Advantage?** To the entrepreneur, this is not a drill in dreaming up slogans and banners to paste on the office walls. This is the deadly serious business of identifying those few values, or operating factors, you absolutely, positively have to be great at in order to achieve your product/customer strategy. And once you've determined what those two, three, or four critical factors are, they must become the operating *values* of your business. The right values for your future company can come from a wide variety of possibilities: innovation, fast action, cost control, global distribution, product quality, customer service, employee relations, etc.

- **How Can I Get Everyone Committed?** Becoming the very best in the world at those few values or practices most critical to your competitiveness requires an uncompromising commitment from you as the leader and your entire workforce. In every way possible you will need to reinforce the values to your people—and even let them know violations will be cause for dismissal. This tough process is the entrepreneurial way to bring business values to life in an organization—and is the best way ever invented to get groups of disparate people to focus on and achieve a common goal.

- **Behavior, Not Words, at the Top.** Your behavior is more eloquent than your words—always. Believe this if you believe nothing else in this book. The moral for new entrepreneurs: Don't expect your customers, suppliers, and future employees to take your company values seriously until and unless you are living them yourself.

- **Few and Simple.** How many things can you be best at? Two or three if you're lucky? Maybe just one. But the good news is, that's all it takes. You're not trying to be all things to all people. You're trying to be the very best in the world at one thing; delivering your product or service to your customers—full stop.

- **Never Compromise.** Here's the really hard part. You just can't go around changing your principles because you're having a bad day, or even a bad quarter. Unfortunately, compromises are often more habit-forming than principles. One well-placed compromise can reverse years of principled effort. So, never means never.

Entrepreneurial business values are, indeed, the most powerful weapons ever invented to beat your competitors and ensure the accomplishment of your product/market business plan. But creating them is the easy part—keeping them alive as the years pass and your company grows is what's hard. So here's a final thought.

KEEPING THEM ALIVE

A philosophy is not only preached but also practiced at the very top of a company . . . sound principles vigorously applied.

LORD CHARLES FORTE, Founder, Trusthouse Forte Hotels

Creating an entrepreneurial culture and values can be challenging. Even more challenging is keeping them alive for decades. In too many companies, slogans and shifting priorities begin to replace the original culture. The deeply held convictions and inspiring personal examples of the founding group just disappear over time. The unhappy fact is, corporate culture can, and often is, trivialized beyond recognition. This all flies in the face of the entrepreneur's hands-on, lead-by-example style. Great entrepreneurs like Watson, Matsushita, and, yes, Richard Branson, maintained their corporate cultures for decades by being the best example of the values themselves.

For sure, it's easier to say than do. I learned from firsthand observations of 85-year-old Lord Charles Forte, the founder of Europe's largest hotel chain at the time, just how tough and frustrating it is to be the last entrepreneurial role model in the company. The energy he and other great entrepreneurs have to put into keeping their original values and cultures alive is awesome. He told me he spent half his time trying to keep the entrepreneurial spirit alive in the company and the other half warding off all the latest management theories and fads his MBA-trained management team wanted to implement. The good news is, if you work hard enough and long enough at keeping your values alive, you do get very good at it.

Of course, you have to get the business going before you start worrying about keeping it alive. But in the spirit of taking "an ounce of prevention," a final thought on how to maintain your business values may be worth its weight in gold. Obviously, those things you determine should be the core values of your business have to keep working day in and day out, year after year, to keep you growing in the future. If your values are indeed "those few operating factors critical to the accomplishment of your business plan," letting them die is exactly what you can't afford to do.

So for your future reference at least, following are the three greatest influences on keeping your entrepreneurial values alive. If these all-important cultural influencers support and reinforce your company values, you can be sure the values will stay alive. If they don't support your values, or even worse subvert them, your values will be quickly lost—and with them, the best insurance you could ever have for maintaining your entrepreneurial dreams.

- **Your Daily Behavior.** Maybe Lord Charles Forte was right. It's not a fair world. The founder is "on stage" every minute of every day. Your personal daily behavior will set the standard for your entire company. Your most insignificant behavior will be of intense interest to employees, customers, suppliers, and even investors. So, surprise everyone and actually behave, all the time, as the best example of your company's values. If customer service is a core value of the company, you had better be first in line to show love for customers. If product quality is the value, you have to be the one who never, ever, allows junk to go out the door. It may not be a fair world, but it's a price most entrepreneurs gladly pay. The fact is, the single most powerful factor in keeping any company's values alive is the founder's daily behavior.

- **The Rituals and Practices You Follow.** Everyone knows the written policy manual or even the Mission Statement hanging on the wall are not what the culture is all about. Your company's true values actually reveal themselves in the mundane rituals and practices of daily operations. For example, the Mission Statement says that innovation is a core value, but do you ever talk about it, offer seminars on creativity, or even have an active suggestion program for new ideas? You state that employees are your most important asset, but how are workers actually treated on the line? And what's the reaction to losing a customer? Does everyone just shrug their shoulders, or does all hell break loose to regain the client? It's at this level that the culture of any company lives or dies. Not reinforcing your values in the daily rhythm of the business is a damaging failure. You are actively destroying, day in and day out, the very things that you say will give you enormous competitive advantage in the marketplace.

- **What You Reward and What You Penalize.** How do I get promoted around here? And what does it take to get fired? Your answers to these eternal employee questions will directly and powerfully set the true values of the company—for all employees. Keeping your company's values alive ultimately depends on what actions get rewarded and what actions get penalized. Say, for example, "loving the customer" is the big value in your company. Employee X is widely recognized as Mr. Customer Service who will do anything to keep customers happy. Employee Y hates customers, and everyone knows it. At the end of the year, X and Y both get a slap on the back and the across-the-board 8 percent raise. Goodbye "loving the customer" as a corporate value. The most frequently violated practice in keeping values alive is that they are not part of the reward and penalty system of the company.

It should be clear by now that having an entrepreneurial sense of mission isn't rocket science. It's all straightforward, simple stuff: creating simple plans, picking markets and products you really care about and know about, determining the few critical values needed to support your market/product plan, and then keeping those values alive year after year. It's simple stuff, but it's also powerful stuff. So whether you're an entrepreneurial dreamer, or a doer just starting up, or one of the dazzling few already on your way, it's absolutely critical to remember that having a powerful sense of mission about your business is *entrepreneurial practice number one.*

Complete the following Applications at the end of this book:
  Application 2: CREATING ENTREPRENEURIAL BUSINESS PLANS
  Application 3: PICKING MARKET/PRODUCT WINNERS
  Application 4: IT'S START-UP TIME!
  Application 5: CREATING ENTREPRENEURIAL BUSINESS VALUES
  Application 6: KEEPING THEM ALIVE

JA ALUMNI INTERVIEW

Steve Case
Founder, America Online (AOL), JA Alumnus, Hawaii, USA

Our goal was to get America and the world online.

My JA Experience:
"I was growing up in Honolulu, Hawaii. I heard about the JA program and signed up for it. I think it's a great program for a lot of people. It gives them a first exposure to business, to know what business is.

I'm sure a lot of kids never heard the word *entrepreneurship* or *start-up company* before—so it's helpful. I know it has helped a lot of young people over the years. I'm also aware that JA has changed and enlarged its programs with a lot more on ramps for different people with different skill sets and different interest levels—so I think that's all good."

My Career / Business:
"I did know by the time I was in high school and college I wanted to do something entrepreneurial. First, I did a bunch of different businesses, the music business, selling greeting cards, a bunch of different things, even a lemonade stand. Then in college I became interested in what we now think of as the Internet. I remember reading a book by Alvin Toffler, when I was a senior in college about 1980, called *The Third Wave*. Toffler was essentially talking about the Internet, although he didn't call it that at the time. I was mesmerized by it, so I knew I wanted to do that, but when I graduated there were no Internet companies to go to because they didn't yet exist, and frankly there was not much of a start-up culture back then coming out of college. So I ended up working for two big companies: Procter & Gamble in Cincinnati for a little while and then PepsiCo in its Pizza Hut division out in Wichita, Kansas. Then I moved to DC in 1983 to join a start-up, that sadly failed, but with two of the people I met at that company, I ended up starting America Online in 1985. That was 32 years ago—and our goal was to get America and the world online! At the time, only 3 percent of people were online, and those 3 percent were online an average of one hour a week, so we knew it was going to take some time. It actually took us a decade to really get traction.

"We went through several phases. One of them was when we got the PC companies to build modems into PCs. When we got started the users had to have peripheral devices to connect, and not many people had them. Second was when the World Wide Web emerged as a broader platform, and third was when we were able to reduce the cost of communication substantially. When we started it cost $10 an hour to be connected, and we had to get it to pennies an hour and then to unlimited use pricing. So, we had to make it easier to use, more useful, more fun, and finally more affordable—to go from being a niche business to being a mainstream mass business. That's why it took us

10 years. As I said, only 3 percent of the population was online, and nobody cared about it. That was the first wave. But by the end of the first wave, roughly the year 2000, everybody was online and couldn't live without it. We eventually did the merger with Time Warner in 2000, which closed in 2001. Then I stepped aside as CEO and a couple of years later got off the board. So, that was the AOL experience.

"And now, for the last 15 years, I've been doing other things. My activities today include Revolution, our investment company, a venture capital operation called Revolution Ventures, and a later stage growth company called Revolution Growth. We also have an initiative called Rise of the Rest, which is promoting regional entrepreneurship pitch competitions. We're doing pitch competitions and bus tours all over the country to stimulate entrepreneurial ecosystems around the country. We're bothered frankly that last year, as an example, 78 percent of all venture capital went to three states: California, New York, and Massachusetts. So how do you support the entrepreneurs in the other 47 states? The Case Foundation, which my wife runs, is focused on inclusive entrepreneurship and is trying to level the playing field so that everybody everywhere has a shot at the American dream. So it's all sort of an evolution from the first 15 years or so of being an entrepreneur and the last 15 years of being more of an investor, mentor, evangelist if you will around entrepreneurship."

My Advice to Young People:

- "It's important to be curious and flexible and try to imagine how things might change in the future and try to position yourself to be where things are going. Also it's important to have some sense of the areas you are interested in, or passionate about, and where you have some competence.
- "Great entrepreneurs connect the dots in interesting ways, and imagine new possibilities in interesting ways and see things that other people don't see. So that skill set that some call creativity or connecting the dots is critically important.
- "Entrepreneurship is a team sport. So collecting the right team that has a shared passion about what you're trying to accomplish, with a complementary mix of skills, and diverse mix of perspectives, is important. If you have the right team, anything is possible. If you don't, nothing is possible.

- "I also think that partnerships are going to become really important. It's not just about what you do, the product you build, the service you create. It's also about how you can partner or collaborate with other people and companies who can take your idea and give it life and momentum that wouldn't be possible if you just try it on your own.
- "Finally, we're involved in some programs for people coming out of poverty, and the question is always, how do you give them exposure to business, some of the required skills, and some of the mentoring that is critical—and also figure out ways to get them access to start-up capital—so they at least have a shot. Obviously, this is the kind of thing JA tries to do also."

JA ALUMNI INTERVIEW

Monica Rivera
Founder, Madersolda, JA Alumna, Colombia

> *Success does not come as a miracle. I knocked on doors, spent time planning my future, worked very hard, and now I'm living the life I hoped for.*

My JA Experience:

"I joined the JA Colombia Mujeres Emprendedoras (Women Entrepreneurs) program in 2014. I was 25 years old and had just been married. When I signed up I was thinking that I wanted and needed economic independence and to start creating a future for the family that I wanted to have. The program gave me the tools to consolidate the business idea I had back then. It also motivated me to continue training to ensure I had the skills to reach my goals—and show people that a woman who knows what she wants can be a successful entrepreneur! With the experience of the course, I began to project my personal image and my business as a successful and happy life experience. It has taken some sacrifice and a lot of effort, but the results have shown me that the undertaking has been very worthwhile.

"Before the program I only had a high school degree. But I realized that my company role would demand another profile and more knowledge. I already had the natural strength which characterizes most women, but having managed to consolidate my business idea, I needed to study more. Today I'm a certified technologist in customer service and sales."

My Career / Business:

"My business is Madersolda, an enterprise dedicated to the manufacture of wood furniture for the home and office. The business concept was that my husband would provide the manpower and I would manage the people side including sales and service. I decided to risk it all because I was sure our business could become a good source of income and savings. And after learning how to calculate revenue and costs, I knew we could produce a product that would sell well and create a few jobs—which would be a good thing for our entire community.

"Today we have our own well-assembled factory and machines, and have legalized the company. With the demand for our product, we are able to employ three people to whom we offer stability and all the benefits workers have by law. It makes me proud to know that through my business, there are other families that have the possibility of having a better quality of life. Thank God I have managed to keep my business going for three years—and it's growing nicely!"

My Advice to Young People:

- "To young people who may not yet know what to do with their lives, my advice is to find a way to study so that they can be useful and competitive people.

- "Second, if young people have clear goals and are well grounded, it's much more likely that their dreams will come true. It's worth little to dream if nothing practical is done to materialize those dreams.

- "Third, success does not come as a miracle. I knocked on doors, spent time planning my future, worked very hard, and now I'm living the life I hoped for. Of course, I haven't fulfilled all my goals and

I continue to work hard to achieve them. But I rise every single day knowing that everything I have, I have earned, and that I must take care of it.

- "Finally, something that has helped me a lot as a person and as an entrepreneur—I convinced myself that if I believed I could do it, I would succeed. Sometimes I risked being different and bold, but my belief in myself has become like my personal brand."

JA ALUMNI INTERVIEW

Sergey Borisov

Founder, Apps4All / Apps4Ads / Ads4All, JA Alumnus, Russia

> *It was an amazing place—the monastery in the desert—it was a powerful and interesting experience for me. I recommend it to everyone.*

My JA Experience:

"My experience in the JA Company Program was good. Our team was great and very enthusiastic. Working with the team showed me how entrepreneurs can solve the problems of their business. I was in the program only one year, but it was exciting and we had a great education from it. Later my friend and I made the JA dream come true by founding our own business. The main thing I learned from JA is that entrepreneurship is the best way for a person to succeed in life—it actually changed my life."

My Career / Business:

"Today I am kind of a serial entrepreneur. I believe that all entrepreneurs try to solve problems by trying to find new ways to do things. That's what I am doing today. I'm still trying to find the main business of my life even though we already have several companies, all in the IT marketing area. For example, Apps4All, started in 2011, is the biggest app developer online community in Russia. It's become one of the most popular platforms for online app developers. Through it we work with Fortune 500 companies like IBM, Samsung, LG, Google, Intel, HP, and others. We help them reach our developer community and to improve their developer relations.

"We also have Apps4Ads, a digital marketing agency. In Russia our digital agency is quite successful; we work with big companies and we are currently ranked number 72 out of 1,200 agencies in the Russian Federation—even though the company is only two years old. One of our new clients is the biggest online poker company in the world, and they have big plans for the Russian market. They already have around 8,000 people playing poker online with huge prizes, around $20 million, for the winners. We're proud that they work with our agency to advertise their brand across Russia.

"Ads4All is a Russian company of course which we tried to start in the United States last year. We went to Silicon Valley to plan the start-up, but it wasn't successful because our organization and platform weren't really ready. But like good entrepreneurs we are planning to start up again next year in San Francisco. We now have a U.S.-registered company and we look forward to start working in the huge USA market. I learned in JA there are always new opportunities in the world. So as we say in Russia, just keep your 'nose to the wind' and you will find those opportunities."

My Advice to Young People:

- "I think the main advice for young people is to not be afraid to try new things because the opportunities are always changing and the main thing for the entrepreneur is to seize the future opportunity and follow that idea.
- "From seeing the idea until the end, commitment and execution of the idea is the main thing. A good idea without good execution won't work.
- "The third thing is to always try something new—don't stick to one idea, it may not be successful or it may not be in the right place at the right time. But if you feel the situation is not so good then you should try a new opportunity, and one day you will find the business of your life, which will give you satisfaction and of course profit for your life.

- "Finally, Larry, I see that you are in Arizona. Believe it or not, I've been there. I actually spent a full week at an Orthodox monastery in the desert in Arizona. It was an amazing place—the monastery in the desert—it was a powerful and interesting experience for me. I recommend it to everyone."

JA ALUMNI INTERVIEW

Titus Mboko
Founder, Grain Solutions, JA Alumnus, Zimbabwe

I founded Grain Solutions with the mission to reduce hunger and poverty of the rural poor.

My JA Experience:

"As a youngster who grew up in rural areas, I believed that JA programs offered the best opportunity for people with my background to understand the principles of business and economics. The programs simulated the real world of business, and to me it was the right way to be slowly but carefully introduced to the business world. The programs initially prepared me to be a versatile employee who understood how business works from production, to sales, to financial management.

"However, I soon discovered, through the programs, a whole new world of entrepreneurship. From that experience, I eventually formed my own small, but growing business along the agriculture value chain. The solid ground set by the JA programs has given me the strength and the skill to run my own venture."

My Career / Business:

"Having been raised by peasant farmers, I initially shunned a career in agriculture largely because I had witnessed my parents struggle to just put me through high school. So when my sister later on took over the responsibility to pay for my university fees, I chose to study accounting. I graduated from the University of Zimbabwe with an honors degree in accountancy, and I worked for a number of organizations across many sectors of the economy for seven years. But I began to think that my future should be in agriculture. I had actually been a financial manager for an agribusiness, and I realized there was so much value that could be created, added, and delivered across the agriculture value chain. I also learned that peasant farmers (smallholders) actually represent over 70 percent of Africa's food production, and much more could be done by the agri-industry to lift them out of poverty—socially and economically.

"I founded Grain Solutions with the mission to reduce hunger and poverty of the rural poor. In 2013, I voluntarily resigned from the corporate world to become a full-time entrepreneur and started Grain Solutions as a grain trading company, sourcing agricultural commodities from small farmers, for resale to large agro-processors. Over the years the business has grown to include transport and logistics as well as stock-feed manufacturing through a partnership with an Indian agribusiness.

"Working in the agribusiness sector allows me to impact a lot of people living at the bottom of the socioeconomic pyramid—while working toward the challenge of feeding nearly 9 billion people by 2050, when the world will need to produce 70 percent more food to avoid starvation. Everyone needs to work hard to improve food production, nutrition, and income security for the rural poor, but the idea of young people driving agriculture's revolution really excites me. The future belongs to the youth of the world, and according to the UN's Food and Agriculture Organization, the agriculture industry is 11 times more effective in reducing poverty in sub-Saharan Africa than any other activity. So I chose to work in the agriculture sector because of the amazing impact metrics it produces.

"Since I graduated from university with a degree in accounting, I actually ventured into agribusiness without the requisite undergraduate qualifications in agriculture. However, my experience with JA cultivated in me the skills to build a business regardless of one's educational background. The success of Grain Solutions has largely been the result of the rigorous and meticulous training I received from the JA program."

My Advice to Young People:

- "To young people I would say innovation and technology drives any business forward. Youth should therefore embrace technology and continuously seek innovative ways of doing business. Innovation, in particular, creates new, cheaper, cleaner, and more disruptive ways of doing things.
- "In addition, investing in collaborations, partnerships, and joint ventures helps in up-scaling and growing the business and creates added value for consumers and stakeholders.
- "Finally, young people should participate in programs like JA to learn about entrepreneurship and innovation. This will foster *The Entrepreneurial Attitude* at a young age!"

JA ALUMNI INTERVIEW

Munjal Shah

Founder, Health IQ, JA Alumnus, California, USA

> *I think in life you don't always find your mission—sometimes it finds you and you have to be open to it.*

My JA Experience:

"I did JA as a high-schooler. It was a wonderful experience. I was CEO of my JA company. We were a first-year team and came in second place against all the other JA company teams. We made little cornucopia things that we sold to people as wreaths to go on their doors. They were glued together with plastic flowers and whatnot. I think they cost us five bucks to make and we sold them for $20, so we were doing good. The program was at Cupertino High School, Steve Jobs's old school, by the way. I not only live in Silicon Valley today, but I'm one of those rare people who actually grew up in the area and hearing about all the famous entrepreneurs. I remember going to the JA annual dinner at the Fairmount Hotel, and they seated the

JA company CEOs next to real CEOs. I got to sit next to David Packard of Hewlett-Packard who was being honored that night. I ended up giving a speech to the 500 guests, which was all very inspiring. I also went to the National JA Conference that summer, so it was all a wonderful experience for me.

"I always thought I would start a company someday. I had conceptualized it but had never actually started a little company until my JA experience. The main thing for me was learning about leadership. I got to run the little team of five or six kids. It was just a great opportunity to work with the marketing person, the finance person, to sell the products, and it was all profitable! So from my earlier conceptualizing about being an entrepreneur, the JA program actually made it a reality and solidified everything for me—and I said, oh, I really enjoyed this!"

My Career / Business:

"I'm a serial entrepreneur. I've founded three companies so far. The first one was called Andale. It provided tools for people selling on eBay. I ran that from when I was 26 until we sold it about five years later. It was a convoluted sale, and the company eventually ended up at Alibaba, the giant Chinese online retailer. My second company was called Like.com, and it used computer vision to search photographs to get the color, shape, and pattern of a picture from which we built a shopping engine for clothing, shoes, handbags, watches, etc. We sold that company to Google for over $100 million in 2010.

"Starting my third company has been a little different. The day after I sold my company to Google, I was 37 years old, I began having chest pains and ended up in the emergency room of the hospital. So at the pinnacle of my entrepreneurial career, achieving the big payday, the thing I had been working for all my life, I ended up in the ER. I didn't have a full heart attack, but it was something serious. So I lost 40 pounds, changed my health habits, started running marathons, and decided that my next company was going to be something useful around health. It's called Health IQ. We built a health IQ test that measures not how healthy you are but how health-conscious you are and how much responsibility you take for your own health. We use that to get cheaper life insurance rates for people who do take care of their health—celebrating and rewarding healthy people versus the usual thing of just berating and penalizing unhealthy people. I've spent the last decade building this third company. It's become my life's work. Everyone says you should do something you really have a passion for, and I really agree with that now, particularly in building my third company. The only caveat is, since I didn't really feel that way until now, I think in life you don't always find your mission—sometimes it finds you and you have to be open to it. In any event it's very exciting to be doing something I really believe in."

My Advice to Young People:

- "There's real power in exploring your life to be the entrepreneur you want to be, and then just listen. Listen to the market, to your customers—listening can change your whole business direction—as it did mine.

- "Don't get hung up about finding your mission on day one. It may come and find you. You don't need to connect all the dots at first. As you move forward in life you will see the grand scheme for yourself and it will all come together—as it has done for me with my third company.

- "Work with the absolute best people you can find. Don't compromise on the quality of people you work with. I can't stress this enough. It's really worked for me. My cofounders and partners have been absolutely fabulous for my businesses.

- "Finally, because I had the luxury of taking some time off, I took a class for a month at Second City Chicago, the famous comedy school. I wasn't terribly funny, mind you, but I had always wanted to try that. I would say if you learn how to do it, humor can be a superpower skill! You can get so much further with humor than with so many other leadership skills. You can guide people with humor, it allows you to deliver difficult messages, you can use it to break tension in meetings—it's just a superpower, so learn to use it!"

CHAPTER 2

Customer/Product Vision

My Customer, My Product, My Self-Respect

> *The computer is the most remarkable tool we've ever*
> *built.... but the most important thing is to get them*
> *in the hands of as many people as possible.*
>
> **STEVE JOBS,** Founder, Apple Computer, NeXT Inc., Pixar

In his famous quote above, Steve Jobs wasn't talking about how to manage, or the latest marketing technique, or even how to grow Apple Computer. He was obsessed with the two most fundamental ideas in enterprise: customer and product. He said the only thing more important than making computers was having satisfied customers actually use them. Of course, along the way, Apple reached the Fortune 500 roster faster than any company in history and today is the most valuable company in the world.

What was the big secret? Jobs had a big vision. A vision of "the most remarkable tool we've ever built." But then he says "the most important thing" is to get them used in every office, in every home, and by every child in every classroom. Like no other computer maker, Jobs understood the needs of naive users. That's why Apple made computers inexpensive, easy to learn, and fun to use. Jobs was an expert on both products and customers—the classic vision of an entrepreneur.

The really important lesson of Jobs and most great entrepreneurs is that at heart they are craftspeople. They have a single, integrated vision of customers and products. They don't functionalize them. They know they need both to survive. They are, in fact, obsessed with making products that customers will buy. The trick for you, then, is to become a passionate expert on your own products and customers. After all, they are the two most important words in business.

And speaking of entrepreneurs with world-class customer/product vision, let's turn our attention to the leading candidate for that title for the entire twentieth century—Walter Elias Disney.

THE REAL MAGIC OF DISNEY

The inclination of my life has been to do things and make things which will give pleasure to people.

WALT DISNEY, Founder, The Walt Disney Company

Beyond our opening example of Steve Jobs, go down any list of famous entrepreneurs. Think of old-timers like Thomas Watson, Karl Benz, and Konosuke Matsushita. Or newer faces such as Richard Branson at Virgin, Amazon's Jeff Bezos, or Sergey Brin and Larry Page of Google (who were big fans of Jobs, by the way). They all share a finely tuned passion for producing things exactly the way customers need them and want them. It's a rare skill when you think of the hundreds of businesses you've dealt with that just don't seem to get this simple concept. And there's never been a better example of 20/20 customer/product vision than Walt Disney.

Disney had it right in his famous quote above. When he said: "do things and make things which will give pleasure to people," he wasn't thinking about the latest management theory or getting another stock option. He was thinking about the two most important ideas in enterprise; products and customers. So the real magic of Disney is clear. Like Steve Jobs, he was a product expert *and* a customer expert at the same time. A scientist *and* a salesman. It's the beautiful balance between these two basics of business that we call being an Entrepreneur—Disney style. How could it be otherwise? Well, unfortunately it can, and often is. There are at least three other possibilities. You'll recognize them all in Figure 2.1. We call them the Scientist, the Salesman, and the Bureaucrat.

| Figure 2.1 | **Disney Magic** |

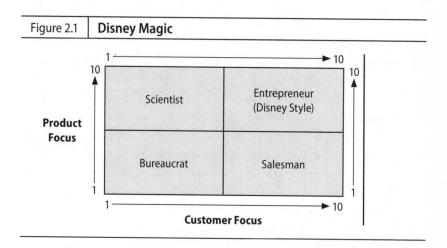

- **The Scientist.** Ever come across people, or even whole companies, who are so into their technology or product, they forget they're creating it for someone else to use? We call this the *scientist syndrome*—or loving the product and hating the customer. In the world of Disney, it could be the filmmaker who loves to make films but doesn't care if anyone pays to watch them. In the world of Steve Jobs, it's the computer scientist who builds the world's most elaborate machine, but it takes an Einstein to figure out how to use it. This is more common than it at first appears. It ranges from user "unfriendly" products, to simply unusable products, to the adding of so many bells and whistles to a product that no one can afford it. The scientist often has a peculiar disdain for the need to sell and satisfy customers. This is the scientist syndrome—or loving products but hating customers—and it isn't exactly the focus you're going to need to grow your new business. The remedy—get refocused on the customer side of your business and try to remember they are the ones paying your salary.

■ **The Salesman.** Is it possible to love your customer but hate your product? You bet it is. Most of us run into the *salesman syndrome* every day. This is the professional salesman who loves to sell but doesn't give a damn what he's selling. Cars last year, computers this year, and Hawaiian time shares next. The fact is most salespeople know how to sell. They're trained *ad nauseam* on how to sell. But that's the problem. They know 10 times more about selling techniques than they do about their product. The number one customer complaint about salespeople today is not that they don't know how to sell. It's that they can't explain their darn product! Substituting courtesy for competence is a common variation on this theme. It's the ever-courteous voice on the phone who never solves your billing problem. Or the smiling baggage attendant at the airport who announces that your luggage just went to Karachi. The bottom line is, nobody even wants to see a salesman. They want to see real product and service experts—who really care about the product and really know how to make it work. For the entrepreneur about to fall into the salesman trap, forget about more marketing and sales training, and start spending a lot more time making yourself into a product expert.

■ **The Bureaucrat.** If you hate both your product and your customer, consider going to work for the government or a huge company. You'll never make it as an entrepreneur, but you'll be a perfect bureaucrat. The *bureaucrat syndrome* is so common you might think it's the driving force of most of the large organizations we deal with. Bureaucrats demonstrate zero excitement about customers or products. They have little interest in even being around the people who make the products and sell the customers. This is a crazy state of affairs—but it may not be entirely their fault. There are plenty of "good employees" who have never seen a customer or touched the company's product. Unfortunately, most bureaucrats spend their 40 years in their cubicles passing papers and e-mails back and forth and praying for five o'clock to come. In the bargain, they miss out on the joy of working with customers or products—the two really exciting things about any business. So, maybe they're bored with good reason. As a new entrepreneur, you might think you won't have to worry about the *bureaucrat syndrome* until you are much larger and many years into the business. But be warned, it just ain't so. Any company with three or more employees can become a raging bureaucracy. So stay vigilant on this, and make sure you and *all* your future employees are intimately involved with both customers and products.

- **The Entrepreneur: Disney Style.** How about "loving" the customer *and* "loving" the product? Of all the characteristics of entrepreneurial behavior, this dual focus on customer and product best illuminates the difference between entrepreneurs and professional managers. Like the craftspeople of old, entrepreneurs are intimately involved in both making products and selling customers. This entrepreneurial vision produces appreciation, expertise, and even respect for both customers and products. It also produces great competitive advantage in the marketplace.

  Of course entrepreneurs are close to their products. They're intensely interested in the design, manufacture, and usage of their product/service. They take it personally. They're ashamed when the quality is bad, and they're proud when they get it right. They love their product and make no bones about it. They are clearly product experts.

  Entrepreneurs are also very close to their customers. They have to be. They know their paycheck depends on it. They listen carefully to customers, not because someone told them to, but to pick up any new idea to improve their product or service. If a customer is unhappy, it's a major crisis. If the customer is happy, it makes their day. They are clearly customer experts.

"LOVING" CUSTOMERS AND PRODUCTS

Think about it. Was Steve Jobs a great scientist or a great salesman? Was Walt Disney a product genius or a marketing genius? How about Soichiro Honda? Did he just love cars, or did he understand that the world really wanted smaller, more efficient, and more reliable automobiles? Did Ray Kroc at McDonalds have a great product concept—or a great customer concept? The truth is, all great entrepreneurs are both—product experts *and* customer experts. In our vernacular, they "love" their customers and their products.

The most expensive MBA in the world can't give you this entrepreneurial passion. The entrepreneur's timeless adage says it all: "My customer, my product, my self-respect." Creating a passion for both customers and products is the driving force of great entrepreneurs everywhere. They go to sleep thinking about them. They dream about them. They wake up thinking about them. They are truly obsessed with their customers and products. And so it should be for you and your start-up business. There are hundreds of things you can do to create this passion and instill it in every employee you hire. Here are several of the most important and common ways entrepreneurs do just that. We call it "loving" the customer and "loving" the product.

"LOVING" THE CUSTOMER

> *I solemnly promise and declare that every customer*
> *that comes within ten feet of me, I will smile, look*
> *them in the eye, and greet them, so help me Sam.*
>
> **SAM WALTON**, Founder, Walmart (Employee Pledge)

One day during 2001, a recession year, Walmart Stores, that down-home retailer from tiny Bentonville, Arkansas, became the biggest company in the history of the world—in less than 40 years since its start-up. With sales of $219 billion, the amazing customer-friendly discount chain had literally galloped past all rivals for the top spot.

Sixteen years later, and another much worse recession, it's still on top of the world. Its current revenues are a staggering $482 billion, with solid profits of $14.7 billion. But there's more: Walmart, now 55 years old, still covers less than half of the U.S. market, and just a fraction of the global retail market—in both the store and Internet sectors. It's gone from one store in 1962 to 11,500 today, employs an incredible 2.3 million people, and it's just getting started. As amazing as it sounds, this is a company with a lot of room to grow.

How did all this happen? How could a five-and-dime retailer from Arkansas become the biggest business ever? Well, thanks to its super-duper information systems and hard-nosed purchasing—it does indeed try to give customers the lowest prices in town. However, that can't be the main reason. After all, Target, K-Mart, Costco, and a dozen more discount chains also offer consumers some very competitive, bargain-basement prices these days. What I, and I suspect millions of other customers, really like about Walmart is: It's the one big company that really and truly makes you feel welcome. Like the famous Walmart employee pledge quoted above, everyone and everything at Walmart says: "We love our customers!"

Take the official Walmart job of "People Greeter." The idea, which came from an employee, is that when you visit a Walmart store, it should be like visiting a friend's home. So there are People Greeters to greet every visitor, at every door, of every store. Essentially what they do is smile, say hello, give you a cart, and wish you a good visit. Each of the 11,500 big stores must have eight or more People Greeters to cover all the doors and all the shifts. That's about 92,000 employees standing around, doing nothing much but saying hello to customers who enter the stores. They don't sell, stock the shelves, check out customers, or even sweep up. They just say *hello* and *welcome to Walmart.* There's no doubt the first thing any efficiency consultant or cost-cutter would do at Walmart would be to get rid of all these "nonproductive" employees. And in one fell swoop, they would cut the legs out from under Walmart's number one competitive advantage.

As Sam Walton demonstrated his entire life, the entrepreneurial approach to customers is full of caring common sense. As an up-and-coming entrepreneur, you should also have a lot of built-in motivation to love and respect your customers. However, instilling the same behavior in your employees may be your bigger challenge. The really nice thing is that every minute you spend on this challenge, as you start hiring people, will be money in the bank. There is nothing you can do that will be more valuable than making sure you and your people "love your customers," just like Walmart. Of all the ways you can do this, here are four of the most important.

- **Knowing Your Product.** The number one complaint in the world today about marketing and salespeople is they don't actually understand their own products. After all, how can you really take care of your customers if you don't know how your product works, how to fix it when it's broken, and how to squeeze the most out of it to make life easier for your customer/user? What's the message you're giving to customers when you can't even explain how and why your product will solve their problem?

There's also a very practical consideration. No one really wants to see a salesperson anymore. Think of the last time you chose a doctor. Or wanted to buy a car. Or needed to acquire outside help to solve a business problem. Who did you want to see? A sales type? Of course not. You wanted to see a product/service expert—someone who really knew the nuts and bolts of solving your problem.

Enter Ray Kroc, lowly traveling salesman of milkshake machines, who fell in love with the products of one of his customers—the McDonald brothers in Southern California. Kroc couldn't believe that the single McDonalds burger shop ordered eight of his multi-mixers, capable of making 48 milkshakes at once, so he went to take a look for himself, and the rest is history. And it was all started by a salesman turned product fanatic. As Ray Kroc loved to say: "You gotta see the beauty in a hamburger." The idea behind those words could also be the winning customer sales and service strategy for your own company.

- **Responding Immediately.** The number one complaint in the world today about service people is they are always so busy with other things, you have to wait, and wait, and wait some more . . . Think of the last time you needed a quick answer from a tech support call center, or when you tried to find a clerk in a big-box department store, or stood in the "customer service" line at the airport, or e-mailed your credit card company to correct a billing error—or God forbid tried to renew your driver's license on your lunch hour. Doesn't it seem that service people know every trick in the book to avoid getting sucked into serving you promptly? Whatever the reason for this behavior, the message the customer gets is crystal clear: "I've got something a lot more important to do than wait on you."

Of course this is all very good news for you as a new entrepreneur—it's a constant reminder of what *not* to do. To entrepreneurs, responding immediately to customers is one of the greatest weapons ever invented to beat the competition. This is why Sam Walton insisted that every employee take the

Walmart pledge. It's also why he put Walmart People Greeters in every store. It's not very scientific, but this is the kind of immediate customer response "stuff" that's made Walmart the fastest growing retailer in history and the biggest company in the world today. And it can do wonders for you too—if for no other reason than you'll be all alone—the only place in town doing it.

- **Being Courteous and Competent.** "When we answer the phone, we're very courteous. That's the good news. The bad news is we don't answer the phone." Famous last words from Ramon Cruz, former CEO of Philippine Airlines, lamenting the lousy telephone system in Manila. What he was really saying was that courtesy without competence will get you nowhere. The most courteous airline in the world (which PAL may well be) can't overcome chronic lost baggage problems and reservation systems that don't work. The opposite is also true. Competence without courtesy isn't going to get you in the winner's circle either. Lufthansa may get you and your luggage where you're going on time, every time, but who wants to be served by the cabin crew from hell?

  Entrepreneurs should have a huge advantage in this area. Courtesy has a certain ring of sincerity from people who run their own shop. When they thank the customer for making a $200 purchase, you get the feeling they just might really mean it. And if the product doesn't work, they take it personally—and know exactly what to do to get it fixed. This double-barreled behavior, so rare in bigger companies and government agencies, is just another area where entrepreneurs and their young companies can have a built-in advantage over the bureaucracies of the world. The entrepreneurial message here is clear: Even a little bit of courtesy and competence can give you a huge competitive edge because you will be the only company around providing both. Just be sure you don't lose this competitive edge as you grow bigger.

- **Keeping Current Customers Forever.** Thomas Watson, the founder of IBM, liked to say: "The most important customer we'll ever have is the one we already have." The message was clear. Don't lose current customers. And in the early days he put his money where his mouth was. IBM had a sales commission system that actually penalized salespeople for losing existing clients. Now that's a powerful way to get the "loving the customer" message across.

Your most important prospect for future sales is a current customer, always, always, always. And with the sky-high marketing costs of acquiring new business, all of the profit for the year will likely sit in your current customer reorder base. Losing just one or two current customers can be an unmitigated disaster—to be avoided at all costs. Therefore, the most important marketing job in any business is to resell and expand those current customers.

This is not an argument against new business—just a commonsense look at growing your revenues and profits. Repeat business literally keeps you alive. Make sure "keeping current customers forever" is your first sales and service priority as you grow your business.

All the above suggestions can help you employ the same entrepreneurial practices around "Loving the Customer" as Jobs, Disney, Walton, Kroc, Watson, et al. These simple practices may end up being the most powerful sales and marketing tools you will ever have.

"LOVING" THE PRODUCT

Her name is Mercedes.

GOTTLIEB DAIMLER, Cofounder, Daimler Benz Company

Karl Benz was the "product man" of one of the greatest teams in the history of business. He invented the two-stroke gas engine and was in fact the product genius behind the first commercially viable automobile. Historians rank his contribution alongside electricity, antibiotics, computers, and space travel as one of the most profound scientific and technological advances of the twentieth century. Of course, this made him the perfect partner for Gottlieb Daimler, the "customer man" of the team and the first of the great car salesmen and tire kickers.

If you have to boil it all down to one thing, the single most critical element in any successful start-up is the entrepreneur's ability to come up with a better mousetrap. The mousetrap could take the form of a breakthrough product, an innovative new service, or even a new and improved version of an existing mousetrap. But here's the catch: The final judge of the worth of your efforts will be the customers, not you. So again, it's the bringing together of the scientist and salesman in yourself and your start-up team that is required to produce winners. Here, straight from the entrepreneur's handbook, are four of the most basic practices for loving your products—starting with, as you may have already guessed, knowing your customer.

■ **Knowing Your Customer.** Gottlieb Daimler is usually hailed as a great maker of engines and cars. But in reality, he was a near-fanatic on knowing exactly what his customers wanted. It was Daimler, more than his partner and technical genius Karl Benz, who understood that knowing your customer is the essential first step in producing great products. He was technically competent to be sure, but he was first and foremost a salesman, who just happened to love his product. Fritz Nallinger, the German biographer of both Daimler and Benz, wrote: "Daimler was completely possessed with the idea of equipping every conceivable vehicle with Benz's engines."

For Daimler, the whole point of making cars was to please and even astonish the customer. Even the great brand name Mercedes came about to please a customer. In the early 1900s the largest distributor for the Daimler automobile was in Vienna, Austria. This dealer threatened to switch to another carmaker in France, so Daimler rushed to Vienna and promised him the company would do *anything* to keep his business. As a joke the dealer told him he'd only stay with the Daimler car if the company put his 11-year-old daughter's name on the hood. And what was her name? You guessed it: "Her name's Mercedes" . . . and the rest is history. Probably no customer will ever ask you to put his daughter's name on your product, but what would you do if he does ask? Hopefully, something as clever as Daimler.

There has never been a great product company, Apple Computer, Daimler-Benz, or Matsushita Electric, that didn't give its customers exactly what they wanted. Knowing exactly what your customers want, and then actually delivering it, is the crucial first step in becoming a world-class product company.

■ **Feeling Old-Fashioned Pride.** Entrepreneurs obviously have a strong sense of personal ownership in the products they make and the services they deliver. This creates old-fashioned entrepreneurial pride, an enormous natural advantage over their competition. The important question for entrepreneurs is, can they pass on their natural advantage of old-fashioned pride to their employees?

During our interview in Tokyo, Tetsuo Chino, the founding president of Honda USA and a lifelong friend of Soichiro Honda, told me one of Mr. Honda's favorite stories about a retired Honda worker who had gained some local celebrity for shining the chrome on any Honda he saw parked on the streets of Tokyo. When asked by the local press why he was doing such a strange thing, the elderly retiree's answer was classic: "Because I can't stand to see a dirty Honda." This may be the ultimate example of feeling old-fashioned pride for your product—and goes to prove that some big companies can and do instill it in their people. It takes effort, however. One of your most important and challenging tasks as an entrepreneur will be to make sure your employees acquire some level of entrepreneurial pride about your company and your products.

A lot of useful techniques are available to put pride back into employees' work: job autonomy, quality of work life, face-to-face meetings with real customers to hear their positive and negative comments, and of course it always helps if workers have some actual ownership and stake in the business. If you can't do this, to some degree, you'll be in danger of ripping the pride out of your employees' work—and quite possibly the growth out of your company's future.

■ **Making It Better Than the Next Guy.** Lord Charles Forte, an Italian immigrant to the United Kingdom, grew Trusthouse Forte from one sweet shop on Oxford Street in central London to over 900 hotels and 93,000 employees worldwide. When I first met him several years ago, he gave me the best definition of "making it better" I've ever heard. Forte said that when his managers proposed opening a hotel in a new city or country, he asked them just three simple questions:

1. Can we make the hotel cheaper and better than the competition?
2. If not both cheaper and better, at least better?
3. If not better, at least cheaper?

If he didn't get a strong yes to at least one of those three questions, the conversation was over. That simple system seemed to work rather well over the years as he built Europe's largest hotel chain from scratch. Most entrepreneurs, like Charles Forte, don't get too caught up in concepts like Six Sigma, TQM, Kaizen, Lean Manufacturing, and the ISO 9000 certification. Too often the missing link in quality theories and techniques is the word *competitive*. The entrepreneurs make their living by beating the competition, and as Charles Forte said, you can beat the competition in just three ways: higher quality, or lower costs, or both.

In the modern entrepreneurial age, when the life cycle of products and services can be six months or less, we may have to add one more question to Lord Forte's list: Can you, in your new venture, also *make it faster*? And that leads us to the next entrepreneurial practice for loving the product.

■ **Making It Faster Than the Next Guy.** Ross Perot, that quintessential entrepreneur from Texas, really hit the nail on the head on this point. After selling Electronic Data Systems (EDS) to General Motors for $2 billion cash and joining the GM board of directors as its largest stockholder, he was stunned at how slowly everything moved in what was, at the time, the biggest company in the world. After six months on the board, he went public with this famous complaint: "I just don't understand it. It took us four years to win World War Two—but it takes these people seven years to produce a new Buick." Touché!

In fields like electronics and software, where product life cycles can be as short as six months, the competitive advantage of *making it faster* is well known. But in our global economy, *making it faster* will be an increasingly critical issue for all companies. As Dr. Ed Penhoet, the great biotech entrepreneur, told me: "The entire biotech industry has been a horse race. The winners are the ones who get to the finish line first with FDA approved products." So from Big Macs, to iPhones, to finding the cure for cancer—the entrepreneurial winners will indeed be those who "get to the finish line first."

All the above ideas can help you employ the entrepreneurial practices of Daimler, Honda, Forte, Perot, and Penhoet. In a sense, it almost doesn't matter which specific actions you take in "Loving the Customer" and "Loving the Product." It's virtually impossible to go wrong spending time on these ideas. So here's a final, very important thought on the power of focusing on customers and products: We call it growing your business the old-fashioned way.

GROWING THE OLD-FASHIONED WAY

My mind started going kind of wild at that
point with all the possibilities.

BUEL MESSER, Founder, Messer Landscaping

Providing more products to sell to more customers used to be the way all companies grew. But today, there seems to be a lot of ways to grow. Mergers and acquisitions, strategic alliances, pushing accounting rules to the limits, getting bailed out by the government, and even outright fraud (think Volkswagen, Toshiba, Bernie Madoff, etc.) are some of the current-day favorites.

The old-fashioned way of growing is easier to understand. All you have to do is make more products and sell more customers. To do this, you don't need M&A specialists, strategy consultants, investment bankers, accountants, or lawyers. You do, however, have to know the answer to a very important question: Where exactly are my best opportunities for growth?

Fortunately, we have the answer, which was inspired by Buel Messer, the founder of Messer Landscaping in Virginia, one of the most unforgettable entrepreneurial characters I've ever met. For starters, he was born dirt poor and blind (born with optic atrophy leaving him with 5 percent vision in just one eye), became a wrestling and track star in college, and began his career as a teacher. Then he made the worst decision of his life and tried his hand at cattle rustling to make a few extra bucks. He got caught and went to prison. After paying his debt to society, he worked hard at redeeming his character and reputation. He eventually founded and ran a very successful landscaping company. Naturally I wanted to learn how he did it and went to meet him. At the end of our interview I couldn't resist asking him this burning question: "How in the world does a blind man rustle cattle?" His classic reply: "Not very well, that's why I got caught—so I went into landscaping." As a master of keep-it-simple business thinking, it became obvious to Messer over time that the most important reason to focus on customers and products is that they hold the key to all future growth of the business.

What follows is Buel Messer's commonsense analysis of the (only) four ways to grow your business—graphically displayed in Figure 2.2 and then followed by full descriptions.

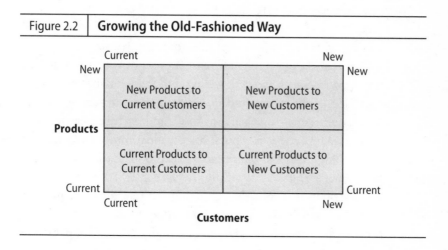

| Figure 2.2 | **Growing the Old-Fashioned Way** |

	Current	New	
New	New Products to Current Customers	New Products to New Customers	New
Products			
	Current Products to Current Customers	Current Products to New Customers	
Current	Current	New	Current
		Customers	

■ **Current Products to Current Customers.** After prison, Messer started rebuilding his life by shoveling snow with his two small boys in the winter of 1980. He had a small group of customers lined up for the season. He quickly realized that in his existing business, his income was going to be determined by how many times he could provide this same service to the same group of customers. It didn't take a genius to figure out that the more it snowed, the more money he would make. Messer discovered the first way to grow any business: selling current products to current customers, more often. Creating growth this way, which could eventually hit a limit, takes a tremendous amount of attention to the ongoing servicing and selling of your existing customers.

- **New Products to Current Customers.** By March of 1981, the snow shoveling business was finished and Messer wondered how he would make a living during the summer. Since he had developed a good relationship with his snow removal customers, he asked a few of them if he could mow their lawns during the summer. They liked his work, trusted him personally, and quickly agreed to employ him for the summer. So, Messer discovered that another way to grow his business was to sell a new service to his satisfied current customers. Growing this way, constantly producing new and improved products for your current customers, typically requires focus on, and investment in, new product research and development.

- **Current Products to New Customers.** Once he was up and running with year-round work, he got the expansionist bug. He began to look around for new market areas in which to offer his existing services of snow shoveling and lawn maintenance. He advertised in the paper, and to his delight, he began to acquire new customers in other parts of town and even in nearby communities. Messer was now pursuing the most common method of growing any business: offering current products to new customers. Growing this way typically involves geographic expansion, new distribution channels, exporting, and so on. It requires a heavy dose of solid marketing and selling.

- **New Products to New Customers.** Finally, Messer hit his stride and became a full-service landscaper. What it meant was developing completely new products and services for completely new customers. Managing tree farms, creating large tracts of shrubs, and buying earthmoving equipment and dozens of trucks was a far cry from owning a snow shovel and a lawnmower. Likewise, bidding for multimillion-dollar landscaping projects for government offices and corporate headquarters is hardly the same as becoming friends with a few homeowners in your end of town.

What Messer did, of course, was to use the fourth way of growing his business: offering new products to new customers. This avenue to growth, similar in most respects to actually starting a new business, requires intense focus on both new product development and new customer marketing and selling.

In pursuing all the possible ways to grow his business, did Messer once think about mergers, acquisitions, strategic alliances, or fancy accounting techniques? Of course not. Messer and virtually all entrepreneurs grow their businesses the old-fashioned way: making more products and selling more customers. Since we now know there are only four possible ways to do that, it isn't all that complicated.

The following Applications at the end of the book are designed to record your first brainstorming sessions on loving customers and products, and growing the old-fashioned way. Enjoy!

Application 7: "LOVING" CUSTOMERS AND PRODUCTS
Application 8: GROWING THE OLD-FASHIONED WAY

JA ALUMNI INTERVIEW

Karoli Hindriks
Founder and CEO, Jobbatical, JA Europe Board of Directors, JA Alumna, Estonia

> *It turned out to be a unique idea that could be patented, so I became the youngest person in Estonia to ever receive a patent!*

My JA Experience:

"I am from a small town in Estonia. I was in a very average government school, nothing fancy. Actually everything in my life was very average. But my school gave us the opportunity to choose an extra class in the arts or in economics—and I chose economics. I didn't have a dream to become an entrepreneur, and I didn't have any understanding about the economy. I just was an average teenager from a small town in Eastern Europe.

"During my second year with the JA program, we created a student company. The first thing we did was to choose a president. I went to the board to write down the names everyone called out, we counted the votes, and suddenly I saw I was the president! I didn't understand why they chose me, but I got so inspired by being named president. Then we had to figure out what we were going to do. We brainstormed a lot. It was October, and getting dark early. Suddenly I had the idea that we could use the same reflective fabrics that we had on our sports clothing and create a fashionable little badge to attach to your clothing or your hat, as a cool accessory—and it could also be worn as a safety feature at night along the roads. So that became our product idea. We made and sold reflective accessories to hang on your clothing, your belt, or your scarf. We also had a version to put onto the fabric of your hat.

"There is another part of the story. When I went home and told my father and mother about my idea, they could have told me it was nonsense and just go study your lessons. But my father said, 'What a great idea, I wonder if you can patent it.' So, the next day I went to the patent office in my small town. They had never seen a young, small girl there, and they became so excited about the whole situation that they did all the research on the patent for free. It turned out to be a unique idea that could be patented, so I became the youngest person in Estonia to ever receive a patent! We started up the business, and everyone was really excited about it. We approached sponsors like Opal and Ford, telling them we would put their logos on the reflectors, and we got our first clients that way. We sold a lot. Of course it helped with the marketing that I was the youngest inventor in Estonia. We got a lot of press coverage. Finally, our student company won the JA Estonia competition in the spring. We were all so proud of our achievement.

"I learned so much from that JA experience. I saw that a 16-year-old from a small town in Estonia could make a difference. I don't have to have a PhD and come from a big city to be successful. The JA program was my inspiration, but my family was very supportive also. If my parents had told me to forget about it, you need to have a degree, you're just a woman, I would not be sitting here today. So, I think it was the combination of JA and my parents' support that was really important."

My Career / Business:

"My life started in a world full of borders—in the Soviet Union. We had no knowledge or understanding of the outside world. Ironically, the mission of my company, Jobbatical, is to help build a borderless world. When we got our independence in the 1990s, we got information from the media, and I got really inspired watching American TV about American schools and all the freedoms. I dreamed about going to study in America. So it was great when I actually got a scholarship and went for my senior year to New Hampshire, a beautiful part of the USA. I really got into the local life and culture there. Then one day I was sitting in a café and thinking about my experience and how I had changed. It was the first time that I felt if everybody could just live a year abroad, we would have a better world.

"I came back to Estonia and decided to start my own business, based on my JA student company. We actually sold hundreds of thousands of reflectors across the Baltics and also some in Scandinavia and central Europe. I was only 18 and of course I made mistakes, but it was a good learning experience. Then I helped launch MTV in Estonia as their first CEO. Next I helped build up the National Geographic and Fox channels in Estonia. Altogether I worked about seven years in Estonian television.

"After my work in television I was thinking about my friends in America and realized that my friendships were more rooted in mutual interests than in geographic location. I was ready to take a 'jobbatical' myself at the time, as I would have loved to move to another country to work for a while. These were my earliest thoughts on creating a business to make it easier for people to work and live anywhere in the world. That's how I came up with my original idea for Jobbatical. I did a Google search on the name 'Jobbatical,' a combination of 'job' and 'sabbatical,' and found nobody had the name, so I had created a new word that reflected my new business.

"We launched in 2014 and had our first round of angel investing. I was just the second woman in Estonia to raise a round of venture capital. Then in 2016, Union Square Ventures, one of the top VC firms in the U.S., led a $2 million capital round for us. We were their first investment in Eastern Europe. Jobbatical is primarily focused on the tech talent market. We do business around the world from Tallinn but are concentrating on Southeast Asia and some European countries. The biggest groups of talent are today coming from the U.S., Brazil, India, and the Philippines. Right now Southeast Asia seems to have the most needs and job openings. In Jobbatical today, I have a team of 24 people from 10 different nationalities and we are working across 38 countries.

"We are a marketplace for cross-border jobs. For companies which are hiring and cannot find the skills locally, we have the platform for them to find people internationally. And for individuals who want to move overseas, we have the platform for them to find jobs abroad. Our service is to connect people to jobs around the world. We want to make cross-border hiring as easy as local hiring."

My Advice to Young People:

- "The first thing is to be absolutely focused and become good at saying no. I always ask myself, does this new idea help my company? If it doesn't I just say no. Some people think I'm really negative, but it helps keep me focused on my business.

- "Another thing is, if anybody says you cannot do something, don't take them too seriously. Believe you can do it, whether you're starting a career or you're starting your company. Of course your career and your life will have ups and downs and you may have some self-doubt. But don't worry. Just take the self-doubt as a normal way of learning things.

- "Today you have to learn how to learn new things. At Jobbatical, for example, everywhere we operate companies are looking for 'app developers.' This is a job that didn't even exist 12 years ago when we started. I tell young people you must learn to learn—because we have no idea what jobs will be needed tomorrow."

JA ALUMNI INTERVIEW

Edward Lee

Founder, COL Financial, JA Asia-Pacific Board of Directors,
JA Alumnus, Philippines

> *We like to say to our customer base: "Can you imagine, the biggest and best corporations in the Philippines are all working for you?"*

My JA Experience:

"In 1972 I joined JA in the Philippines. I never really enjoyed school, so I was looking for other things to do. I was interested in joining the JA program because it was an after-school activity—on a voluntary basis. On the first day, we organized the company and I was elected president. We were a very confident team, and we had a good group of mentors to help us organize the business. I was just 17 years old, and I think when you're exposed to entrepreneurship at a very young age, you learn a lot of things that the books don't teach you. I really believe I learned how to become an entrepreneur from that early JA experience.

"There's another important benefit of JA. Even though I was not strong in academics, my parents never said to me you're stupid, you can't do this, you can't do that. I was always being encouraged. I felt loved and inspired. But maybe some families can't do this for their children; they have to work so much, or they're struggling in other ways. So one of the main benefits of JA *could be* to give students the confidence and values that will help them the rest of their life—added to whatever their families can or cannot also give them.

"One of our mentors invited us to visit his office, and there were a lot of stock charts on the walls. I asked him, 'What is all this?' and he explained it a bit and gave me a book to read about stocks. That was my first exposure to the stock market, and it actually introduced me to what we're doing today. So I have to thank JA for actually getting me interested in the business I'm in today."

My Career / Business:

"In 1978 I was working for a computer company and getting married. I thought it was time to begin setting up my own business. I started with two of my best friends, and we each put in $3,000 to set up a company selling wallpaper, of all things. Over time we continued to add different products and services until we finally hit upon the stock brokerage business, which of course has become our most important activity. Ever since my exposure to the stock market back in JA, I had been interested in the market. I should add that after 39 years, I'm still with my two original partners who, believe it or not, were actually in the same JA program with me so many years ago.

"We set up the brokerage business in 1986, and because we were also in computers, we built the first software platform for stock trading in the Philippines. That was the beginning of the online stock trading business here. Our name was CitisecOnline, now shortened to COL. We were very early in Asia with online trading, and here in the Philippines we promote to the mass market, not the sophisticated investor. So we have to educate people about the stock market, teach financial literacy, and explain how the market works to individual Philippine investors. For our not-so-sophisticated customers we advocate long-term investments in our exclusive funds of blue-chip Filipino companies like SM Investments, Ayala Corporation, and Jollibee Foods. We point out that all the companies in the funds are run by families who will be around for generations. We like to say to our customer base: 'Can you imagine, the biggest and best corporations in the Philippines are all working for you?'

"When we started we had just 272 customers and today we open 20,000 to 30,000 new accounts a year. We've become the biggest online trading company in the Philippines. More than 95 percent of our customers are local Filipinos, and as I said we specialize in well-known Philippine stocks, not global stocks. We're very dedicated to the Philippine market, and still today less than 1 percent of the Philippine people are invested in the stock market—so we have a lot of room to grow."

My Advice to Young People:

- "First you have to build good relationships.
- "Second, you need to have integrity.
- "Third, you need to have the ability to evolve.

- "Fourth, you need to have strong financial literacy.
- "And finally you need to dream big—with real purpose."

Fernando Tamayo
Founder, Yaqua / Fighter Club, JA Alumnus, Peru

> *People said, "Are you crazy? Why are you doing that—selling water— then giving all the profits away?"*

My JA Experience:

"It started with my motivation in high school to learn about enterprise. I was 15 years old when my teacher said our school was going to participate in the JA Company Program national competition. About 15 of my friends and I met and named our company Innova Peru. I was made worker number three. I was not the CEO or CFO—I was just employee number three on the factory line, making our product. I had no leadership position, but I enjoyed it so much. Actually I was very shy in high school, and my JA experience got me into trying to stand out a little bit more. It worked. When the competition fair came, I was right there selling our product to everyone from our booth. We didn't win the JA Company Program competition—I think we were in the top 10—but the experience gave me the tools to make sure I could be successful in my future entrepreneurial activities.

"So yes, the JA program had a big impact on me. For example, I learned that everyone matters. I was only employee number three on the production line, but my contribution was important to the company. Second, I learned a lot about selling. I learned it's not just about the products, it's the value you give the products—and the story you use to present it to the customer."

My Career / Business:

"Today I have two businesses. Yaqua, our branded bottled water company, is the largest. It's a social enterprise company, selling over 300,000 bottles of water a month with 100 percent of the profits invested in infrastructure projects for clean water development in rural communities of Peru. The need is great. There are 8 million Peruvians without access to clean drinking water. I started Yaqua when I was 21 years old, but it took me two years to secure the investment money, the alliances, and the partnerships. People said, 'Are you crazy? Why are you doing that—selling water—then giving all the profits away?' Anyway, this is my first and biggest business. I'm very proud of what we are doing, and it's going very well. Last year I started a second social enterprise business called Fighter Club. My cofounder is Jonathan Maicelo, the Latin American lightweight champion, and we have a partnership with Everlast, the world's leading boxing equipment company. Fighter Club is a chain of training gyms for young people who live in vulnerable communities and are in danger of becoming drug dealers and criminals. We give them scholarships to train in boxing and the martial arts to give them the personality and character to say no to drugs and a life of crime."

My Advice to Young People:

- "First, live the problem you want to solve. Some people want to start a social enterprise, but they don't necessarily understand the problem they want to tackle. I always say, for example, if you want to help people who are blind, you should at least try living one day being blind yourself. This will give you more commitment and more understanding of the problem. So, live the problem you want to solve.
- "The second advice is—don't take too seriously all the negative responses you may get to your ideas. For example, many people told me my idea could not work and would just mess up the bottled water market in Peru. It's good to remember, we went to the moon after a thousand years of people saying it could never happen."

JA ALUMNI INTERVIEW

Tang Keng Hong
Founder, ImageFarm Productions, JA Alumnus, Malaysia

> *Of course you have to love what you do, but you also have to make sure that what you love is going to add value to your work or to your product.*

My JA Experience:

"I was in the pioneer batch when JA started in Malaysia in 1991. Actually, when I signed up for the JA program, I had no idea what I was getting into. But I said, 'Hey, here's a chance to learn how to run a business.' It was kind of cool really. So that's how I got into it. I was 18 at the time.

"Before the JA program, my English was not very good. I had all my schooling in Chinese, but in the JA program we had to speak English during our presentations and with the outside mentors. So the first benefit was that my English improved. The other important benefit was that it really boosted my confidence level. Suddenly we were learning a lot of things about business that our peers at school didn't know. It gave us a confidence level we didn't have before. And there's one more thing that maybe should be off the record, but I also met my wife in the JA program. So that is another reason why I have such good memories of JA.

"We still have contact today with JA Malaysia because ImageFarm, our production company, does a documentary video for them every year. JA has offices in both Kuala Lumpur and Penang, where my company is located—so we stay in touch frequently."

My Career / Business:

"I was always interested in photography and creating beautiful visual images. I started making money out of my camera at 13. If we had some school or family activity, I would take my camera and start clicking away. I would print the photos myself and sell them for a little money to the people who attended. So after graduating from the University of Malaysia, I decided to give photography a shot. I became a commercial photographer in 1998. But by 2001, along with a partner, I decided to go into my current business of video production. From day one I wanted to do premium video production because that's what I love. Photography, video, and video production is the passion of my life. Today we do professional video production for big companies and governments around Asia and TV documentaries for Asian and European broadcasters. The business is good, and I will continue to do this for the foreseeable future—always helped by the confidence I learned so many years ago in JA."

My Advice to Young People:

- "First and foremost is to do what you love. Don't think about money first—do what you love to do and the money will come later.
- "Second, of course you have to love what you do, but you also have to make sure that what you love is going to add value to your work or to your product.
- "Also you need to have a very clear direction of what you want to do. Sometimes it's not practical to have the perfect idea or a very specific plan from day one. That's very difficult—but nonetheless you have to stay true to your overall direction and be very persistent about that.
- "Finally, don't fear failure. As they say, failure is the mother of success, so you need to keep on trying. It's OK to make mistakes and take some calculated risks. Just keep on trying."

Lars Johansen

Founder, Unicus SA, JA Alumnus, Sweden / Norway

> *In terms of national economics, it's a no-brainer. For every autistic person we can employ, society saves about 12 million Norwegian kroner, almost $2 million.*

My JA Experience:

"I joined the JA program in high school in Sweden. I live in Norway now, but I'm actually Swedish. In the program my high school classmates and I started a trading company, importing goods, which we sold to friends and family. It was quite a simple company, but it gave us the best possible insight on how to run a business. We learned how to handle revenues, costs, capital expenses, and come up with a profit at the end. I was intrigued by the JA program, and I found it very interesting and practical.

"I always thought I might start my own company someday, but first I went to do my military service, next I got a job, and then I went to the university. The real impact the JA program had on me, that I know now but did not understand then, was that it actually lowered the bar for starting a company. After being in JA I never thought of starting a company as being such a complicated thing. I know that many people believe starting a company is so complicated—almost like brain surgery. But in the JA program, I saw I was able to do it, I saw it was fun, and I saw it was not so complicated really. Certainly in this way, JA has had a great impact on me."

My Career / Business:

"After school I worked in finance for 10 years. I was in equity sales, kind of a Wall Street job, in Norway. It was very interesting, but after 10 years I was really done with it. I was thinking what to do next when I heard about a Danish company that was the first in the world to combine autism and the software testing industry. I got so inspired by that story that I decided to try it myself in Norway. So I started my company Unicus, Latin for unique, in Norway, and we expanded to Sweden just last year. The idea, or DNA if you will, behind the company is to employ people with autism. That is, to employ autistic people and get them contract jobs in the software testing industry. So we are actually an IT company which happens to employ people with autism.

"The rationale for our approach is twofold: First and most important is that autistic people have strong competitive advantages in software testing. Autism gives them special skills and characteristics for these jobs. They are very logical thinkers, analytical thinkers, they see details that others may not see, and they have strong pattern recognition skills. These are all really good skills for software testing. They are also very honest. They don't lie, which of course is a really good trait for any employee. Because our employees have these unique skills and characteristics, our clients keep coming back to buy our services.

"The other reason behind our business is to give employment to people with autism because they have difficulties in the ordinary job market. This is the social part of our business. In terms of national economics, it's a no-brainer. The calculation is that for every autistic person we can employ, society saves about 12 million Norwegian kroner, almost $2 million. For example, during their adult life, instead of paying people to stay at home and do nothing, our employees work, provide for themselves, and of course they pay taxes. There are also secondary savings on healthcare and other things, so it's a no-brainer economically. If you take people who are not able to participate in the ordinary workforce, and provide them with work they can do, it's good for them and good for the country.

"Of course we are still a small company, with offices in Oslo and Stockholm. We started in 2008 and have made a profit every year, except for a small deficit in 2012, so our business and financial record are good. This year we have 25 employees, and 22 of them have autism. So the business has been progressing well for 10 years. We hope to expand throughout the EU with our good track record. We certainly have proof of concept—we have proved the concept works, we can make a profit at it, and it provides a good service and economic return for the country."

My Advice to Young People:

- "I tell young people to really follow their interest. That's a cliché maybe, but I tell them that because the world is changing so rapidly. It's about being able to catch up, stay on top of things, and find out what's coming to fulfill your interest.

- "Second, focus on your competitive advantage. We learned that in our business. As I mentioned, people with autism have a strong competitive advantage and you should take special advantage of your competitive advantage whatever it is.

- "Finally, young people already have one big competitive advantage—they are not bound by conservative thinking. They can and should be innovative, and even destructive in their thinking. For this I like to quote Einstein: "We can't solve the problems by using the same kind of thinking that created the problems." We need new ways to solve old problems, and young people really have an advantage in doing that."

CHAPTER 3

High-Speed Innovation

The Necessity to Invent, the Freedom to Act

The DryWash process was invented because I felt guilty wasting that much water and electricity . . . just washing one car.

LITO RODRIGUEZ, Founder, DryWash

High-speed Innovation is the entrepreneur's secret weapon—and it's virtually free. In today's world you cannot find a better and cheaper way to give your start-up an enormous competitive advantage. So what exactly is it? There are two golden rules for high-speed innovation: First you and your people must see innovation as an absolute necessity, and second, there must be a high sense of urgency to take actions and implement new ideas. We call it the *necessity to invent* and the *freedom to act*.

Innovative action can work wonders in all industries, and certainly those in the booming "green economy." Take Lito Rodriguez, Brazil's young car wash king, who figured out how to wash cars without a drop of water, and with a 99.5 percent reduction in electricity used per vehicle. He became disgusted with wasting freshwater and electricity in his traditional car wash facility: "I didn't really have to be a chemist to create this product—which was lucky since I failed chemistry in school! The most important thing I discovered is that water doesn't wash anything. Friction cleans things, not water. The DryWash process is based on that principle. I also learned that if you really feel the need to improve, if you do a lot of experiments, and work at it seven days a week, you will eventually come up with a better way." With over 500 locations in Brazil and a backlog of 14,000 franchise applications from around the globe, Rodriguez certainly did that. And in a world where many countries are facing freshwater shortages, he also proved that a small, relentlessly pursued invention in a car wash in São Paulo can help solve a very big problem around the world.

We all know that necessity is the mother of invention and that more gets done in a day of crisis than a month of complacency. The trick then is to learn how to keep this sense of urgency alive in your business— so that innovation becomes a necessity, and everyone has the freedom to act, and act quickly. High-speed innovation could be your secret weapon too. And why not? All it takes is feeling the necessity to do it better—and the freedom to do it faster.

THE TWO GOLDEN RULES OF HIGH-SPEED INNOVATION

Failure is an option here. If things are not
failing, you are not innovating enough.

ELON MUSK, Zip2, XCom, PayPal, Tesla, SpaceX, Solar City, Hyperloop

By now you may be saying, "My business idea is pretty normal, perhaps even a bit mundane. Who is going to feel such a great need for speed or innovation in my business? Where's our feeling of necessity and sense of urgency going to come from?"

Elon Musk would be a great person to answer that question. He creates new companies the way other people create new products. Look at the lineup of companies above—and he's only 46 years old. His famous explanation on why he keeps creating new products and new companies is that one day in the shower, many years ago, he asked himself what are the five things that would be most likely to affect humanity in a positive way. He came up with his list (the Internet, sustainable energy, space exploration, artificial intelligence, and rewriting human genetics), and decided to try his hand at each. As of today, he's developed companies around three of the five. This could be labeled the big picture method of coming up with ideas, but it contains some very practical tips about being innovative and action oriented. Especially when Musk also says the number one reason he has been successful is that he "works a lot." Combine these two activities, imagining what's needed to make things better and working a lot to get them done—and you end up with the winning combination of innovative thinking and taking a lot of action. And then throw in Musk's other idea, from the quote above, that some failure along the way is a necessary part of the process—and you have a perfect definition of what we like to call high-speed innovation.

Unfortunately, there's no free lunch on instilling the idea that high-speed innovation is a necessity in business—any business. So the impetus for it has to come from you, the founder. You have to build it into your business. It comes from your own perceptions of the challenges you face and what needs to be done to succeed. Regardless of your circumstance, whatever your business, doing it better and doing it faster has to be made into an exhilarating race against time. Beating your customers' expectations and beating the competition is a noble challenge for any company. Even beating your own personal best can be thrilling—and sometimes even more important than beating the next guy. For sure, you can't just sit around hoping something big and exciting happens to your business. Fortunately, you *can* make it happen. You absolutely *have* to make it happen if you expect your company and your people to respond with great speed and great ideas.

Akio Morita, the great founder of Sony, liked to say: "Taking innovative action is the entrepreneur's secret weapon . . . and the best thing about it is it's free!" He was right. Just consider this: A landmark study of California companies found that the cost of innovation, as measured by new products and patents, is an astounding 24 times greater at large companies than small companies. If you're the CEO of a giant bureaucracy, this statistic could keep you awake nights. If you're a start-up entrepreneur, it's the best news you'll ever hear. Few people today need statistics to convince them that speed and creativity are major competitive factors in our global economy. And even fewer would disagree that young, entrepreneurial companies can, and regularly do, beat the socks off their larger competitors. The number one reason: they are both faster and more innovative.

The question, then, is: How do you do that? What is it really that makes entrepreneurs and their start-ups so fast moving and innovative?

And can you keep it alive as your company moves along its life cycle—getting bigger and more bureaucratic year after year? These are terribly important things to know—we might call them the "genetic mutations" of the entrepreneurial company. Fortunately, unlike decoding the human genome, entrepreneurial practices are not so complicated. At the heart of all high-speed innovation are just two golden rules: feeling the necessity to invent and having the freedom to act.

THE NECESSITY TO INVENT

We did it because we believed we had to.

LARRY HILLBLOM, Cofounder, DHL

Remember this bit of old-fashioned wisdom: *Mater artium necessitas?* If your Latin is a bit rusty, it means "Necessity is the mother of invention." And we've all been saying it since the time of Caesar—because it's absolutely true. History is replete with evidence that anyone can be innovative if their life depends on it. And one of the greatest illustrations of this in the world of business is the amazing story of Larry Hillblom.

He was a young law student in Northern California who worked as a freelance courier on weekends. At the time there were no courier companies. Hand delivering time-sensitive documents, cash, traveler's checks, and even vaccines around the world was an individual and disorganized business. It had been done that way for decades. For Hillblom, being a courier was a great way to spend a weekend. He got a lot of studying done and pocketed a few bucks. On his long flights across the Pacific, he began to wonder why no company provided this valuable service. On one of his 15-hour trips to Asia he scratched out an idea to create an international courier company. He got two of his buddies, who were also freelance couriers, to join him. They called it DHL (for Dalsey, Hillblom, and Lynn), and they literally invented an industry.*

Hillblom quickly learned that creating a DHL global network was an absolute necessity to getting the business up and running. An office

---

* DHL was founded as a worldwide courier business in 1969—Fed Ex was founded initially as a domestic U.S. courier business two years later in 1971.

here or there wouldn't be very interesting to Bank of America and Deutsche Bank or Toyota and IBM. This meant that DHL would have to create a worldwide network of offices—overnight. But how could three freelance couriers with no business experience and no money possibly do this? Hillblom told me that they pulled it off for one reason only: "We did it because we believed we had to. No network, no business. And we didn't know there was any other way than bootstrapping it, which was lucky for us. If we had spent our time writing business plans, lining up bank financing, and using headhunters in 50 countries, there would be no DHL today." And what a network they built! They opened an amazing 120 country offices in the first 10 years of DHL's existence—still the fastest international expansion of any company in history!

They started in Asia. Their method was pure *mater artium necessitas*. On every courier trip each of them took, they signed up anybody they could find to be their local partner. They weren't too discriminating. They got a taxi driver at the Sydney airport, the manager of an A&W Root Beer stand in Malaysia, a toy salesman in Hong Kong, and so on. There were no plans or systems or procedures, and zero external financing. Handshakes sealed all the deals. Thus was born the worldwide network of DHL partners and mini-entrepreneurs.

Larry Hillblom (Dalsey and Lynn opted out early) did indeed create quite a network, without resources or experience, because he believed he had to. By the time of his early, mysterious death,* he had created a $3 billion company with 40,000 jobs, spanning the globe. These things can happen when you, and your start-up team, truly feel the necessity to invent. To make sure the spirit of *mater artium necessitas* is alive and well in your start-up team, and stays alive as your business grows, here are four key practices to keep in mind:

- **Feeling the Heat of Necessity.** It's hard to beat great stories like DHL's, or for that matter, the story of the six Minnesota miners who in 1906 faced bankruptcy after putting their life savings

---

* Larry Hillblom was killed several years ago while flying his own plane. It disappeared without a trace into the Pacific Ocean near his home on the island of Saipan. Larry shunned publicity all his life and became a virtual recluse by the time he was 40. He died as he lived—doing his own thing in his own way. I only met him twice, but like everyone who knew him, I was fascinated by this rebellious business innovator.

into a "worthless" gravel pit. They hoped it would yield valuable minerals, but all they could find was sand. They tried to figure out what to do with all the sand they now owned. Out of desperation they came up with the creative product idea of gluing sand onto paper to smooth out metal and wood objects. They called their invention sandpaper—the first product of the great 3M Company—and the rest is history. Facing the necessity to invent is a lesson 3M has never forgotten. Product innovation remains its single corporate value—and it has the highest ratio of new product revenue (around 30 percent) of any big company in the world. By the way, 3M says its three biggest sources of new product ideas are accidents, failures, and mistakes—not exactly the kind of things taught at business school.

Innovative companies like DryWash, Tesla, SpaceX, DHL, and 3M all know that "feeling the heat of necessity" is a big part of keeping their creativity alive. There are many things you can do: Make it a visible strategy to employees. Use creativity training, innovation newsletters, suggestion programs—whatever you can to keep the idea alive throughout the company. Ensure everyone has face time with customers to feel some personal heat from the people who pay their salary. The ultimate "feeling the heat" moment may come from employees understanding that their job, and the company's survival, are on the line every day.

■ **Create Crisis and Urgency.** Akio Morita, the founder of Sony, also said, "A little crisis is a good thing." And so it is. Everyone knows that more gets done in a day of crisis than a month of complacency. But how will you get this notion embedded in your future organization? Are there any positive ways to create a little crisis and a lot of urgency?

Creating a sense of crisis and urgency can be done most powerfully by that old-fashioned technique of leading by personal example. The best example I've ever seen is my longtime acquaintance up north, Jimmy Pattison, the founder and sole owner of The Jim Pattison Group. With over US$7 billion in revenues and 33,000 employees, it's Canada's second largest privately owned company. As you might guess, Pattison has a knack for getting people's attention.

The first time I addressed his company conference was in beautiful British Columbia. Upon my arrival at the site, I noticed the schedule showed I was to open the conference the next morning—at the bewitching hour of 7 a.m. At dinner that night, to make sure it wasn't a misprint, I asked Jimmy if 7 a.m. was really the starting time. He said matter-of-factly, "Yes we like to start all our meetings by 7. And by the way, Larry, would you mind showing up a little early, because I really don't like to start late." So I got to the conference room by 6:30 the next morning and noticed everyone was already seated waiting for the conference—and my address—to begin. Jimmy grabbed my arm and walked me toward the stage, saying, "I think everyone's here, so let's just start now." I cleared my throat, took a quick gulp of water, and started presenting to the 300 managers in the audience. I glanced at my watch. It was 6:31 a.m., and The Jim Pattison Group annual conference was rolling! I'll never forget it as long as I live. And that's the point, of course. It's the Pattison way of sending a powerful message.

There are other ways to create a little crisis and a lot of urgency: Establish real deadlines and stick to them. Make it a really big deal if a good customer is lost. Ditto for product/service complaints. Finally make certain all your employees know you are dead serious about making the business a success. The trick is to dole out these messages in small, regular doses. The entrepreneurial message is clear—a little crisis a day keeps complacency away.

■ **Do Something, Anything, Better Each Day.** Thomas Edison, still the all-time record holder of U.S. patents and the founder of scores of companies, was famous for this pearl of wisdom: "Invention is 10 percent inspiration and 90 percent perspiration." So what can you do to make sure the "perspiration level" in your future business is high? For starters, you and every employee you hire have to believe that the most important task you have every day is to find a better way to do the job. It's called continuous improvement in human performance—and it's one of the most visible differences in behavior between the hungry entrepreneur trying to survive and the complacent bureaucrat counting the days till retirement.

For a dramatic example of this behavior, let's take a final look at Elon Musk. He's raised the bar on "doing something better each day"—he's creating a new company every few years. Look at the string of great, futuristic companies he's founded in just two decades: Zip2, X.com, PayPal, Tesla, SpaceX, SolarCity, and Hyperloop. That's seven successful companies in just 20 years. This serial innovator was so eager to start creating companies, he left Stanford's PhD program in applied physics after just two days of classes to start his first company—and he's never looked back. Elon Musk has the practice of "doing something, anything, better each day" down pat.

How can you get every employee to come to work every day thinking, "What can I do today a little bit better than yesterday?" First, get this notion into every job description. Then put real teeth into it and make it part of everyone's performance goals. You could even run a half-day workshop on why it's critical and provide simple examples of what you want people to do. Remember, if every employee comes to work every day and actually improves something in their work area, you are talking about a miracle in company-wide improvements. So try it. It may end up being the biggest competitive advantage of your future business.

THE FREEDOM TO ACT

The trick is to get to the finish line first.

ED PENHOET, Founder, Chiron Corporation

Innovation without action might get you a Nobel prize, but it won't get you a customer. Most entrepreneurs agree that in today's world, fast action is even more important than innovation. The biotech industry is a perfect place to learn about this. And Chiron Corporation's founder/ CEO, Dr. Edward Penhoet, is the perfect entrepreneurial leader to ask. Some 25 years after its founding, Chiron had grown to be one of the big winners in the biotech race. Its first blockbuster product, which put it on the map, was the hepatitis B vaccine—now estimated to have prevented millions of cases of hepatitis and hundreds of thousands of deaths. It also created products for the treatment of kidney cancer and melanoma, pediatric vaccines, and blood tests for HIV and hepatitis. It became the number three biotech firm in the world—after Genentech and Amgen—with about $2 billion in revenues and healthy profits. It's market value had risen to some $9 billion—making it a charter member of that elite family of biotech firms that produced big products and big profits. With such impressive numbers, it got gobbled up by Novartis, the giant Swiss pharmaceutical firm—and Chiron's remarkable entrepreneurial journey ended. Even so, the entrepreneurial lessons from Chiron are profound and worth recounting here.

Ed Penhoet and I were both speakers at a conference in San Diego. As I listened to this articulate scientist/entrepreneur, with PhDs in both biology and chemistry, I knew I had to interview him. A couple of months later, I went to Emeryville, California, Chiron's headquarters, for a tour of its famous labs and a long interview in Penhoet's office. I didn't quite know what to expect, but I had assumed, given the incredibly high-tech nature of the biotech industry, success would depend primarily on how smart your scientists are.

It turned out that I was in for a big surprise: "We're all smart. In our field we've already been preselected, in the sense that by the time you get to people who have PhDs from major institutions like Harvard, UC Berkeley, or UCSF, it's a given that they're smart. In this group, there are very few people who are really very much smarter than the rest— damn few. In the beginning it was just a race. We all knew what had to be done. We had to be able to hit the ground running and stick with it. Everyone is now talking all about speed, right? Well, certainly in biotech . . . the trick is to get to the finish line first."

Who would have imagined that speed is a more critical competitive advantage than IQ in the ultimate high-tech business of biogenetics? If high-speed action is a defining advantage even in biotech, what are the odds that it will also be a critical competitive factor in your business? If you're thinking about a thousand to one, you're probably right on the mark. So how are you going to make that happen? To create such a bias for action, your people have to have the freedom to act, the freedom to experiment, and the freedom to make mistakes. It's not any more complicated than that. Here are three proven ways to get you started.

■ **Freeing the Genius of the Average Worker.** Soichiro Honda was never part of the blue-blood establishment in Japanese industry. The son of a blacksmith, he started off as a mechanic and became a race car driver, before he designed and made one of the world's all-time great products, the Honda scooter. With just a third-grade education, he was the original blue-collar "automobile man's man." And he believed that the best ideas in the company came from the people who actually made the cars. Honda called it the "genius of the average worker." Tapping this genius was the reason for Honda's famous employee suggestion program, which still today produces a staggering 15,000 suggestions a month—all of which are read, evaluated, and acted on within 30 days.

As mentioned earlier, I got the inside scoop on this great entrepreneur when I met and interviewed Tetsuo Chino at Honda's headquarters in Tokyo. Chino was the former president of Honda USA and grew up in the car business with Mr. Honda. Chino told me wonderful stories of how Honda got on with the rank and file: "Honda initiated many policies and actions that endeared him to the average workers: He built three Honda plants in Japan just for handicapped workers. The employees really appreciated that. Also, he had a very unusual rule for a Japanese company—neither he nor any top executives could have any of their relatives working in the company. He said he didn't want a dynasty because it would be unfair to the rest of the employees. Mr. Honda really believed the genius of the company was in the workers. And they knew that he trusted them. This was very much appreciated by the employees, and it was very unusual in big Japanese companies."

So who will be the geniuses of your company? Who will you turn to for good ideas, and who will you encourage to take action on those ideas? It should be your average workers if you apply the moral of the Honda story: Free the genius of your average workers, and you will create a miracle in your company—a miracle of good ideas and actions.

■ **Action with Customers, Products, and Inside Your Organization.** Where should you aim your innovative actions? The entrepreneurial answer would be, on the core of what keeps you competitive. And that, of course, leads us right back to customers and products. You'll never go wrong by taking actions to improve your products and deliver better services to your customers.

Actions directed at the internal workings of your business are surefire winners also. This covers actions to improve the key processes of the enterprise such as hiring, employee development, financial and accounting systems, overall administrative efficiency, IT systems, cost control, purchasing, legal, etc.

It really all boils down to taking action on the things that make or break the company. Kathy Prasnicki Lehne, a soft-spoken entrepreneur from East Texas, learned this on day one in the "tough man's business" of wholesaling and delivering gasoline. She founded Sun Coast Resources at age 23, with just $2,000. She says: "From the beginning, the company was driven by meeting challenges with innovative solutions. Every day I have to find little things to improve and ways to save time and money. It's the only way to win in a 3 percent margin business." And win she does. Sun Coast Resources, with $1.8 billion in sales, has become the largest distributor of gasoline in the state of Texas. And Kathy, who plays high-stakes poker in her spare time, is now the proud founder and CEO of the largest woman-owned company in all of Texas.

Actually, there's a long list of recommended actions for improving organizational efficiency: one page only e-mails/memos, simplified forms, 24-hour response time to complaints, tighter supply chains, fewer levels of management, etc. But the all-time winning tip comes from Robert O'Brien, the president of Carteret Bank in New Jersey. To cut down on the seemingly endless meetings in the bank, he had all the chairs removed from all the conference rooms throughout the bank. He told me: "Larry, it was a miracle. Today we have very few meetings, and they never last more than five minutes. Our people loved to sit for hours in those big, comfortable leather chairs—but they just hate stand-up meetings." A little extreme, perhaps, but just the kind of eye-catching action you may need to improve "the little things" inside your own company.

■ **Battling Bureaucracy.** Bureaucracy wouldn't seem to be a problem for entrepreneurs and their start-up companies. But consider this: If you are successful, and start growing bigger and bigger—and begin drowning in bureaucratic policies and practices—wouldn't it be better to start off on the right foot by not letting bureaucracy get started in the first place? We call it "battling bureaucracy" from day one.

To learn how the battle against bureaucracy can be won, there's no better role model than Norman Brinker, who single-handedly invented the full-service chain restaurant business in the United States. He did it all: from serving burgers at Jack in the Box, to being the chairman of giant Burger King, to creating one famous chain after another—Steak and Ale, Bennigan's, Romano's Macaroni Grill, and his flagship brand, Chili's Grill & Bar. Along the way Brinker became a living legend in the restaurant business and rewrote the book for battling bureaucracy in the food service industry. A few years ago I had the pleasure of meeting and talking at length with Brinker, in Singapore of all places. Here's Norm Brinker's proven recipe for battling bureaucracy:

- **It's a Lifelong Challenge.** "The larger you get, the harder it becomes. Imagine changing one menu item at 30,000 McDonald's locations."
- **Direct Customer Feedback Beats Reams of Market Research.** "I waited for people to come out of our restaurants and asked them: 'How was it? Is this place any good?' This is how you get great customer feedback in the restaurant business."
- **Direct Employee Feedback Beats Personnel Surveys.** "We spent a lot of time just talking to our people. I liked to wander into someone's area and explore any new idea on their mind."
- **Decentralized Action Taking Always Beats Corporate Control.** "Cutting out all the red tape and pushing decision making down to the lowest possible level is the best answer."
- **Conduct Annual Bureaucracy Audits.** "Just as companies have annual financial audits, you need an annual 'bureaucracy audit' to weed out unnecessary and outdated procedures and forms."
- **Don't Become Part of the Problem.** "Whenever someone suggests a new procedure, a new committee, or another system, ask yourself: 'How exactly is this going to contribute to

beating the competition?' If you can't come up with a clear, convincing answer, kill the new idea."

We'll close the chapter on "High-Speed Innovation" by taking another look at the biggest, hottest, and most hi-tech entrepreneurial sector of all—the biotechnology industry—which operates in a race against time with an insatiable need for innovation.

CHANGING THE WORLD WITH A GOOD IDEA

We are studying the most sacred information that exists.
The information that goes into designing you.

KÁRI STEFÁNSSON, Founder, deCODE Genetics

In 1980 there was not one biotech company in the world. Late in that year the United States Supreme Court ruled that genetically engineered organisms are patentable—and one of history's most important, fastest growing entrepreneurial industries was born. Today there are over 3,000 biotech firms around the globe, with a total market value approaching $1 trillion, and total revenue of $150 billion. The pioneers of the industry have been companies no one had even heard of 25 years ago. Companies like Genentech, Amgen, Chiron—and now deCODE Genetics, a fabulously interesting and innovative member of today's biotech elite, founded in that faraway Viking land called Iceland.*

One of the dazzling stars of this dazzling industry is Dr. Kári Stefánsson, the founder and CEO of deCODE Genetics. I had the pleasure of doing two long interviews with him in Reykjavik, over a very cold January weekend. He's progressed from young Harvard Medical School professor, to world-class entrepreneur, to Iceland's richest and most famous man—in just the last two decades. Here's Stefánsson's own story on how it all started: "I was a professor at the Harvard Medical School studying the genetics of multiple sclerosis when I first started to see the confluence of two very important things. First was the technology being produced to allow one to study genetics in a systematic

---

* In 2012 deCODE Genetics was acquired by Amgen, the world's largest biotech firm. By all accounts the acquisition has been quite successful—with deCODE operating independently and Kári Stefánsson remaining as CEO.

manner. Second, I began to think about the incredibly important qualities of the Icelandic nation that could be mined once this technology was in Iceland. So I began to sense the danger that foreign companies and universities would go to Iceland and do "helicopter science." By that I mean transporting the material abroad from Iceland for the studies. So I looked at the possibility of setting up a facility in Iceland. I put together a business plan, we raised enough money to start the company, mostly from the government, and we started up in the fall of 1996."

By way of context, Iceland, a country with a grand total of 270,000 people, has the most homogenous population in the world. It's made up entirely of the original Vikings from Norway and a few Irish slaves they brought with them in the ninth century. There has been virtually no new migration into Iceland since then. (Visiting in January gave me a clue as to why!) It's the only country in the world where the phone books are listed by people's first names, as there are too few last names in the population. This twist of history, near total homogeneity in the country, is at the heart of Iceland's greatest entrepreneurial company. As the genealogy is incredibly well documented all the way back to 874 AD, Iceland is a geneticist's dream laboratory. deCODE Genetics was founded on the premise that the only way to discover the genetic basis of complex diseases like cancer, Alzheimer's, schizophrenia, and multiple sclerosis is by finding the genetic mutations in homogeneous populations, thereby eliminating the wide genetic variability found among different racial and ethnic groups. Only by comparing the DNA of people with the particular disease to very similar people who don't have the disease can we hope to isolate the disease-causing genetic mutations. Iceland is by far the best place in the world to do this.

The results have been spectacular. As confirmation, deCODE Genetics and its founder have received extraordinary press. Stefánsson has actually achieved what few scientists ever will—three blockbuster stories on the front page of the world's most important paper, the *New York Times*. Likewise, a *Wall Street Journal* headline read: "If This Man Is Right, Medicine's Future Lies in Iceland's Past." And the *Financial Times* in London reported: "Iceland Cashes in on Its Viking Gene Bank." The reason for all this unprecedented blue-chip press coverage is that the medical breakthroughs just keep coming from deCODE Genetics. Completely new genetic markers have already been discovered for schizophrenia, Alzheimer's disease, multiple sclerosis, and various cancers.

Stefánsson's own quote from our interview showcases his personal dazzle and passion: "We are studying the most sacred information that exists. The information that goes into designing you. It is by far the most powerful way of looking for new knowledge in medicine, and it has worked wonders for us. We are convinced this is going to be the mechanism whereby we institute a new revolution in medicine." That's it. Kári Stefánsson came up with a good idea, went for it—and changed the world. And so can you.

The following Application at the end of the book is designed to record your plans for increasing innovation, speeding up action, and battling bureaucracy. Enjoy!

Application 9: CREATING HIGH-SPEED INNOVATION

JA ALUMNI INTERVIEW

Sanjay Gupta
Chief Medical Correspondent—CNN, Associate Chief of Neurosurgery, Emory University School of Medicine, JA Alumnus, Michigan, USA

Finally, if you feel good about what you're doing, and you're helping your fellow man at the same time, everyone benefits.

My JA Experience:

"JA was a very formative experience for me, and I haven't had a chance to talk about it. I was living in a small town in southeastern Michigan. My parents were engineers in the automotive industry. They were immigrants to this country, sort of entrepreneurial people, in search of economic and educational opportunities. My mom first heard about JA through her colleagues at work, and she brought home some information about it. This was the first spark of interest. I was really at a stage where I didn't know what I was going to do in the future, but there was something about the entrepreneurial and collaborative aspects of JA that were quite attractive to me. I went to a very small school, so finding like-minded people was challenging and broadening the ocean a bit was interesting. So that was how I got into it initially.

"I did two and a half years of JA. We had a couple of JA Company Program businesses and products over that time. One I remember well was using the school yearbook, with everyone's picture in it. In what I can only describe as really rudimentary photography, with a little bit of editing, we took pictures of the student pictures in the yearbook and then adorned them as cards to essentially sell to the families of the kids who were just finishing school. So we were selling those cards to parents, then other people wanted some, and we took orders for those also, and ultimately that was the business. I was voted the Outstanding Young Businessman for the JA region that year. There was a competition where you presented your product and sales data to three businesspeople, and I won the award. My mom still has that trophy somewhere.

"There were a lot of takeaways from my experience in JA. One of the more subjective things was that socially it was a very good experience for me. I had been living a more insular life, educationally certainly. And I think it was good to be around more people. You know when you come from a small town, your eyes get opened to the fact that there are other people who have some of the same interests as you.

"There are other things that are more tangible. One that I still use to some degree even as a doctor is that people are more likely to do something that makes their loved one happy, more so than themselves. In healthcare decisions, for example, people are more likely to encourage their loved ones to get screened or tested than they are to have the procedure for themselves. Back then to JA with the photography product, it was essentially parents who wanted to do this thing for their child, to have the nice adornment card. And I remember thinking you really have to understand who your customer is, and that they're buying it for someone else. So everything we said, our sales pitch, our promotion, had to reflect that.

"Another takeaway, which is also reflective of medicine, is that technology should play an additive role, not just make existing structures more efficient. Back to JA, we could've taken that yearbook picture and just photocopied it and said to parents, here's 100 copies of your kid's picture for this price. But they could have done that themselves. But, because we were editing it and adding personalized features, our simple technology was adding value to the cards that they couldn't automatically get themselves. We talked a lot about this in the JA Company—back in the tenth or eleventh grade. What is the real value of this product, and why would anyone pay money for this thing? That's a pretty significant lesson even if you're not an entrepreneur. Certainly as a doctor, I have to ask, why am I ordering this test, recommending this procedure? What is the value really to the overall care of the patient? Same question—just a different time frame and circumstance. So, for me, the value of JA is obvious—it did a lot for me."

My Career / Business:

Author's note: Because Sanjay's career is so well documented elsewhere, as the globe-trotting, Emmy Award–winning medical correspondent for CNN, I used our interview time and the space here to record his thoughts on being a "JA kid" and his career advice to young people.

My Advice to Young People:

- "Well, this has become a more personal question now that I have three daughters of my own. But I think that some of the basic advice I received still holds up today. That is, you really need to find something you love because you will be much more likely to do it and you will also be more successful at it. Your passion will actually help you find your path forward—and make your life and career as meaningful as possible.
- "Also, the jobs by which you may measure your aspirations today are changing so fast. I'm not saying anything novel here, but the jobs that my kids will want probably don't even exist yet. That can be a little frightening, but I think overall it's a good thing because

you will really have the chance to create the career or job that you are most likely to find meaningful and joyful.

- "I don't want to speak in platitudes, but I must say that what's happening in the world today, the big global issues as well as smaller regional issues, is really important. And we see over and over again that everybody has a role to play. So figuring out what your role is should also drive your thinking about your future. It doesn't need to be a big, stressful thing like 'I have to be out there curing cancer' or 'I have to be negotiating peace in the Middle East.' But everyone can have some impact on the world, and keeping that in mind, as well as how you want to be remembered in terms of your impact, is really important.

- "Finally, if you feel good about what you're doing, and you're helping your fellow man at the same time, everyone benefits. I think that's why the human species has been able to survive and thrive, because ultimately it's been about reciprocal altruism as opposed to simply rugged individualism. I believe it's a good thing for young people to keep this in mind."

JA ALUMNI INTERVIEW

David Darmanin
Founder and CEO, Hotjar, JA Alumnus, Malta

> *We are closing in on 11,000 customers, with 300,000 sites using Hotjar. So yes, we are one of the fastest growing digital companies in the world today.*

My JA Experience:
"I am a living, walking advertisement for JA. Since I was young I always had the desire to build something, sell it, and make a profit. That is the concept, right? But in Malta everything was career based. Even at the age of 12 you're given a survey, you answer some

questions, and based upon what you say, you're told what you are most likely to be: a lawyer, a doctor, whatever. For some reason they said I was on the road to be a lawyer.

"Now fast-forward a few years. I was 15, had made it into a college, and still had this bug in me to build and create something of value and profit from it. Then I heard about the JA program. I said this is fantastic. I'd love to do this. Keep in mind that I had already committed myself to the law, which was coming two years down the road. And I came from a family background where you play it safe in life, you get the salary, you're loyal to the company, and everyone's happy. But to make a long story short, I participated in the program and loved it. It was completely new to me. Basically it was an intense crash course in business. It put me on a particular path and triggered certain events in my life—and we were lucky. We won the JA Company competition in Malta and went on to win the JA Company of the Year award for all of Europe in 1998. That was also the first opportunity I had to compete with other students and companies from around the world. It was character forming for me. It was a wonderful experience.

"So my story began to take an entrepreneurial twist following my JA experience. Of course my family's views still had a bearing on me, and I ended up finishing my law degree, but I actually started a company while I was studying at the university. It was called Start-Up Malta and was a business competition at the university. Upon finishing my law degree and graduating from the university, I determined to become an entrepreneur and not practice law as a career. So as you see, the JA experience influenced everything. It was an awesome experience which changed me forever—yes, forever."

My Career / Business:

"After graduating, for a short time I worked for a Swedish software company, then moved into consulting to help other businesses use enterprise software. Soon the entrepreneur bug came back to me. I approached the best people I worked with in software and said: 'Listen, this software industry where we all work is terrible, it really sucks. So let's completely democratize it and disrupt the entire industry.' We started Hotjar to do exactly that.

"In my early exposure to the software industry, there was no way to measure whether what I was doing, building sites for clients, was working or not for them. Back then the way we measured client satis-faction was whether or not they paid you. Or they might be pleased if the site won an award for 'best website of the year.' I hated it that we couldn't measure our own work. So our idea at Hotjar was to build a very easy-to-use platform which would allow anyone from a Fortune 500 company down to student companies to very quickly and very cheaply understand how their site was being used. What are people clicking, what are they doing on the site, asking them for instant feed-back on what they liked or disliked, and why they left the site. The most basic information any client, large or small, needs to know. And we wanted to do this for a really low monthly cost, which any com-pany, big or small, could afford. Accomplishing this would fill a gaping need in the market, and would be a really big opportunity for us.

"That was our vision. It was a very ambitious plan to take very expensive tools and make them very cheap by changing the model of how you collect data. We introduced Hotjar as a premium trial ser-vice, and it just exploded. We got traction immediately from day one. After seven to eight months in this beta program, we had acquired a massive fan base. We had users from some of the biggest brands in the world, who loved it and started selling us internally and to other companies. It's been nonstop growth ever since. We are closing in on 11,000 customers, with 300,000 sites using Hotjar. So yes, we are one of the fastest growing digital companies in the world today."

My Advice to Young People:

■ "My final word would be, I can't thank JA enough. And my final advice would be, participate in JA yourself. Everything I learned back in JA still lives with me: The product quality aspect, the team-work aspect, the confidence building, everything. I attribute much of my success to that small step I took when I was young."

JA ALUMNI INTERVIEW

Eleonora Arifova

Founder, Fun Chulan Children's Art Studios Network,
JA Alumna, Russia

> *Thanks to JA I understood at an early stage that entrepreneurship would be my career path and way of living.*

My JA Experience:

"I grew up in the village of Bavly, Tatarstan, some 1,200 kilometers east of Moscow. I dreamed of freedom and independence since my childhood. I was interested in *making* a job rather than simply *taking* a job and was seeking possibilities to do what I liked and was passionate about. JA was key to boosting my desire and intention to become an entrepreneur, showing me what opportunities were possible and that setting up my own business was both feasible and doable. Participation in the JA Company Program played a vital role in teaching me the basics and skills required to become an entrepreneur. It also provided a step-by-step plan for implementing ideas, making decisions, solving problems, and working as a team. Most importantly, JA helped me understand that nothing is impossible and everything depends on me."

My Career / Business:

"Thanks to JA I understood at an early stage that entrepreneurship would be my career path and way of living. And it's been a highly rewarding and enjoyable life. My first business, launched after graduation from school, was inspired by my JA Company Program experience. It was engaged in the planning and organization of children's parties and special events. My entrepreneurial dream had become a reality, but I continued thinking about building a large network of children's creative centers.

"In 2010 I found the way to develop my idea and started the first children's art studio, named Fun Chulan. It was in a special space inside a shopping center where children, aged 3 to 14 could experiment with art while their parents went shopping. Setting up and running the new business was a challenge—it has taken a huge amount of hard work. But I had confidence in the potential of my business idea and the mission of the new enterprise to deliver engaging art experiences to children and help parents admire the creativity of their children. The last few years have brought even better than expected results. Currently Fun Chulan is an established brand with branches in eight cities plus a network of some 40 franchisees across Russia from St. Petersburg to Vladivostok.

All our children's art studios offer a variety of activities, materials, and tools to help children unleash their creativity and enterprising ideas."

My Advice to Young People:

- "Being entrepreneurial can be applied to any chosen path in life. The ability to spot opportunities and implement ideas benefits everyone. So unlock your enterprising talent and follow your dreams.
- "Don't take the well-beaten path and don't be afraid of any lack of skills or experience. Learn all you can, create new things, bring them to life, inspire and lead and build strong relationships with customers, with employees, with partners.
- "Most importantly, be positive and optimistic in all situations. Have self-belief and aspiration. Whatever you decide to do, take charge for getting where you want to be and just go for it!"

JA ALUMNI INTERVIEW

Bill Herp
Founder, Linear Air, JA Alumnus, Kentucky, USA

> *So, I've always been fascinated with the potential for using disruptive technology in highly regulated industries, and I saw great entrepreneurial opportunities there.*

My JA Experience:

"Why did I join JA? Well the honest answer is that I went to an all boys' Catholic high school and I joined the JA program so I could meet girls . . . but more seriously I was also attracted to the concept of being my own boss. As a kid I had the usual paper route and a couple of other work experiences like that, so I joined. I was in the JA Company Program. It was an extracurricular activity, and we had JA volunteer advisors from companies. We started our company, ran it during the school year, and I did that for three or four years in high school. Many of my friends were also in the program, and we got to meet people all over Louisville, Kentucky, where I grew up. It was a great way to expand my horizons. I managed to be successful in JA and was elected to the national student office in 1980 so I also got to meet people nationally. I went to the JA national convention with 3,000 kids from all across the country. That was very exciting to me. The most important lesson for me from JA was validating that it's possible to have your own company. We learned all sorts of things about starting a company: employing other people, making payroll every week, taking certain kinds of risks. We saw all that in the JA program—and I learned that being an entrepreneur could be a potential career path for me."

My Career / Business:

"Most of my friends in high school went to college and studied engineering and things like that. I went to Notre Dame and actually hatched out my plans to become an entrepreneur while I was in college. I got an accounting degree, which was not really my career choice but was a stepping-stone to being my own man and having my own business. Right after college I worked briefly for Price Waterhouse in Chicago and then went to the Harvard Business School. It was right after HBS that I decided to take the entrepreneurial plunge. I became interested in the application of technology to highly regulated industries. That's why I went into the various industries I did: first the telecommunications industry, which is heavily regulated, then the wine distribution industry, which is also heavily regulated, and now air travel, which is a very heavily regulated industry. I founded Linear Air in 2004, and today we're the dominant player in the "air taxi" marketplace throughout the U.S., Canada, and the Caribbean. Our goal is to make affordable private air travel a reality for more people than ever before. Since I'm also a pilot, an added perk with this business is that I actually get to fly some of our clients once in a while. So I've always been fascinated with the potential for using disruptive technology in highly regulated industries, and I saw great entrepreneurial opportunities there."

My Advice to Young People:

- "The first piece of advice I would give young people is—put your phones down—don't get too sucked into the social media world with the supercomputers you have in your hands. You still have to develop the ability to communicate with real people and operate outside of the virtual world of Facebook and Instagram. It's very rare to have a job that involves no physical interaction with other people, unless maybe you're going to be a weather observer in the South Pole. So put down the phone and get in the real world. By the way, this is another advantage of the JA program—actually interacting with real people.
- "The second is you absolutely need to have an education. You can't really expect to be an entrepreneur or get a decent job without an education. And it doesn't necessarily mean going to university; it could be technical or vocational or professional. The important thing about education is it allows you to become an expert in some area or multiple areas. People who don't have that expertise have unhappy lives working in minimum-wage jobs.

- "The last thing is, if you feel like you want to be an entrepreneur, the best advice I can give you is to get some cofounders. It validates what you're trying to do, it probably fills some gaps in your own experience or skill set, and frankly it's just a lot more fun to have a team of cofounders working with you."

JA ALUMNI INTERVIEW

Eric Chen

Founder, Vitargent Biotechnology, JA Alumnus, Hong Kong/China

My two main goals for Vitargent are to make our technology the standard for food and drink safety testing around the world, and to create a go-to source and portal for safe products.

My JA Experience:

"In addition to entrepreneurship and business skills, the JA program also taught me to be ethical in conducting business. Nowadays, many people only pay attention to winning or losing financially, but not enough attention to being right or wrong. I really think that is the biggest takeaway I have from JA.

"After secondary school and JA, I went on to college and graduated from the City University of Hong Kong with degrees in engineering and marketing. I was actually studying for my master's in economics at the University of Hong Kong when some very bad news came along, which led me into my entrepreneurial career."

My Career / Business:

"In 2008 the melamine scandal hit the Chinese mainland; six babies died and 300,000 fell ill after drinking milk powder tainted with an industrial chemical. Parents were horrified. How could the main source of food for so many babies be so dangerous? Actually China had experienced many toxic food and drink crises over the years. Even though I was studying economics at the time, this news caused me to start thinking about food and drink safety, and what could be done about it.

"Fortunately, I discovered that new food testing technology was being researched and created right at City University. So I teamed up with one of the scientists there, Dr. Chen Xueping, to start up a commercial activity built around the research. We founded Vitargent in 2010 and set up the firm in the incubation program run by the Hong Kong Science and Technology Park, which provides a business network and laboratory for participating firms.

"Current food testing mechanisms only reveal around 30 percent of toxins in food and drink. Through Vitargent we hope to bring about a revolution in how food, cosmetics, and other products are tested. We use genetically modified embryos from transgenic medaka and zebrafish, as an alternative to traditional animal testing. Some of our specially designed fish embryos turn fluorescent green in the presence of toxins, while others develop abnormalities and tumors. Our tests can screen for more than 1,000 toxins at one time, compared to 5 to 10 toxins using current technologies. Our ultimate goal is to build an innovative and efficient platform to test and certify the safety of all foods, drinks, and cosmetics.

"In 2011 we initially raised 10 million Hong Kong dollars, about US$1.3 million, from angel investors and the Hong Kong government. We achieved profitability last year, and closed a second round of financing led by venture capital firm WI Harper Group in San Francisco—whose founder, Peter Liu, has now become Vitargent's chairman.

"In the future, we see huge needs in China and elsewhere, as food and drink scandals continue to shake consumer confidence. It seems businesses are so creative they will add anything you can imagine to our food and drink. Both regulations and testing technology need to catch up. My two main goals for Vitargent are to make our technology the standard for food and drink safety testing around the world, and to create a go-to source and portal for safe products."

My Advice to Young People:

- "My first advice is to follow the '3H' principle; stay humble, stay hungry, and stay helpful. Stay humble and stay hungry were of course said by Steve Jobs and are well known. I want to add 'stay helpful' as it's become such an important part of my company's strategy.

- "Second, to expand and emphasize, 'stay helpful' means you have to help your team members realize their career goals, help your customers solve their problems, help your partners develop the business, and finally help your investors get a better return. You do this, and all these people will help you succeed."

CHAPTER 4

Self-Inspired Behavior

Love What You Do and Get Very Good at Doing It

> *If you don't give up, you still have a chance.*
> *Giving up is the greatest failure.*
>
> **JACK MA**, Founder, Alibaba

Self-inspired behavior is perhaps the sharpest difference of all between entrepreneurs and bureaucrats. But what are entrepreneurs actually self-inspired to *do*? When I think of legends like Disney, Lever, and Honda, or modern-day entrepreneurial icons like Jack Ma, a couple of images come to mind. First, they love what they do—they're highly committed to their work. And second, they constantly try to get better at what they do—their performance is high. These two ideas, high commitment and high performance, are the backbone of an entrepreneurial approach to work. And it's damn tough to beat people who love what they do and are damn good at doing it.

Entrepreneurs are so self-inspired because they face the consequences, positive or negative, of their performance every day. Those consequences come directly from their customers, and they are timely, accurate, and extremely powerful. To inspire your employees, you will need to instill similar consequences, positive and negative, for them, too. The fastest and surest way to inspire your people will be to create an "entrepreneurial performance system" across the entire company.

To start your own business, you have to be self-inspired—and never give up. Then to grow your business you have to inspire others—by instilling real consequences for them, too. No company leader is doing a better job at this today than Jack Ma—who applied and was rejected 10 times at Harvard University—and then founded China's most famous company, Alibaba, the largest IPO in history on the New York Stock Exchange with a market valuation of $231 billion. And in the process Ma developed an incredibly loyal (high commitment) and incredibly hardworking (high performance) group of executives, managers, and employees who will follow him to the ends of the earth. This is why mastering the final entrepreneurial practice of self-inspired behavior, for yourself and your future employees, is the underpinning of all entrepreneurial success.

Jack Ma's life provides a textbook, rags-to-riches example of "loving what you do" and "getting very good at doing it," the two qualities that underpin all entrepreneurial behavior. We call them high commitment and high performance—and you'll never find a better example of using them to create giant companies than the great Texas entrepreneur Ross Perot.

HIGH COMMITMENT AND HIGH PERFORMANCE

I'm looking for people who love to win. If I run out of those, I want people who hate to lose.

H. ROSS PEROT, Founder, EDS, Perot Systems

I first became intrigued by Ross Perot way back in 1979. But it wasn't because of this Texas entrepreneur's business exploits—even though he had already made a name for himself as the founder of Electronic Data Systems. I had a more personal reason. Like some other Americans working in Iran around that time, I had gotten trapped in the wild and woolly Iranian revolution. I was held for a period of time, guarded by wild-eyed Iranians with AK-47s, and only escaped with the brave help of Air France personnel—who were allowed to bring all of us one airline meal a day. They eventually managed to sneak me out to the airport and put me on an Air France flight to Bangkok, with no ticket, no passport, and no money. To this day I have a very soft spot in my heart for the French.

After returning home, I was watching the TV news when Ross Perot's face popped up on the screen with the incredible story of how he had just rescued two EDS executives from Evin Prison in central Tehran. Perot had organized and paid for a commando team of ex–Green Berets, a couple of planes and helicopters, and plenty of ransom money to bring his two employees home. All this made great headlines and even a great book and movie: *On Wings of Eagles*. I was, of course, personally fascinated by this daring exploit in the same place I had just escaped from—with zero help from my employer, by the way. It was stunning that a company CEO would put so much on the line to save a couple of employees. I still ponder, and you might also—*if you ever get thrown into a foreign jail, or taken hostage, who would you want to be working for?*

And that's the point. Entrepreneurial leaders who demonstrate high commitment toward their people get that commitment returned back to them and the company—in spades. Think about it: What would your commitment be to a CEO who hires commandos to rescue you from a foreign prison? Or to a CEO who built a company worth billions, but set his own salary at $68,000 in year one and never gave himself a raise? The fact is, few CEOs anywhere had more respect and loyalty from employees than Perot. After EDS was sold to General Motors, one executive gave up $900,000 in GM stock to go back and work for him when he founded Perot Systems. The corporate motto at Perot Systems is "One for All and All for One." It may sound corny to some, but if history is any guide, this slogan on mutual commitment really means something when you work for Ross Perot.

Perot's history as a high-performance businessman is also well documented. In his first job—after graduating from the Naval Academy at Annapolis and serving in the U.S. Navy—as an IBM salesman, he met his annual sales quota by the end of January. When he discovered he had maxed out on the commission system and would receive no additional sales commissions for the next 11 months, he quit his job and founded EDS with $1,000 borrowed from his wife's savings account. After selling EDS to General Motors in 1984 for $2.5 billion, he founded and grew Perot Systems to $2.8 billion in revenue over the next 20 years, and in 2009 sold it to Dell for another $4 billion. In the process, he became the first entrepreneur in history to found two companies that ended up on the Fortune 1,000 list. Today, Perot is obviously in the twilight of his remarkable career—but his legacy is secure as an all-time champion of creating companies just brimming over with high commitment and high performance.

The self-inspired behavior of great entrepreneurs like Perot rests on two basic qualities—*high commitment* and *high performance.* In plain English, entrepreneurs "love what they do" and they're "very good at doing it." And the best of them work very hard to instill these qualities in their employees. Figure 4.1 shows the four possible combinations of these two characteristics. You can find managers and workers in any of the four quadrants. A quick definition of each follows the figure.

Figure 4.1	**Entrepreneurial Commitment and Performance**

- **High Commitment/High Performance.** The upper right-hand corner is entrepreneurial territory. "I love what I do and I'm good at doing it" is the clarion call of all self-inspired entrepreneurs.
- **High Commitment/Low Performance.** In the lower right-hand area are those people who love what they do but aren't very good at doing it. It's not unusual to find new employees here. They can be bursting with enthusiasm for their new job, but they just don't have enough knowledge or experience yet to do the job well. You can also find, unfortunately, long-term employees occupying this spot. They're loyal and they do love the company—but they stopped learning and improving a decade ago.

- **Low Commitment/High Performance.** The upper left-hand area houses the exact opposite type of worker and is much more common. These are the folks who hate their job but are very good at doing it. They're usually highly skilled people who don't like the environment, or company, in which they have to perform. Airline pilots come to mind. Flying tourists to Orlando has to be pretty dull compared to combat missions over Iraq and Afghanistan. You can see this type everywhere, especially in large bureaucracies, which can drive the commitment out of even the highest skilled workers.

- **Low Commitment/Low Performance.** What can we say about workers who hate what they do and are no good at doing it? If you make such a blunder and hire this type in your business, don't compound the problem by wasting months or years trying to "fix" the person. Cut your losses and say sayonara.

Successful entrepreneurs, by definition, fit squarely into the high commitment/high performance area of behavior. Their biggest challenge may be passing on and instilling the same behavior in their employees. The first mistake you can make is to wait 10 years to get going on this. The time to start is with your first employee. Having an entire company full of mini-entrepreneurs is the goal. Think about it— if you hire and develop a band of people who absolutely love what they do and are very good at doing it—well, you're going to be one tough competitor. Read on to examine how you can instill entrepreneurial commitment and performance in your own business.

CREATING ENTREPRENEURIAL COMMITMENT: "I LOVE WHAT I DO"

18,000 employee shareholders by 1925.

WILLIAM HESKETH LEVER, Founder, Lever Brothers (Unilever)

To set the record straight, employee stock ownership wasn't invented in Silicon Valley in 1990. Way back in 1909, William Lever announced the Lever Co-Partnership Trust, the world's first employee stock ownership program. By 1925 an amazing 18,000 employees were members of the trust. Was Lever a man ahead of his times? Probably. If nothing else, he put his money where his mouth was in urging workers to cast their lot with his company.

Lever was an early believer in entrepreneurial "tough love"—doubly inspired by Victorian England's rock-hard work ethic and the belief that workers should get their fair share of the pie. In 1900, Lever Brothers was the largest company in the world. Today, Unilever* is ranked fifty-sixth in worldwide market value and forty-first on *Fortune's* Most Admired Companies list. This amazing 115-year performance makes Unilever—hands down—the most consistently successful big company in the world over the past century. No other company even comes close. It is the shining example of how to beat the deadly Life Cycle of Organizations. It must have been doing something right all these decades. And most people who have researched the company, including yours truly, agree that the single most important reason for its astounding long-term record is that Unilever has always been, and continues to be, an absolutely great company to work for.

Here's how it started. When it came to business performance, William Lever was a very tough competitor indeed. He traumatized the gentlemanly world of London commerce with massive and outlandish American style advertising. He literally invented consumer goods packaging, brand recognition, the concept of market niches, and the production of multiple brands to compete against each other. By 1910 Lever Brothers had 60,000 employees in 282 operating companies spread across five continents. He also demonstrated an autocratic model of leadership, demanding hard work and high morals from employees, insisting they were the root of all success in business and in life. His personal performance standards were very high and never compromised—and he insisted on the same with his workforce.

Beyond his high performance standards and demands, we also find caring words and radical deeds in his commitment to employees. Creating the first employee stock and profit-sharing program was truly revolutionary for the times. Taking this giant step toward the creation of mini-entrepreneurs within the organization was among his proudest achievements. In addition to the Co-Partnership Trust, Lever instituted

---

* Unilever was formed in 1929 through the merger of Lever Brothers and several smaller Dutch companies. It operates today as a Dutch/UK group, with headquarters in both countries.

many employee benefit programs we all take for granted today. Unilever was the first company on record to provide company training, sick leave, annual paid holidays, and pension plans. These were all radical steps.

So what are we to make of this industrialist, philanthropist, politician, and self-inspired entrepreneur? The legacy of Lever's "tough love" approach to employees is clear: The company has enjoyed a high-commitment/high-performance workforce for well over a century—and is still overwhelming the competition. The bottom line may be, like most things in life, getting commitment and performance from your people is a two-way street.

Here are four key practices that will help you develop those super levels of entrepreneurial high commitment in your own company.

- **Love What You Do.** Ray Kroc, the legendary founder of McDonalds, said: "You gotta see the beauty in a hamburger!" That was his version of the number one rule in commitment: "You gotta love what you do!" Entrepreneurs really do love what they do. It comes with the territory. They're proud of their enterprise, and they see noble purpose in every mundane step they take. They love it so much that they'll work night and day to see it succeed. A little of this will go a long way in any growing company.

   It will be your job as the founder to define that noble purpose and pass it on to your employees. It actually starts with hiring people who are interested in what you do. Then, every job will have to be made important. Challenges will need to be built into even the most mundane tasks. Whether you're in landscaping or finding a cure for cancer, the long-term payoff for getting your people to like what they're doing, and be proud of it, is simply enormous.

- **Give Autonomy, Demand Accountability.** One surefire way to build commitment is to give people some autonomy and freedom to do their jobs. In an entrepreneurial environment, empowering people, or giving them autonomy, also means they're accountable for results. It's very much a two-way street. Employees not only understand this, they like it. For some it may be the first time they've ever been treated like a responsible adult at work. The results can truly be astounding.

   A wonderful example of doing this would be Norm Brinker's company, Brinker International, which owns famous restaurant chains like Chili's Grill & Bar. Brinker had this down to a science. He told me: "The restaurants are highly decentralized and spread out into hundreds of little entrepreneurial style businesses. We *really* do delegate, decentralize, and give a lot of autonomy. And the field stays focused on what they're doing because it's in their self-interest. Everyone's in profit sharing. Everyone. The wait staff runs their own profit sharing with tips. All the managers in the units get bonuses based on what their one restaurant does in profitability. So they're all self-contained little businesses. Each restaurant is like a little $2 to $3 million family-owned business. And when they hit their goals, they all get their bonuses. So they're very focused to make it happen."

Every company must find its own particular way to focus on employee autonomy and accountability. Brinker International's amazing record says it has found a pretty good way: energetic commitment from the top, a completely decentralized organization with self-managing entrepreneurial units, and every employee, top to bottom, on profit sharing.

■ **Share Fortune and Misfortune.** As an entrepreneur, you will have little choice but to pin your hopes and fears on the future of your company. You will have to share the fortunes as well as the misfortunes of the business. And so it should be for your employees. What's good for the company should be good for the workers. And if it's good for the workers, it should be good for the company. Conversely, if it's bad for the company, there has to be some negative consequence on employees. It's called having a shared destiny, and without it, you can forget about a committed workforce. So do yourself a huge favor and start developing your plan now for doing just that.

Of course it's easier to share the good times than the bad. But for sure, no employees will be ready to share any company misfortune if they haven't experienced along the way a fair share of the company's good fortune. Some of the greatest examples of "sharing fortune and misfortune" actually come from employee-owned companies. And the historical record is clear: When employees have an ownership stake in the business, commitment and performance go through the roof. The only question on this isn't whether or not it works—but why do only about

15 percent of companies have meaningful employee ownership plans in place? Of course you will have your chance to raise that percentage a bit.

- **Lead by Example, Never Compromise.** Leading by example typically comes with the territory for entrepreneurs. Many of them believe it's their most powerful people management tool. Being the customer/product guru of the business obviously goes a long way in the "leading by example" arena. But this doesn't mean you always have to be the greatest product developer or the best salesperson in the company. On the other hand, you cannot take a second seat to anyone in terms of commitment to the mission—if you hope to create entrepreneurial high commitment in your own staff.

  Remember, your people are watching you like a hawk, so never be shy in showing that you love what you do, even on a bad day. Openly demonstrate your pride in the company's products. And publicly proclaim that the customers pay everyone's salary including your own. Leading by example, and never compromising, could be your most powerful people management tool.

There are hundreds of specific policies and programs you can initiate to foster high commitment. Whatever you do, from major steps like employee ownership to the most mundane of personnel practices, remember that the underlying goal is to make people feel so important in their job and so proud of their company that loving what they do will just come naturally.

CREATING ENTREPRENEURIAL PERFORMANCE: "I'M GOOD AT DOING IT"

If I can't sell better than anybody in the company, I don't deserve to be president.

JOHN JOHNSON, Founder, Johnson Publishing (Jet, Ebony)

Would the Harvard Business School hire a professor who said he believed the most important management principle of all is hard work? You doubt it? Well, that means it wouldn't hire the entrepreneur who founded and ran for many years America's largest black-owned and operated company. Meet John Johnson, who built the great media and cosmetics empire Johnson Publishing.

Johnson said he only had two important jobs in the company: First was to know exactly what his employees thought of their jobs and the company, so he personally interviewed every new employee and every departing employee. His second job was to sell a lot of advertising space, which he learned on day one was the only way to stay alive in the magazine business. He actually believed CEOs and presidents of companies are supposed to be able to sell their product. Johnson took it even further with his motto that if he couldn't sell the product better than anyone else he didn't deserve to be president. This is performance aimed squarely at the heart of the enterprise—the kind that really interests entrepreneurs.

John Johnson's high-performance career—his never-ending effort to be good as what he did—brought him fame and fortune. Born dirt-poor in Arkansas, as a young boy he moved North to Chicago with his mother during the Great Depression. The dual goal was to find work and further his education as there were no high schools in Arkansas for blacks. He flourished in public school being voted class president in both his junior and senior years. He also became an avid reader and noticed there were not any magazines or newspapers in the Chicago area catering to the interests of the sizeable African American market. So at just 24 years of age, he borrowed $500 from his mother (to get the money she had to put up all her furniture as collateral) to start up *Negro Digest*, the first ever black news publication in Chicago. That was followed three years later by *Ebony*, which has been the largest circulation black-owned magazine in the United States every year since its founding in 1945. Numerous other successful ventures followed: *Jet* magazine, book publishing, radio stations, syndicated TV shows, and of course the hugely successful beauty and cosmetics business.

In all this, John Johnson worked night and day, doing any job necessary from chief salesman to chief floor sweeper, to make Johnson Publishing the world's largest African American–owned publishing house, and Fashion Fair Cosmetics, the world's largest African American–owned cosmetics firm. On a personal level, Johnson was the first African American to land a spot on the Forbes 400, the annual listing of America's wealthiest people. And most important of all to Johnson himself was President Clinton's bestowal upon him, in 1995, of the Presidential Medal of Freedom, the nation's highest civilian award. These are the kind of achievements and accolades super high performance can deliver—even for a poor black boy from Arkansas.

To entrepreneurs, high performance is an on-the-job fight to the finish—not scoring points for their next performance review. And their performance is highly focused on what matters most—making more products and selling more customers. In other words, you want your people to perform like entrepreneurs—and actually move the business forward. Here are four key practices to help you develop and maintain entrepreneurial high performance in your business:

- **Get Better at What You Do.** Continuous improvement in performance becomes a habit with entrepreneurs. This happens when you know you're in a competitive battle for survival. If raising the bar to stay competitive is the lifeblood of enterprise, shouldn't it also be the lifeblood of everyone in the enterprise? Of course it should. And you can make it happen if it's crystal clear to everyone that "getting better" is every employee's most important job.

  Examples of entrepreneurs who continuously seek to get better at what they do are legion. For starters there is Karl Benz, who spent his entire life designing and engineering improvements for his revolutionary engines and beautiful cars. And what about Akio Morita, founder of Sony, who spent four years of his life knocking on doors in the United States to learn how to make and sell electronic products for the American market? More recently, we had the wonderful example of Steve Jobs going to work every day at Apple to inspire his teams to find the next great product. And right up to today, we see Elon Musk overcoming every small failure with heroic product advances. On and on it goes—as it should for you and the employees in your own company.

  An obvious way of getting better is to provide ongoing training. Whether it's on-the-job training or classroom seminars, the focus should be on the core skills that actually help grow the business: how to make better products, find and sell more customers, and deliver superior customer service. At the end of the day, getting better at what you do requires both working harder and working smarter. Show me an employee who is constantly doing that, and I'll show you a high-potential mini-entrepreneur for your company.

■ **Winning at Quality, Quantity, Speed, and Cost.** The entrepreneur's shorthand for performance comes down to asking: "How well can we work, how much can we do, how fast can we do it, and how efficient can we be?" The answers to these four commonsense questions will define the competitiveness of your employees and your company. Instilling these fundamentals in your people, constantly getting better at them, and measuring every employee by them, will give you the performance standards you'll need to end up in the winner's circle. Following is an entrepreneurial dream team that illustrates extreme achievement in each of the four parameters of high performance:

- **Quality—How Good.** Gottlieb Daimler and Karl Benz set out to make the highest quality car in the world every year. One hundred years later, their great company is still doing it.
- **Quantity—How Much.** Ray Kroc started a hamburger empire that has grown to 30,000 locations around the world and each day sells enough food to feed 50 million people. How much did he accomplish? A lot!
- **Speed—How Fast.** Think about Larry Hillblom and DHL's expansion to 120 countries in a decade—still an all-time record.
- **Cost—How Efficient.** Lito Rodriguez' DryWash technology in Brazil uses not a drop of water, saving 316 liters of freshwater per car and uses 99.5 percent less electricity per car than its traditional competitors. Now that's efficient!

Such a list could go on and on, but I think you get the point. So why not aim for the stars and create your own Daimlers, Benzes, Krocs, Hillbloms, and Rodriguezes across your workforce?

■ **Save Your Best for Customers and Products.** Entrepreneurs save their best efforts for making great products and selling real customers. As an entrepreneur, you should have this kind of focus in spades. But Walt Disney may have been the first person in any business to really understand that caring for the customer and the product is every employee's responsibility.

Disney people, from janitors to Snow White, aren't employees—they're performers, members of the cast. When they work, they're on stage. A cast member's sole reason for being is to make guests happy. In this special relationship between cast members and guests, little is left to chance. Disney training is intense and absolutely explicit on how to make guests happy.

On the other hand, Disney's focus on making the product/service picture perfect was legendary, right down to the details of every cast member's appearance. In an extraordinarily frank employee pamphlet, *The Disney Look*, appearance and grooming for cast members is covered in detail from the length of fingernails to the use of effective deodorants. The opening message to employees makes it clear that their commitment to Disney's customer/product vision is a condition of employment:

> *Each guest who makes up our audience is our boss. He or she makes our show possible and pays our wages. If we displease our guests, they might not return, and without an audience, there is no show. For this reason, anything that could be considered offensive, distracting or not in the best interest of our Disney show, even a conspicuous tattoo, will not be permitted.**

Disney's rules and expectations of employees may appear strict and even unrealistic in today's world. But creating the best products in the world and the best customer service in the world doesn't come easy.

■ **Lead by Example, Never Compromise.** As the creator of the company, you have to personally show the way on performance. This doesn't mean that you have to be, or even should be, the top performer in your company. It does mean you have to be ready, willing, and able to roll up your sleeves and give it your all—side by side with your employees. Seeing the founder of the company putting the product together or personally delivering the service

---

* *The Disney Look*, Walt Disney World, The Walt Disney Co., 1986.

can be an inspiring sight to employees. As John Johnson believed when he was building *Jet* and *Ebony* into the world's leading black magazines, you can't build a company without hard work. And you can't get your employees to follow you if you don't get out of the office and do real, frontline work yourself.

Your biggest challenge may be to keep it up, especially after your company moves beyond the start-up phase. A million things will come up to keep you off the shop floor or prevent your customer visits. If this happens, watch out. You're losing your most powerful tool for fostering high performance in your people.

THE ALMIGHTY POWER OF CONSEQUENCES

There is only one boss. The customer. And he can fire
everybody in the company from the chairman on down,
simply by spending his money somewhere else.

SAM WALTON, Founder, Walmart Stores

New entrepreneurs must be self-inspired to get the business up and running. That's a given. The tougher challenge will be passing on your own entrepreneurial self-inspired behavior to others—to the future employees of your enterprise. As you grow your new venture and start hiring people, can you develop mini-entrepreneurs across the company? A company full of people who love what they do and are very good at doing it? Fortunately, the answer is yes—and this section explains how.

The essence of self-inspired entrepreneurship still rests on an old, simple truth about human behavior. That is, people behave in their own self-interest—taking actions that they perceive will result in some positive consequence, and avoiding actions they perceive would result in negative consequences. Figure 4.2 is the classic model of entrepreneurship—squarely based on the power of consequences. If you're looking for the number one difference between entrepreneurs and bureaucrats, here it is. Entrepreneurs feel the consequences of their performance every Friday night when they count the money in the cash box. If it's full they feel on top of the world. If it's empty their kids won't eat. These are powerful, timely, and accurate consequences—which would affect anyone's behavior.

| Figure 4.2 | **Classic Entrepreneurial Behavior** |

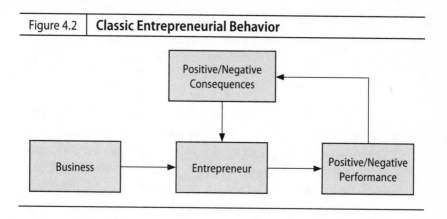

Bureaucrats, on the other hand, rarely feel any consequences, positive or negative. I learned how this works in my very first job, years ago, at American Express Company in New York. My salary was $1,250 a month, a princely sum to me at the time, and I was very excited to be working in the Big Apple. American Express was and is a great company, but it taught me a very frustrating lesson about consequences—or the lack thereof. It quickly became apparent that if I worked very, very hard for a month and brought in several big, new customers, I got $1,250. If during the next month I took it a little easier, more of an average month, I again got $1,250. And finally I realized, if I did practically nothing for a month, just showed up and stayed awake at all the meetings, I got—you guessed it—$1,250. The message was loud and clear. The company was practically screaming at the employees: "It really doesn't matter what you do!" If this seems a far-fetched example to you—good. Hopefully that means you'll never tolerate such a crazy system in your own company.

Entrepreneurs are indeed self-inspired. It comes naturally to them. But they have a mixed record on fostering high commitment and high performance in others. Like great natural athletes who make lousy coaches, entrepreneurs often have a hard time passing on their "natural" ability as self-inspired enterprisers. But it's not hopeless. There is a way—three ways actually—to instill entrepreneurial behavior in workers in any company. They can become owners or shareholders of the company. They can, along with a small team, create a new, little company within the company as "intrapreneurs." Or they can be entrepreneurial in their own job or department—by working under a companywide "entrepreneurial performance system." Any combination of these three approaches is guaranteed to help. Here's a brief description of each.

- **Workers as Owners.** Miracles do happen when workers become owners, and start facing the same positive and negative consequences as entrepreneurs. In recent years more and more companies have become employee owned—from China and India to Spain and the United Kingdom. Leading the movement is the United States with about 12 percent of all American workers now working in employee-owned companies.

    A great example is Walmart. Even a charismatic, entrepreneurial leader like Sam Walton found that company slogans and hoopla can only take you so far in the business of inspiring employees. That's why Walmart, the fastest-growing and now biggest company in the history of the world, has an across-the-board employee stock ownership program for its 2.3 million employees. And just to remind everyone they are indeed owners of the company, you'll find a Walmart stock quotation screen in the employee break room of every store. Because Walmart believes so strongly that workers should be shareholders, they've even made the level of employee participation a part of every manager's annual performance review and bonus.

    Whether it's W. L. Gore, Andersen Consulting, and Walmart in North America, or Thomson/RCA and John Lewis in Europe, or even some of the newly privatized state industries in China, the result is the same. Any form of employee ownership has to instill some level of entrepreneurial consequences in the company, generating more self-inspired behavior by employees. There's no mystery to it. The only mystery is why 85 percent of companies around the world still don't do it.

- **Intrapreneurship.** This is an old idea with a new name. Give a small group of highly committed, top performing employees a little seed money, a lot of autonomy, participation in the financial results, and ask them to create a new business for the company—but operating outside the normal bureaucracy. For some big companies like Xerox and Levi Strauss, this method provided the chance to create new entrepreneurial businesses and motivate the new "corporate entrepreneurs" running them. The upside possibilities for the company are enormous—while the only downside of intrapreneuring is that only a few can play. The other 90 percent of your people will not be involved. Even so, it's a terrific way to create entrepreneurial excitement—and growth—in your business.

■ **Entrepreneurial Performance System (EPS).** If making workers the owners isn't for you, and if intrapreneurship affects too few people, what else can you do to instill powerful consequences and foster the entrepreneurial spirit in your employees? Here's the answer. We call it *The Entrepreneurial Performance System*, the third proven way to inspire entrepreneurial commitment and performance in all your people.

The Entrepreneurial Performance System diagram in Figure 4.3 expands on the Classic Entrepreneurial Behavior model illustrated in Figure 4.2. The point is to duplicate for your workers, to the extent possible, the real-world performance environment of entrepreneurs.

Figure 4.3	**The Entrepreneurial Performance System**

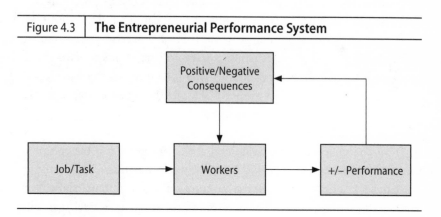

The EPS helps explain the eternal question, Why is some employee performance good, and other employee performance bad? The sales clerk sees a customer enter the store and responds with courteous service—or turns her back on the customer. The shipping clerk gets a customer order and ships out the product the same afternoon—or puts it on the shelf and sends it three days later. Why the different responses? Or in our words, why do some employees behave in an entrepreneurial self-inspired way, while others behave in a more bureaucratic way? Fortunately there are only four components to worry about in any performance system—and any one of them can break down and cause poor, or bureaucratic, performance. The following chart illustrates the four possible causes of bad performance, the required solution, and the percentage frequency that each is the culprit.

COMPONENT	CAUSE	SOLUTION	% FREQUENCY
Job	Job not clear	Clarify job	10%
Workers	Lack of knowledge	Train workers	15%
Performance	Lack of resources	Provide resources	10%
Consequences	Out of balance	Rebalance	65%

Use this chart, and Application 11 at the end of the book, to troubleshoot any performance and commitment problems you may have with future employees. The causes and solutions are straightforward. Obviously, the lack of powerful consequences, positive or negative, is the primary culprit—causing two-thirds of all performance problems. This is why we say consequences represent the biggest single difference between entrepreneurial and bureaucratic behavior.

If all the charts and explanations above are getting a bit complex, you can also just keep in mind Sam Walton's warning: The customer can fire us all. Or you can listen to Jannie Tay, entrepreneurial superwoman and Chinese *mamacita* to a sprawling watch and jewelry empire from Monte Carlo to Tokyo to Sydney—and a master at describing why entrepreneurial inspiration is good for us all.

SELF-INSPIRATION: GOOD FOR THE BUSINESS, GOOD FOR THE SOUL

Self-inspired behavior is not only good for the business, it's also good for the soul.

JANNIE TAY, Founder, The Hour Glass

My longtime friend Jannie Tay was recently named one of the "Fifty Leading Women Entrepreneurs of the World."* In the tough, discount-crazy Asian retail market for watches and jewelry, you have to be doing a lot right to hit $600 million in revenues and 25 straight years of growth. Today The Hour Glass has some 15 retail outlets spread over Singapore, Australia, Malaysia, Indonesia, and Hong Kong. They sell the world's top brands such as Cartier, Rolex, Christian Dior, Patek Philippe, and Mondial Jeweler. They have also integrated backward with two joint-venture watch factories in Switzerland, as well as wholesale operations in Tokyo, Singapore, Hong Kong, Geneva, and Monte Carlo.

The Hour Glass has a strong public reputation based on two things: high-quality products and exquisite, upscale service. What the outside world doesn't know, however, is that both the high quality and the great service are, in truth, driven by Jannie Tay's greatest personal asset: her amazing instincts for inspiring herself and her people. Tay actually believes that self-inspiration, the indispensable human quality that underpins the entrepreneurial spirit, carries double-barreled power. Of course it's good for business. That's been true forever. But it may have as much to do with how you live as how you work.

Here's how she described it to me: "In the final analysis, why should you want to inspire yourself? Why should you like what you do and be good at doing it? Partly because you're supposed to—a fair day's work for a fair day's reward is still a fair obligation. But there may be an even more important reason. Think about it. If you have to work for a living, which virtually everyone does, you're going to spend more time in your life at work than with your family. You'll spend more time at work than with your friends, or enjoying a hobby, or just taking it easy. In fact you're going to spend more time at work than on any other activity in

---

* Tay was recognized as one of the "Fifty Leading Women Entrepreneurs" by The National Foundation for Women Business Owners as part of a global research project funded by IBM.

your entire life. This is why it's important to love what you do. It's your *life* we're talking about. And it's also the *lives* of your employees. And God help you, and your employees, if you spend your lives doing something you hate. That's why I say self-inspired behavior is not only good for the business, it's also good for the soul."

So consider that the real purpose of being inspired is not to move mountains—but to move yourself. To motivate yourself to make your life matter and leave some footprints in the sand. It can make you a great entrepreneur, no doubt about it. But even more importantly, it can make you a great person!

Complete the following Applications at the end of the book to raise commitment and performance and instill our entrepreneurial performance system. Enjoy!

Application 10: SELF-INSPIRED BEHAVIOR—RAISING COMMITMENT AND PERFORMANCE

Application 11: THE ALMIGHTY POWER OF CONSEQUENCES

JA ALUMNI INTERVIEW

Donna Shalala

President, Clinton Foundation, former President, University of Miami, former United States Secretary of Health and Human Services, JA Alumna, Ohio, USA

> *In addition to being a good professional, you've also got to be a good person, a good citizen.*

My JA Experience:

"Cleveland, Ohio had a huge JA program. It was the traditional JA. You went to a center, there were advisors from different companies around Cleveland. I started as a freshman in high school, so I spent four years in JA, had lots of different companies, all of which were successful I should point out. One year we made step stools, and members of my family still have some of those stools 50 years later. I was editor of the JA newspaper called *The Achiever* and vice president of JA Cleveland, and I went to NAJAC (National JA Conference) three times, which were all wonderful experiences. I also went to college on a JA scholarship. So I was deeply involved in the JA program all through high school.

"From JA I took away a deep respect for business and for business-people and the guys who volunteered to work with us young people. We were from the inner city and came from working-class families. We were not rich kids from the suburbs. We were all very enthusiastic about forming companies and creating jobs. And it was adults show-ing us how to do it—they didn't take over for us, but they coached us. JA taught me how to organize and how to lead other people. Also I could relate to adults better because I had worked with adults in JA. It all gave me self-confidence and instilled in me forever a sense that I could start something new, that I could be an entrepreneur.

"After high school, and JA, I went to Western College for Women, which is now part of Miami University of Ohio. When I graduated I joined the Peace Corps,* which also gave me a lot of self-confidence. It actually greatly enlarged on my JA experience—the same skills I used in JA I used in the Peace Corps. After the Peace Corps I went to Syracuse University to the Maxwell School to get a PhD in political sci-ence and economics. From there I started my academic career with a strong interest in public policy."

My Career / Business:

"I began by spending more than a decade at Columbia University teaching political science. While I was at Columbia, Governor Carey of New York asked me to help put his budget together and then again to be on the board to oversee New York City's bankruptcy, which we eventually solved. I think my JA experience even helped in this expe-rience because it was an entrepreneurial, out-of-the-box effort. From there I drew the attention of the Carter administration. President

---

* By happy coincidence Donna Shalala and I were both Peace Corps volunteers in Iran, so we had some shared memories to discuss.

Carter was looking for women to appoint, I think, so I went to HUD as assistant secretary for policy in his administration. Next I became the president of Hunter College in New York City, where I was the youngest college president around. I then got a call about the chancellorship at the University of Wisconsin. I thought, my goodness, a Big Ten school, a major research university, so I went and interviewed for this big university position and they hired me. Next, and I should say that I actually knew the Clintons even before they were married, I became the secretary of health and human services in President Clinton's administration for eight years. And after that I spent the next 14 years as president of the University of Miami where I'm still on the faculty. Today I'm the president of the Clinton Foundation, which your readers undoubtedly know is the international foundation President Clinton started when he left the White House. My current assignment was to come here to help run the foundation while Hillary was running for president. So I've been here since 2015, and probably by the time your book comes out I'll be back at the University of Miami.*

"In all these positions I've used the entrepreneurial and leadership skills I first learned all those years ago in Junior Achievement. Most of my jobs have in fact been very entrepreneurial endeavors. As an example, a colleague and I started something called the Launchpad at the University of Miami. It was a student center where any student could come with an idea to start a company and we would help them set up a business plan, get them an entrepreneurial coach, and even help them to set up a board—but we did not give them money. They had to get the money from family or friends, and it was a lot like my JA experience years earlier. And another example: One of the things we promote at CGIU (Clinton Global International University) is social entrepreneurship. So one of my big interests at the Clinton Foundation is getting a whole generation of young people to think like entrepreneurs—about things they can do that in some cases will create jobs, but in every case will create opportunities to make the world a little better."

---

* Shortly after this interview, Donna Shalala left the Clinton Foundation and returned to the University of Miami as Trustee Professor of Political Science and Health Policy. I should add that among all her other accolades, Donna was awarded the Presidential Medal of Freedom, the nation's highest civilian honor, by President George W. Bush in 2008.

My Advice to Young People:

- "First, they have to find something that they have a passion for. Nothing works unless you have a passion for what you're doing.
- "Second, they ought to think about *creating* jobs, not just *taking* a job.
- "Third, Bill Clinton once said to my students: 'You need to be like a sponge, you never know precisely what you're going to need to know.' My education philosophy is that students should not be preparing for their first job, but for their third, fourth, and fifth job. They have to have the quality of mind to absorb new technology and new ideas. So it's very important for young people to become lifelong learners.
- "And in the process of doing all that, we want them to be good citizens at the same time. I always tell young people that part of being a true professional is contributing back to your community, to your city, to your country. For example, identify some organization to volunteer with, or some activity to support, even when you're just starting out on your career. In addition to being a good professional, you've also got to be a good person, a good citizen."

JA ALUMNI INTERVIEW

Ben Towers*

Founder, Towers Design, JA Alumnus, United Kingdom

> *You don't have to be a fully polished machine to start. You can learn a lot as you go along. That's what I did, so I would definitely say—just do it!*

My JA Experience:

"Learn to Earn was the name of the Young Enterprise program. It was all about choosing a career and seeing how much you're going to earn, and then you work out your life around that sort of income. That was my first program in YE, and it was interesting because it made you realize that things do cost money.

"After that I went into the JA Company Program, which was the biggest Young Enterprise program in the UK and I believe the flagship program around the world. We didn't do very well. I'm not going to say we did. We didn't get to the national finals, we didn't get to the regional finals, we didn't even win the school finals. But we did the program and learned a lot about the basics of business. After completing the JA Company Program I completely refocused my own business. It really helped open my eyes at a time when I had the skill and the talent to start a business, but I didn't know how to turn it into a real company. The JA Company Program helped me turn my personal skill, which I was doing as a freelancer, into a growing company. I was 15 at the time, and I needed that to help me start growing my company, which I had actually started five years earlier."

My Career / Business:

"I started my business, Towers Design, at age 11 after a family friend challenged me to build her a website. After doing that I realized I

---

* *Author's note:* At 18, Ben Towers is the youngest person I interviewed for the book. But since he's been running his own company since he was 11, the usual age guidelines don't seem to apply to him.

liked it and I started doing more and more sites. You know, freelancing websites, and I kept doing lots and lots of them—really cheap £50 websites. I turned them out alone, and I got to a point when I was about 13, just after doing the Learn to Earn course, I wanted to make it into a real business. I started to see it being a business, but I didn't know what I was doing. But it was fun being in business. I started telling more people about it, and the media picked up on it. I started to get a lot of sales from that, I think because of me being so young and building all the websites. And it just went on to grow from there to the point where after completing the JA Company Program, I realized I wasn't really focused to make the company really valuable. So I started picking up the business skills and learning as I went along. About this time we also moved away from websites a bit and started doing a lot more marketing jobs. I realized that people wanted to market to young people, and having a company run by a young person was quite a value add for some companies. So we started doing more than just the website work: campaigns, social media, print, all that sort of stuff, and looking at marketing as the key aspect. We continued to grow and picked up some big clients and got to the point where today Towers Design has 23 full-time staff and we're working with some very big brands.

"Meanwhile, one of the visions I've always had was to fold the company into some larger group to be able to make more of a full-service group offering. And our way of achieving that, which just happened last week, was to merge with another marketing agency called Zest The Agency. We'll be forming a larger group and will have a wider offering, so that we can work with larger clients and larger brands in larger projects. So this is all very new. It's our 'next big thing' for the longer term."

My Advice to Young People:

- "I would say just do it! A lot of people spend a lot of time on: 'I don't know this, I don't know that, I'll start when I finish school, I'll start when I finish university.' You have to get over these holdbacks. You don't have to be a fully polished machine to start. You can learn a lot as you go along. That's what I did, so I would definitely say—just do it!

- "Surround yourself with people who share the same ambition as you. I call that my 'build-my-business' village. They all want to achieve, have a similar mindset, so you can bounce ideas off each other and grow together. Having that sort of intense community means you will always have people you can rely on to help each other out.

- "Really stay focused. It's easy to go too diverse, to think in launching the company, 'I need to have this and I need to have that.' Most of the things you think you need just take the value away from what you're actually doing in the business. So really focus on what it is you do, how you deliver it, and how you can add value to your clients—and that's it."

JA ALUMNI INTERVIEW

Adedayo Fashanu
Journalist/Writer, JA Alumna, Nigeria

The parents nicknamed me "Maximum Profit" because I would harass them to buy more shares and promise their investment was assured because we were going to make maximum profit.

My JA Experience:

"I was introduced to JA through Cayley College, my secondary school in Lagos, Nigeria. The concept was for my class to think of a business through which we could make a profit and sell shares. To start the business, we were coached by JA-assigned mentors on how to go about picking roles and departments so the business could function properly. We voted in the heads of all the departments, and I was chosen to be the company's president. This result, being the president, was a great thing, but it could also have been a bad thing. Quite honestly, the experience could have made me totally love or absolutely hate being a leader. I had extremely smart classmates with strong personalities. Today some of them are doctors, lawyers, and artists/celebrities and so on, so just imagine 14 years ago, how they would have mounted pressure on their student leader. They wanted results and did not want to fail. So my first lesson in business quickly became people management.

"Initially, we sold company shares to parents at PTA meetings and anywhere else we could hunt down the parents of students who attended our school. In our company, we made African curated jewelry using local beads and materials. We invented our own style of beads, which we made by hand. Each department head was responsible for his or her own department. The production department would go to the Iyaba Market or the Ogba Market and buy the raw materials in bulk. But then after school we all would sit in class together and help them out, making beaded jewelry and being creative. We would package them nicely, set prices for sale, and so on. We fought over our decisions, we laughed during our production and general meetings, we cried when we made profits, and the principal and our parents were surprised and amused by our drive, hard work, and integrity through it all. The parents nicknamed me 'Maximum Profit' because I would harass them to buy more shares and promise their investment was assured because we were going to make maximum profit.

"JA was my first business school, and being the president meant that I had to learn to be decisive, confident, certain, and assure the team we were not going to fail. I will never forget the pressure I faced. Sometimes I would panic that we would fall behind on production or sales, but everyone on the team learned to pull together. Even in the midst of trying to get their own voices heard, they grew to be more considerate and mindful of others. We liquidated the company and paid our shareholders with a good return. It was a successful venture overall. I could go on and on with more tales—but the bottom line is, JA served as the bedrock for who I am today, and I'm sure my peers feel the same about their JA experience."

My Career / Business:

"Professionally, I am today a journalist/writer. Although I studied psychology as my major, with a minor in chemistry, somehow my natural talent and interests have superseded my educational background. I had over six years of experience in the psychology field, but my journalism career has been more rewarding and given me more opportunities. As an independent journalist, I love that I have a voice. I am a media entrepreneur, and my journalistic activity is all about doing stories that will attract sponsors, getting on the right media platforms, and engaging an audience. Ultimately, I want to have some social impact and of course earn—*maximum profit*.

"I have written for *Forbes* magazine, and I write the Art of Being Alive series on the *Huffington Post*. I founded and run my own media news platform called *TANTV: The Millennial's Voice*. I'm currently working on launching a culture magazine called *Dtara* and a global food and entertainment magazine called *LifestyleWellbeing*. I also have a book in the works based on the theme of my *Huffington Post* series. The bigger picture for my career path is to become a media household brand/name in Africa and across the world. In all this, I will always thank and revere JA for giving me a solid business foundation."

My Advice to Young People:
- "My first advice to young people is to have a business model in mind before starting. But in doing that, don't wait for perfection. You may try out many ventures which might not work out, but know that they are not failures, just part of the process needed to grow and learn.
- "Confidence is key in making progress, but do not just base your confidence on results you achieve, because what happens when you fail in something? Is that a cause to lose confidence in yourself? No, your confidence should be rooted in the 'greater cause' of the work that you immerse yourself in and the positive flow of doing that work.
- "Wishing you success, and remember that 'the art of being alive' is being on the other side of fear."

JA ALUMNI INTERVIEW

Bisman Deu

Founder, Green Wood / Color the World Pink, JA Alumna, India

> *Only 5 percent of big company CEOs are women, and at the current pace it will take 100 years to reach parity in the C-suite.*

My JA Experience:

"The first time I went into JA was when I entered their competition, the Social Innovation Relay. I entered the competition with my idea of Green Wood and won, which was great. That's how my journey with JA started. But the real turning point for me, where I felt a much stronger connection with JA, was when I went to their annual conference in Estonia as a facilitator for winning the competition. It was basically an innovation camp which gathered 120 other JA entrepreneurs and innovators from across the world. I met so many inspirational people through JA.

"JA has helped me realize my ambitions and my dreams. When you meet so many people from such diverse backgrounds, and you see the amount of good work they're doing, it motivates you to be the best you can be. That's one impact it's had on me. It's also consolidated my belief in social entrepreneurship. JA has in total made me realize my actual ambition in life."

My Career / Business:

"Green Wood actually stems from a real-life experience. My family has a farm in northern India where we grow rice and wheat. I've always been a very inquisitive kid, and I was taking a walk with my dad when I saw the burning of rice waste and husks in the fields. When the farmers harvest the rice, they have no use for the waste, so they end up burning it, which causes air pollution. I started thinking about this and started researching the properties of rice waste. I learned that it has great properties like being waterproof and termite resistant and fire resistant and has high silica content. I then decided to turn my mom's kitchen into a research laboratory, and basically that's how Green Wood came into existence—as a low-cost, eco-friendly, and sustainable building material. Through JA's program I got the platform to showcase my idea and right now we are still improving the prototype of the product. I've been approached by people from India to Ecuador who want to fully commercialize Green Wood but we're still in the prototype stage and I don't want to bring something to the market before it's perfected. Of course, I definitely see commercializing Green Wood in a few years. It will have broad application to so many people across the globe.

"Color the World Pink is my second activity today. It sprang from my being so inspired by the different social entrepreneurs I've been talking to, and the fact there is a huge ambition gap for young women. For example, only 5 percent of big company CEOs are women, and at the current pace it will take 100 years to reach parity in the C-suite. Also in India, parents are reluctant to direct their daughters into entrepreneurship because it doesn't guarantee a fixed salary. Anyway, I decided to start a campaign which aims to promote entrepreneurship and leadership among young girls. It's a local school-based thing, and I just want to give them hands-on experience in entrepreneurship to give them a push into it. I also give talks at schools about my own story with the hope that my story would be able to inspire at least one girl. I'll also be talking at the Women's' Economic Forum in Delhi this week. So that's where Color the World Pink is right now.

"I'm currently in my first year of university at Warwick University in the UK and will stay here to finish my degree. My end goal is to definitely go back to India and pursue my business and social entrepreneurship activities in my home country."

My Advice to Young People:

- "A crucial piece of advice for young people is to create opportunities for yourself. We tend to wait for the opportunity to come knocking on our door, but that usually does not happen. So, I firmly believe in trying to create as many opportunities as you can. In my own case, joining and winning a JA competition has led to a ripple effect of other opportunities.

- "Also, if you do plan to go into business, or you do have an idea, there will be so many people telling you 'this cannot work.' But, believe in your idea and don't let others shake your trust in what you have inside of you. I say this because there were lots of people who said no to me, 'this might not work.' But I just believed in my idea more than ever, and that's what led me on.
- "I'd like to end with this. I really believe in this quote by the ancient poet Rumi: 'Live life as if everything is rigged in your favor.' If you stick by that I think you should be OK."

JA ALUMNI INTERVIEW

Alfred Bright

Artist and Professor Emeritus, Youngstown University, JA Alumnus, Ohio, USA

> *I'm Alfred Bright from Youngstown, Ohio, and I'm on the waiting list to go to Erma Lee's Barber School in Cleveland, Ohio.*

My JA Experience:

"I'm still in the throes of my JA experience. It's like the song we sang at the NAJAC Conference years ago: "I Have That JA Feeling All over Me." I came to JA when I was 17 years old in 1957. I was the only African American in my JA program in Youngstown, Ohio.

"I actually joined JA because of some childhood experiences. When I was 10 years old I joined one of the Little League baseball teams in town. I was the catcher on the team. We won the city championship in 1950 and had a hero's parade in downtown Youngstown. They put me on the top of the truck in the parade because I hit the home run that won the championship game. After the parade we had our awards banquet at the public swimming pool. So I arrived at the pool as a hero, but then the manager of the pool grabbed me, slammed me against the fence, and locked me out of the pool. He told my team if I came into the swimming pool area, and so much as put my hand in the water, he would have to drain the entire pool and our picnic and award ceremony would be over. He said it was a city regulation and we had to follow it. At the age of 10, that was a very traumatic experience for me. Of course it was overt segregation and racism, and I grew up in that environment.

"But I came out of that experience, and others, not being bitter. I did not allow for any bitterness or hatred for white people who wouldn't or couldn't help me. Instead, I decided to try to maximize my own potential. One of the things I did was to join every organization I could: the Kiwanis Club, school organizations, and when I got to high school I joined JA. At that time most African American kids weren't even aware of JA, but I was welcomed into the program. I went into JA with the same attitude—I was going to try to maximize my potential. I got really involved with JA and the American free enterprise system and ended up being the president of my first company. We built wooden mailboxes for the suburban homes that were developing all around Youngstown. My second year, which was 1959, I became the president of the JA Achievers Association, which was like the Chamber of Commerce for young people. And I was selected to attend NAJAC, the National JA Conference in Indiana. We were 3,000 high school seniors who had been selected as the top achievers from all around the country and the world. I was one of only three African American kids, out of the 3,000, to attend the conference. I won the conference talent show singing "Stardust" like the famous singer Nat King Cole. And I also won the Reader's Digest Speakers Award for giving an impromptu speech on the American free enterprise system. For a young kid from Youngstown, Ohio, it was all very exciting.

"Many CEOs from Fortune 500 companies flew into Indiana to join our National Awards Banquet the last night of the conference. Because I had won two awards, I was seated at a table with Ed Mosler, the CEO of Mosler Safe Company (later acquired by American Standard), and Bayard Colgate, the CEO of Colgate-Palmolive. After dinner, the award winners had to introduce themselves, announce what city they came from, and what university they were going to in the fall. Because we were JA high achievers, everyone assumed we were all going to college. So all the young achievers stood up and said, Harvard, Yale, Columbia, Stanford, all the schools they were planning to go to. When it came to my turn, I stood up and said: 'I'm Alfred Bright from Youngstown, Ohio, and I'm on the waiting list to go to Erma Lee's Barber School in Cleveland, Ohio.' There was this pregnant pause across the room, and then all of a sudden everybody just started laughing. I sat down, and Bayard Colgate said to me: 'You have to be joking. You won the national talent show and you gave that incredible speech on the free enterprise system—and you mean to tell us you're not going to college?' I said: 'No, I'm not. Nobody has ever talked to me about going to college. I don't even know what I would study if I did go.' Then Mr. Mosler and Mr. Colgate said to me: 'If you will go back to Youngstown and find any school that will accept you, we'll help you go to college.'

"So I went home with this new possibility of going to college. To make a long story short, I applied to Youngstown State University, got accepted, and yes, Mr. Mosler and Mr. Colgate kept their word and sent me the money to get started. Later on, with my good grades, I also got a scholarship. So that's how I started, and I've had a great life and career as an artist and professor of painting. And it all started at that NAJAC Conference so many years ago."

My Career / Business:

Author's note: Alfred Bright is a nationally recognized artist and educator. He's had more than 100 solo exhibits, and his work appears in permanent museum collections across the country. He was also the first African American to become a faculty professor at Youngstown University. He currently serves on the JA Foundation Board of Directors. He describes his role there as follows: "We're very involved in funding scholarships for kids all around the country. These are kids who are in the same position I was 60 years ago—not knowing where they're going and needing these scholarships to go to college. I see myself in all these young people." Alfred's artistic career is well documented elsewhere, and in our limited space here, I've chosen to concentrate on his rich comments about his JA experience and advice to young people.

My Advice to Young People:

- "First, my message hasn't changed. It's to maximize your potential. Go deep inside yourself and find the thing you would do even if you weren't being paid for it. Follow your passion, find yourself, and maximize your potential.
- "My second point is to keep a positive attitude about yourself. That's what I did as a youngster after I had that terrible experience. I kept a very positive attitude about myself, and it made a tremendous difference in how people responded to me. I was never ashamed to be myself in that regard.
- "The third thing is to come to self-realization about yourself, your heritage, your past experiences. You really have to come to grips with those elements to achieve your highest goals and believe that you can be anything you want to be.
- "And finally here's a thought I've tried to live by: Plan your work and work your plan. Life is what you make of it . . . the answer is in your hand."

CHAPTER 5

What's Really Required

The Three Requirements

> *Managing is the easy part. What's hard is inventing the world's next great product.*
>
> **STEVE JOBS,** Founder, Apple Computer, NeXT Inc., Pixar

Whether you're a high school student dreaming about owning your own company, or a freshly minted MBA looking for your first billion, or someone with a burning desire to fix the world, welcome to the *new and improved* world of entrepreneurial opportunity.

If acquiring *the entrepreneurial attitude* is the way to go, what does it take to actually get started? Steve Jobs' quote above is a good warning that conventional wisdom, as usual, has it wrong. As this book emphasizes over and over, the single most important thing that's going to be required is to know how to make something, or deliver something, the world needs. After that it's all pretty straightforward, common sense. You are now well armed with the "four fundamental practices" of successful entrepreneurs, and a ton of great tips from successful JA alumni. There are just three more things you have to make sure are in place. Here they are:

A BIT OF MONEY

I started Dell with $1,000 . . . instead of studying for
finals my freshman year at the University of Texas.

MICHAEL DELL, Founder, Dell Computer

There's something about money that brings out the worst anxieties in people. Many would-be entrepreneurs suffer a particularly bad case of this. Some never get beyond the first step because they can't imagine themselves raising the money necessary to start their own business. Making it even more scary, the hype about IPOs and young Silicon Valley billionaires has blown the public perception of start-up financial requirements out of all proportion. A dose of reality may help.

Our research shows the average cost of starting a business in the United States today is about $15,000. It's probably a bit more in a few higher cost economies and significantly less in all lower cost economies around the world. All in all, it's a pretty good deal when you consider the relative economic or social cost of some other ways people could spend time—or money.

- Average business start-up $15,000
- A year on welfare $30,000
- A year at Harvard $50,000
- A year in prison $75,000

What just jumps off the page from this chart is that funding new entrepreneurial businesses is a bargain. Certainly, politicians and governments everywhere have learned that supporting new entrepreneurs is just about the best economic investment they can make. For example, the government can fund two companies for the cost of keeping a family on welfare one year; it can fund three companies for the cost of a one-year scholarship at a top university; and it can fund an amazing five start-up companies for the cost of keeping one criminal in prison for one year! See more below on government funding opportunities.

Crazy comparisons aside, the point shouldn't be missed. On average, the cost of starting up your own business is modest. And of course the smart way to go is, don't quit your "day job" before you're ready. Even if you agree it's not a lot of money on average, you will likely have to come up with *some* start-up money. Where are you going to lay your hands on $15,000? According to a survey conducted by *Inc.* magazine, the multiple sources of start-up financing used by entrepreneurs breaks out as follows:*

- Personal savings   73%
- Credit cards   27%
- Loans from friends and relatives   14%
- All other cash sources   14%
- Loans against personal property   7%
- Bank loans†   5% (some government secured)
- Equity investments   2%
- Internet crowdfunding‡   1% (growing rapidly)

Finally—while only 2 percent of entrepreneurs get their start-up money in the form of "equity investments," angel investors and the VC community can be helpful to you at various stages of your company's development: seed money, start-up, mezzanine, or scaling up financing, and most certainly "bridge" money to ensure a successful IPO if you decide to go that route in the future. Perhaps the only thing you need to know at this stage are the key questions any VC firm will ask you when you seek its money. The great John Doerr, the "King of Silicon Valley" and the funder of many famous companies, says the four questions he always asks are these:

- What's the People Risk? Will the founders stay or move on?
- What's the Technical Risk? Can the product be made—and scaled up?
- What's the Market Risk? Will the "dogs eat the dog food"?
- What's the Financial Risk? Can capital be raised again if needed?

The bottom line is, entrepreneurial seed money just isn't that much of an obstacle for start-ups in today's world. There are in fact, thousands

---

* The total adds up to more than 100% as many entrepreneurs use more than one source to finance their start-up.

† Government (SBA) type loans, available in most countries, can be very useful.

‡ Crowdfunding wasn't on the magazine's list as it's so new, but it's so promising we've added it here.

of famous, bootstrapping companies started for less than $2,500, including many profiled in this book such as Sony, DHL, Virgin, Microsoft, Apple, Chiron, and DryWash. While these great companies didn't need a lot of money to get started, they all did have the one asset that is absolutely essential—the knowledge to create a product or service that customers needed and were willing to pay for. This brings us to the second requirement.

A BIT OF KNOWLEDGE

General graduates of the university are twice as likely to start their own businesses as the MBA graduates of Wharton.

IAN MACMILLAN, Professor of Innovation and Entrepreneurship,
The Wharton School, University of Pennsylvania

The number one reason for new business failure is not a lack of money. It's more basic than that. It is, simply, you haven't come up with a product or service that anyone wants to buy. So you need to learn how to make a product or provide a service that the world needs and will pay for. And where are you going to learn that?

One place you won't learn it is at the leading business schools of the world. Ian MacMillan, the iconoclastic South African innovator, who heads Wharton's highly regarded Entrepreneurial Research Center, developed the first entrepreneurship studies program at a blue-chip business school. And why did Wharton approve his pet project? Because MacMillan's research revealed huge shortcomings in the MBA program, powerfully summarized by his mind-bending statistic quoted above. His well-documented argument was clear: Graduates from the "nonbusiness" departments of the university—the sciences, engineering, health services, and even liberal arts—were two times more likely to become entrepreneurs and start a business than the MBA graduates from the business school. Eureka! Steve Jobs was right when he said, "Managing is the easy part. What's hard is inventing the world's next great product."

So, if learning management theories won't help, then what kind of education would be helpful? The bedrock essential of entrepreneurship (and all enterprise for that matter) is being able to come up with a great product or service. As Jobs said, this is the really tough part of business.

Managing is kid stuff compared to being able to create a better mouse-trap. The simple truth is you have to become very knowledgeable about something—very good at designing and making some product or service that answers a real need in the marketplace. It could be simple or complicated, high or low tech, but you must become expert at it. And where can you learn this? While not essential for every entrepreneurial possibility, university schools of engineering, computer science, biotechnology, and even the arts can be terrific places to get started. Certainly technical institutes and vocational trade schools are also great places to learn how to make something—and in fact are real hotbeds for creating new entrepreneurs. And of course, regardless of your formal education, there is always on-the-job-training in existing companies—which just happens to be the number one source of product/service knowledge for today's largest category of new entrepreneurs—those millions of corporate refugees who have been downsized out of their livelihoods and turned to entrepreneurship to feed their families.

The important lesson in all the examples that fill these pages—from self-educated Soichiro Honda, to high-school dropout Ray Kroc (McDonalds), to university no-shows and dropouts like Richard Branson and Bill Gates, to Yale Drama School grad Jodie Foster (actress, director, and producer) and PhDs in biochemistry like Ed Penhoet—isn't where and how they acquired their knowledge. The one mighty thing they do have in common when it comes to knowledge is that they all managed to become very good at something. They understood that what's required to create great companies is not becoming great at managing, but becoming great at making products or delivering services that a lot of people in the world need and will pay good money for. And that, indeed, takes a bit of knowledge.

AN ENTREPRENEUR-FRIENDLY CULTURE

*I decided to run the big company the same
way I ran the small company.*

FRASER MORRISON, CEO, Morrison Construction

Beyond acquiring the necessary *bit of money* and *bit of knowledge*, entrepreneurs still have to play with the hand they're dealt in terms of the environment in which they operate. Or do they? Of course you can't, by yourself, change the macroeconomics of the day or control the polit-ical/social fabric of your country. For example, North Korea or Somalia might not be the best location right now to start up your business. But you can do a lot about the immediate environment you choose to work in and the culture you design for your own company.

For starters, your family and friends can be strong, supportive allies in your venture. Co-opt their support any way you can. There are other, obvious people to cultivate and activities to engage in: entrepreneur networks, seminars on starting up businesses, funding sources, legal advisors, and actual entrepreneurs as mentors. Beyond all these possibil-ities, the single most important resources of all may be those individuals and organizations who can help make you more of a *customer/product expert* in your chosen field—the next Steve Jobs, or Richard Branson, or Jack Ma of your industry. Take every seminar available, attend every conference and trade show scheduled, and join every professional associ-ation you can find, linked to the customer/product field of your choice.

Actually the more difficult challenge may be to maintain an entrepreneur-friendly culture in your enterprise after it's launched and begins to grow. Remember the dreaded *life cycle of all organizations*? Your start-up enterprise will not be immune. Learning how to avoid the perils of the life cycle can mean the difference between entrepreneurial success and failure. Here's a real-live case of how to do that.

It's the story of Fraser Morrison in Edinburgh, Scotland. It's an amazing tale of regaining his family's construction business 15 years after they had sold it to a giant construction conglomerate in London—which mismanaged the once-thriving $3 million family enterprise into a money-losing, $300 million bureaucracy. In his own words: "We ended up buying back Morrison Construction. I had finally reached my long-held ambition to restore family control. But we also had to buy the money-losing parent company along with it. So I had a busi-ness with overall sales of about US$300 million but losing very big and hemorrhaging cash. But we owned 100 percent, and I thought I knew how to turn it around. Thankfully my hunch was right. In our first year we increased sales and actually made a small profit. The next year, we pushed sales up again and made a respectable $11 million profit—and have never looked back."

And how exactly did Fraser Morrison change years of losses into profits in just 12 months? He started running the big business the same way his family had always run the small business—in a very entrepreneur-friendly culture. He changed five key factors, which I've transcribed into general principles that anyone can apply to maintain an entrepreneur-friendly culture in their enterprise. Here they are, in Morrison's own words:

- **Keep It Small.** "We split up into relatively small units—between just £5 to £20 million turnover. It's worked very well for us. As we grow, we want to continually feel like a small company."
- **Keep It Personal.** "To the owners in London we weren't important. Our people now have a strong personal stake in the business. They have a more entrepreneurial attitude about the business."
- **Keep It Honest.** "We gave 18 percent of the business to the key managers. We try to run the business in everyone's best, long-term interests. Business needs this honesty and transparency at the top."
- **Keep It Simple.** "The single most important thing that I've learned—and I haven't found a situation yet where it isn't true—if you forget about the nuts and bolts of the business, you're lost."
- **Start over with the Basics.** "When we got it back, we refocused the attention of people back to the basics at the site, which in the construction business is the only place you make money."

At the end of the day, what do you actually have to do to pursue your entrepreneurial dream? To be sure, you need to learn and apply the practices of the world's great entrepreneurs as covered earlier: *Sense of Mission, Customer/Product Vision, High-Speed Innovation,* and *Self-Inspired Behavior.* And then, as this chapter illustrates, you'll need to acquire *A Bit of Money* and *A Bit of Knowledge* and create the most *Entrepreneur-Friendly Culture* you can.

The following Applications at the end of the book are designed to plan for what's really required to start your business and finally develop your own start-up action plan.

Application 12: WHAT'S REALLY REQUIRED?—THE THREE REQUIREMENTS

Application 13: MY "GETTING ENTREPRENEURIAL" START-UP ACTION PLAN

Enjoy and good luck!

JA ALUMNI INTERVIEW

Kim Kaupe
Cofounder, ZinePak, JA Alumna, Florida, USA

> *When we appeared on Shark Tank, we received full offers of $725,000 from four of the five Sharks, and then turned them all down. . . . We needed a phone, a computer, and our brains. Those were the only three things we needed.*

My JA Experience:

"I was first introduced to JA in high school in Florida. What really sparked me about JA was that you learn a lot in high school about math and algebra, but you don't learn a lot about practical, everyday things like costs and taxes and stuff like that. I remember those JA workbooks—it was the first time I actually saw math as something useful and applicable in the real world. And for the first time I heard about revenue, costs, profits, and things like that. You know, in high school you're in your teen years, and you're usually talking about the latest movie and if you're going to get asked to the prom. So I went into the JA program and we actually started a company, and it was all very beneficial and very practical learning for me."

My Career / Business:

"Everything happens for a reason. The girl sitting next to me at the New York ad agency where I had just started working was Brittany Hodak, my future cofounder at ZinePak! One day I was complaining to her, 'This place is awful, I have to leave,' and she said, 'I agree, I don't like this place either. In fact, I have this idea to package published content with music, and I think you would be a perfect cofounder.' She had never started a company and I had never started a company, but Brittany had worked at a record label for five years and I had been working in publishing, so we said, 'Well, what the heck, let's give it a go!' I was 25 and she was 27. We knew we had a good idea, we knew what the product would be, and all we needed was a client.

"Brittany and I spent a month doing risk assessment, and what we figured out was encouraging. We believed we could actually be making money from day one. We also realized we didn't need a glamorous office, or employees right away, or all the bells and whistles—just the two of us on our couch in our sweatpants. We needed a phone, a computer, and our brains. Those were the only three things we needed.

"The timing was right and we had the right idea, so we started up. Luckily for us, both the record labels and Walmart loved our concept. We did deluxe albums for everybody from Kiss, The Beach Boys, and Johnny Cash to Katy Perry, Taylor Swift, and Justin Bieber—young and old, pop and rock. We sold exclusive packages into Walmart in all 3,000-plus Walmart stores from the beginning. Walmart is every merchandiser's dream, and they were big supporters of ours from the very first day.

"After our start-up, we were actually invited to go on the hit show *Shark Tank*. We later discovered it was very unusual to be invited on the show. When we appeared on *Shark Tank*, we received full offers of $725,000 from four of the five Sharks, and then turned them all down. We had sales of $1 million our first year, $3 million by the fourth year, all with no outside money—so we ultimately decided we really didn't need or want investment money from the famous Sharks after all!

"Today we are doing a lot more of what we call Super Fan packages, in other areas beyond music. For example, we do New York Mets super fans, Comic-Con super fans, Starbucks super fans, in addition to the music artists. We're working with different sports teams, with different brands, and still working with our music artists. So we've evolved the business and expanded our markets immensely—and we're particularly excited about the sports market today."

My Advice to Young People:

- "First, for those who always say: 'It's not the right time.' Well, it's never going to be the right time. There's always going to be a reason to delay. You just have to take a deep breath and jump, and hopefully your wings will catch you on the way down.

- "Next, entrepreneurs get a bad rap for being frivolous and taking risks, but they are actually very calculating. I tell people it's like a chess game—you look three steps ahead to see where the pieces will end up so that you can mitigate the risk the best you can.

- "Third, whether you're an entrepreneur or an intrapreneur inside a company, it always smart to ask for help. I think women especially often have a superwoman complex—saying I don't need help. You'd be shocked at how many people want to see you succeed and are willing to lend a helping hand—so don't be afraid to ask for help.

- "Finally, I encourage young women to go for the entrepreneurial life as we've done with ZinePak. But it's hard for the girls seeing images of Mark Zuckerberg and Elon Musk everywhere. They say that's not me. He doesn't look like me. That's another reason why Brittany and I wanted to go on *Shark Tank*. We could say, here we are! And a million young girls might tune in and say, 'I could do that too!'"

JA ALUMNI INTERVIEW

Jimmy Zhou

Founder, Private Equity Fund, JA Alumnus, China

> *My founding team and I are helping the young entrepreneurs of China build their businesses in China and around the world.*

My JA Experience:

"I first joined the JA program in 2003. At that time JA was only in the universities in China—it was not in the high schools yet. I was a sophomore at the university in Shanghai. JA was a very good platform for the students. A platform to know the real business world, to learn more about companies, and to create a strong network. So I got a lot from JA—not only the network, there were also a lot of practical things we did in the activities. And the most important part of the experience was those professional guys who mentored us. So JA was very important for me."

My Career / Business:

"I'm in finance now. I left the university after graduation and joined a Chinese investment bank. I learned a lot from the professionals I met in JA who were working in this area. Then I founded this private equity fund. My founding team and I are helping the young entrepreneurs of China build their businesses in China and around the world.

"We like to work with young Chinese entrepreneurs, not with rich people or big companies. That's because I think the young entrepreneurial people are the future rich people, so we think it's very important to work with them now because they are really the future. This is another thing related to JA. Working with and for younger people is so important. And helping them become successful is the future. That's another thing I got from JA.

"I should mention that both my parents are engineers. Even though my university major was also engineering, I went into finance, which is quite different. But my dad and mom taught me that the way to change the world is with 'our own hands.' So, even though I run a financial business I want to help young people become entrepreneurs, and help change the world in my own way."

My Advice to Young People:
- "First, I think you have to do everything with an attitude of happiness. By that I mean you must have the passion and the motivation. You have to be happy, right? You don't want to be sad. If you're sad, you don't want to get up early, you don't want to go to work, you don't want to do anything.
- "Second, I think you have to focus on the 'what' of your business. Put all your efforts and do the very best you can on *what* you are doing. Even if you have a failure, you have to keep working, and stay focused, and you will ultimately make it happen."

JA ALUMNI INTERVIEW

Samer Sfeir

Cofounder, shareQ / M Social Catering, JA Alumnus, Lebanon

> *I've chosen to be in social entrepreneurship because it's a great combination of creating a successful enterprise while making a sustainable social impact on people's lives.*

My JA Experience:
"My friend and I had worked on a social enterprise idea since 2009 that very few people seemed to care about. I then joined the JA Company Program in 2012 as it opened the door for us, with our idea, to participate in a regional program. During that year, we won the Best Women Empowerment Project among five Arab countries. Today, that project has become M Social Catering, where I now work full-time as a social entrepreneur. Our previous name was MommyMade. JA was

one of the first organizations that actually believed in us as youth—and that we could have some impact. JA continued to support us for years beyond the competition."

My Career / Business:

"I am an active social entrepreneur, and cofounder of both shareQ and M Social Catering. ShareQ is the umbrella organization for M Social Catering, a social enterprise that provides high-quality catering services and food for corporate events. Our corporate catering customers are renowned international and local companies, NGOs, banks, and universities. All of the profits go to support our job placement and integration program that trains and employs women and youth with physical, social, and financial challenges.

"Regarding our social impact level, up through 2017, some 150 women and youth with such challenges have been trained. Approximately 80 of them have already integrated into jobs. In addition, we recently launched the Healthy Food for NGOs Program, which has prepared and distributed 50,000 healthy meals to 2,000 children with social and financial challenges all across Lebanon.

"In addition to being a social entrepreneur, I am currently teaching entrepreneurship at Notre Dame University and giving training and workshops on entrepreneurship for several local and international organizations. I've chosen to be in social entrepreneurship because it's a great combination of creating a successful enterprise while making a sustainable social impact on people's lives."

My Advice to Young People:

- "My one big piece of advice is: You are going to spend most of your waking life at work, so try to seek out your life's vocation and passion using these steps which have worked for me and have become my life's slogan: Pray, Dream, Plan, Go for It . . . Success!"

JA ALUMNI INTERVIEW

Stephen Arinitwe

Founder and CEO, Aristeph Entrepreneurs Centre,
JA Alumni, Uganda

> *I joined JA Uganda because I wanted to become a CEO at an early age, and I made it!*

My JA Experience:

"I'm the founding member and CEO of Aristeph Entrepreneurs Centre. ASTEC is a social enterprise which I started in 2008, while I was in the JA Company Program at the Kololo Senior Secondary School. It was legally registered in 2011. The entrepreneurial spirit I gained in JA led me to become a young CEO at the age of 17. It has also helped me win a number of awards that include the Annual Young Achiever's Award in 2009 and 2011, and in 2013 I received international recognition at the One Young World convention in South Africa; 1,250 delegates from 190 countries attended that event, and both Sir Richard Branson and Winnie Mandela addressed the delegation. I was the proud flag bearer for Uganda.

"I joined JA Uganda because I wanted to become a CEO at an early age, and I made it! Today I am also a proud alumni member of JA. I must thank JA Uganda for who I am today in the business world."

My Career / Business:

"Currently I am a practicing business journalist by professional training. I originally established Aristeph Entrepreneurs Centre because I wanted to help other young people in Uganda develop their future as JA helped me. I came from a humble family with not enough money, but I am now proud to say that JA made me rich. Today I can provide for all my needs while helping my fellow youth find a job and earn a living. At ASTEC we help them get hands-on, income-generating skills. My team and I train young men and women to make a variety of products from local materials ranging from eco-friendly paper bags, candles, and charcoal briquettes to hair shampoo and soaps to various art and crafts. We also provide job training in IT and agribusiness. So far, ASTEC has trained over 15,000 young people.

"With their newly acquired skills, they can pay their school fees, take care of their families, and eventually establish their own companies. Today, Aristeph Entrepreneurs Centre is one of the leading social change organizations in the country. We have three social entrepreneurship academies: ASTEC IT and Media Academy, Entrepreneurship and Cottage Enterprises Academy, and ASTEC Agribusiness Innovations Academy. They all operate under our ASTEC Social Innovation Hub.

"I started all this because we have a big problem in Uganda—that affected me and inspired me to be part of JA. It is that parents have failed to provide career guidance to their children. They have also failed to find a good way to mentor their children. Further, the unemployment challenges faced by so many Ugandans are severely limiting the growth and the development of our entire country. And finally, Uganda's education methodology is more theoretical than practical. The number of graduates who are unemployed after leaving university has reached a crisis level. So, I said to myself, I think I can do something about all this—to help myself and all these young people earn a living. That is what led me to found ASTEC, which I hope has become an enterprising role model for the country."

My Advice to Young People:

- "My advice to young people is to always follow their passion and seek knowledge from people who are professionals in the industries they hope to enter. For example, I had a passion for becoming a CEO, and by learning from the CEO of JA Uganda and other mentors I met in JA, I was able to achieve my goal.
- "Also remember that what you earn does not count as much as how wisely you spend what you earn. I started ASTEC with just $14 in capital. As a nonprofit we always had to be careful with our money, and today we have become a large, successful social enterprise venture. So, to all young people, your future lies in your own hands—and be good stewards of every opportunity that comes your way."

Pedro Englert

Founder & CEO, StartSe, JA Alumnus, Brazil

> *Finally, remember that nobody does anything great all alone—and nobody works hard to realize a dream that is not theirs.*

My JA Experience:

"Since I was a kid, I liked the business world. One day in 1995 I learned there would be a program in my school to develop the students' entrepreneurial spirit. It was called 'Mini Empresa' (JA Company Program). I signed up. It was there that I first met JA, which was just arriving in Brazil. I loved the whole idea and started a very close relationship with the organization. In the following years, I participated in various programs such as 'Mese,' Banks in Action, and the Entrepreneur Shadow Program. I was also one of the founders of Nexa, a group of alumni achievers, in 1996.

"With each new interaction with JA programs, I grew more certain of the path I would like to follow in my professional life. The opportunity to participate in setting up a business, establishing a relationship with a USA school, spending a day with an entrepreneur, or listening to lectures from people we only read about in the newspapers was all very rewarding and stimulating. Certainly this was all fundamental to my preparation for the job market, and it allowed me to meet so many intelligent and competent people whom I still relate to today."

My Career / Business:

"I've worked since I was young because I believed that would improve my qualification. Today I am a graduate in business administration. During college, I worked in several areas, but it was the financial industry that I liked the most. When I left college, I began working in the commercial area of a large company called Ipiranga, which distanced me from my dream of working in the financial markets. Then, four years after graduating, I was invited by a friend to join XP

Investimentos, a new, small brokerage firm that was starting up in my city, Porto Alegre. It had a very aggressive partnership model, and I joined the firm with the goal to help lead the growth of all the branches. Well, just seven years later we had 400 branches throughout Brazil, we changed our headquarters to São Paulo, and we became the biggest broker-dealer in the country.

"In my last three years at XP, I was the CEO of a portal that XP bought called InfoMoney. During that time, I learned a lot about the digital world and realized the impact that technology would exert on our personal lives and our businesses. We next partnered with Bloomberg and consolidated ourselves as the largest financial portal in Brazil, and XP Investimentos became one of the largest companies in the financial market in Brazil. We recently sold half our shares to one of the largest banks in Brazil for approximately US$4 billion. I left the company in 2016 and went with my family to live six months in Silicon Valley. There I graduated from Singularity University and learned a lot more about the entire start-up ecosystem.

"Back in Brazil I decided to restart my career. Today I'm the founder and CEO of StartSe, the main start-up platform in Brazil with more than 120,000 people registered between entrepreneurs, investors, and mentors. I'm an angel investor in eight companies and a partner in five fintechs. In addition, I am on the board of directors at JA Brazil as well as the Brazilian Association of Fintechs."

My Advice to Young People:

- "My first advice to young people is to do something you enjoy, because only then will you be willing to devote the time and energy to make it a success.
- "Understand the new technologies and how they will impact your business. Look for reference points and best practices globally, not just in your region.
- "Do not be afraid to make a mistake, but do not persist when you are wrong, and certainly do not repeat the same mistake.
- "Finally, remember that nobody does anything great all alone— and nobody works hard to realize a dream that is not theirs."

JA's Seven Competencies: The Entrepreneurial Attitude in Action

JA gave me my first opportunity to be an entrepreneur, and have the joy of creating an idea, executing that idea, and turning it into revenue and profit. That was a very powerful thing for me emotionally.

JENS WELIN, Managing Director, Starcom USA, JA Chicago
Board of Directors, JA Alumnus, Sweden

Part 1 of the book described the four fundamental practices of the world's great entrepreneurs, supported by interviews with JA alumni who are exceptionally strong examples of each of the four practices.

In Part 2 we will take a somewhat different perspective. JA Worldwide has recently embarked on a major research project to measure JA student improvement in several critical behavioral areas or competencies. The seven competencies JA has identified, and is measuring in its students, are all critical skills young people will need to become great employees and great job creators—or entrepreneurs.

The interviews here, also with successful JA Alumni from around the world, are organized around the seven competencies to illustrate and bring to life the skills necessary to be a successful employee or job creator in our global economy. The stories, as told by the wonderful JA alumni who agreed to be interviewed for the book, all demonstrate *the entrepreneurial attitude* in action.

In that regard, I am so grateful for the cooperation of JA Worldwide in arranging all of the book's terrific interviews. I feel blessed and enriched by getting to know so many JA alumni and hearing their stories firsthand. It's been an unforgettable experience for me—and I hope you will also feel enriched as you read through these remaining, amazing stories. The seven competencies follow.

CHAPTER 6

Goal Orientation and Initiative

Having a Self-Starting Nature and Proactive Approach

Lia Zakiyyah

Deputy to the Assistant, President of Indonesia's Special Envoy on Climate Change, JA Alumna, Indonesia

> *Even though I'm working in government, I have this entrepreneurial spirit about the work and the challenge we face in keeping the environment safe.*

My JA Experience:

"JA people came to my high school, explained the program, and asked who wanted to join. Later they asked who wanted to be president of the company and I just raised my hand. I didn't know what it was all about yet, but I raised my hand. But I didn't regret it—JA was really exciting. It required a lot of teamwork, and at first we didn't really have any idea what to do. We printed holiday cards, we made dried plants, we organized school events—anything that could make money. I was still learning about teamwork and what the company should or could do. As the president, I had to oversee all aspects of the company: finance, human resources, marketing, but at the same time try to not micromanage the other team members. I didn't really realize how hard that would be, but I learned. I think the two most important things I took away from my JA experience were that I became much more confident in my decision making and I learned how to create teamwork within the team."

My Career / Business:

"After high school I went to university where I graduated in economics. I then worked for a consulting company on social responsibility programs, spent a year traveling in Europe, came back home, and actually worked for JA Indonesia for two years as a program officer. While working for JA I also earned a master's degree where my thesis was on climate change communication. That thesis led to my current job working for the president of Indonesia's Special Envoy for Climate Change.

"I love my job. It's very important work, and I'm passionate about it. I'm one of the youngest in the office and the newest member of the team. Even though I'm working in government, I have this entrepreneurial spirit about the work and the challenge we face in keeping the environment safe. We have to educate as many people as possible. I have to figure out the right way to sell this message to people across Indonesia. I am also on the supervisory board for the Youth Climate Movement in Indonesia, and we are trying to set up a formal Institute for Climate Change. Also, we have just finished a project where we collaborated with UNESCO to increase awareness among youth on climate change and to try to trigger actions from young people. I think when you give young people the information, and the tools, and the power, they can achieve great things. Of course, in doing all this, I must acknowledge again that I got my entrepreneurial spirit and action taking attitude from JA.

"Ever since I was in JA I've always wanted to have my own business, or should I say my own institute. I'm always thinking about that and how I could set up an institute of some kind to continue my work on the environment. Meanwhile I will continue using my current government platform to talk to as many stakeholders as possible with the message that we will not suffer economically by taking good actions around climate change."

My Advice to Young People:

- "First, it's all about knowing and pursuing your vision—and making sure that what you're doing is matched with your own personal values. You can't motivate yourself when you work at things you don't believe in.

- "It's not easy to find that vision for yourself—look for those things you really like to do and those things you're really good at doing. It's in these areas that you will find the right vision for yourself.
- "Consider the search for your career to be a lifelong journey. It may not end with your first job or even your first career. Pursue what you believe in and what you are good at for your entire life.
- "Finally I would say just do it! Some young people are very smart, but they just don't go for it—they think they need to learn more before trying something. But soon you will reach 30 or 40 and you still haven't gone after your own dream. So, act now and just do it!"

Joshuel Plasencia

Cofounder, Project 99, JA Alumnus, New York, USA

How much can I do as a person or entrepreneur, but in a way that makes sense for where I am? It's all about driving as fast as you can without coming off the rails.

My JA Experience:

"JA transformed my life. Before JA I would walk by the large corporate buildings in New York City and had no idea what was going on inside. I could only assume what it was to be a business professional. Both my parents dropped out of school, so I didn't have parents who pushed me. Of course my mom wanted me to do well in school, but I needed the other half of the equation—and that came from JA. I became a JA kid when I was a freshman in high school and stayed in for four years. I attended a JA job shadow program at Time Magazine, which was the first time I was inside one of those buildings to see what was really happening. From my experience as a JA student I got exposure and opportunities that I never had before. In 2012 I won the JA of New York award for Student of the Year. I also won the ALFA (Association of Latino Professionals for America) Student of the Year competition, and Jack

Kosakowski, the president of JA USA, actually came to New York to introduce me at the award dinner—which was quite an honor for me.

"I'm one of those JA kids for life. I'm in Boston now studying entrepreneurship at Babson College, so it's a natural connection to work with JA of New England. The president of JA Northern New England, Radhames Nova, is actually the first Latino to run a JA region in the U.S., and I've worked with him on a few initiatives. I'm also familiar with JA in my home country, the Dominican Republic. Recently we had a meeting between the JA Dominican Republic and JA Northern New England management teams which was great. I'm hoping for more global contacting like that within JA."

My Career / Business:

"Project 99, the nonprofit I cofounded with Meehan Valdes, who is also studying at Babson College, is very much a follow-up to my experience at JA. It's something I'm very passionate about: enabling leadership among underrepresented young people—Latinos and African Americans specifically. We've created a leadership program and go on the road to teach the program to young people of color from poor socioeconomic communities. We're active in the U.S. and got started in the Dominican Republic in 2015, Mexico in 2016, and Chile this year. Our goal is to bridge the leadership gap that exists in the United States and across the world. The USA for example, is 30 percent Latino and African American, but only 3 percent of the senior leadership of the country is from those groups. This is the focus of Project 99, and we plan to work full-time at it when we graduate from Babson this year. The name Project 99 comes from the Human Genome Project, which showed that at the DNA level, 99.9 percent of all people are the same. We may be taller or shorter and have different colored eyes, but the differences between people only represent .01 percent of our DNA.

"We were inspired by that data, which so clearly indicates that everybody is capable of becoming a leader and achieving their own dreams. So that's where the Project 99 name comes from. We use crowdfunding on the Internet and corporate sponsorships such as Delta Air Lines to finance Project 99. We have also applied for grants from government agencies and social enterprise foundations. We are determined to succeed in our mission to provide leadership skills to millennials of color."

My Advice to Young People

- "The number one thing for me has always been pushing limits, but in a smart way. How much can I do as a person or entrepreneur, but in a way that makes sense for where I am? It's all about driving as fast as you can without coming off the rails.

- "Second, don't be afraid of failure. The more I fail, the more I learn. If you're not having some failures along the way, you're probably being too conservative and not aiming high enough.

- "Third, and this is the 99.9 percent point, you have to believe we are all *capable* of achieving our dreams. You may be a young person, you may be underrepresented, there may be socioeconomic barriers—but precisely because you are *capable*, you can in fact overcome those barriers."

Cosmin Malureanu

Founder and CEO, Ascendia SA, JA Alumnus, Romania

> *1992 was the start of capitalism in Romania, so we were very much at the beginning of our new entrepreneurial age.*

My JA Experience:

"I joined the JA program a few years after it started in Romania—about 1998. I was in high school and joined because it was teaching new things related to economics. I was passionate about economics—especially the mix between informatics and economics. They put us in teams for computer simulation games. You made inputs into your factory and then put the goods into the market. It was so engaging. It made students think about how to market goods. You had to think about your capacity to produce, your pricing, the marketing, and how the market works. It was very attractive for me as a student to get engaged with other student teams and do something in business and economics.

"Capitalism was so new to us—1992 was the start of capitalism in Romania, so we were very much at the beginning of our new entrepreneurial age. JA brought a new perspective on how economics should work. In school we learn a lot of theory, but JA came as a more practical approach toward business and the economy. I really liked the program and stayed in it for two or three years. Then several years later, I became a JA advisor. Stefania Popp, the founder and CEO of JA Romania, asked me to go to the schools and teach the children. I found that very rewarding. Whenever you receive help, you should give back. Whenever they need an advisor I go. After all these years I'm still close to JA."

My Business / Career:

"I saw that education had problems in Romania. I believed that through technology I could greatly improve the educational process. In Romania the old paradigms of classroom learning hadn't changed in a hundred years. I thought, the whole world today has PCs, tablets, all kinds of smart games, so why not use the power of these tools to enhance the educational process? This is how I saw the opportunity—to use technology to enhance Romanian education and leave a mark on the world. We started Ascendia in 2007—10 years ago now. We first worked to just break into the education market. We initially subcontracted with a large government supplier to create computerized educational programs all around Romania. We did that kind of business for several years to get started.

"About five years ago we started creating and marketing our own programs directly to clients. We started developing products under our own brand, from kindergarten to adult training. We sold more than 140,000 licenses for kindergarten pupils alone. We have agents presenting our programs in schools. We've had partnerships with libraries, bookstores, and kiosks. We have entire kiosk chains reselling the programs. We even had a partnership with Dannon Yogurt Company where they put commercials on TV showing our program in with their yogurt packages. And today we have a good partnership with Samsung for marketing our programs. So we have various ways to market and distribute to the retail education market.

"Our next programs were developed directly for the Ministry of Education, to be used in public school classrooms. They came to us and said they wanted to digitalize the curriculum and have digital textbooks to complement the printed texts. We now provide our own e-learning programs for the ministry, which are being used in all public schools. So we are leaving a mark on the young people of Romania—which was the goal I had when I started Ascendia.

"The government is actually less than 5 percent of our turnover today. We are much more in the B2C retail markets and the B2B commercial markets. In our B2B business, we offer e-training for company employees. We resolve the big cost and logistics problems all companies have with widely dispersed business locations. For example, they can't bring 2,000 people into one place to train them in a new product. So we solve their problem with customized e-learning.

"Along the way, we've also won a few awards. In 2010, I won JA Europe's Young Entrepreneur of the Year award, and in 2014 Ascendia received the European Union's Digital Entrepreneurship award. Today we have 30 people here in Bucharest. While Romania is our main market, we also have clients abroad. Our original programming is in English, but we make multilanguage versions in Russian, Greek, Arabic, etc. In 2015 we listed on the stock market of Romania, so we're a publicly held company now. It's good for a Romanian company to be listed on the stock exchange for local credibility and international recognition. Our turnover is growing nicely and currently exceeds €1 million. The market value of the company on the Romanian stock exchange is about €4 million."

My Advice to Young People:

- "Travel as much as you can abroad. Learn about the world and how others live and think. If possible, study or work abroad a few years.
- "The entrepreneurial journey is a viable option for anyone who has some tolerance for risk, a free spirit, a ton of ideas and doesn't run away from 'mopping the floor' of the workplace. Try it if you can.
- "Learn how to learn. The world is changing at a fast pace. You must avoid getting stuck in a job or career with no future. You must challenge yourself to learn new things and remain competitive.
- "Finally, I've built my company on two pillars. One is my family—my brother and my wife are both partners in the company. The other pillar is my team. I have people working with me for 10 years now, who I completely trust. Without these two pillars, I could never have achieved what we have today."

Jens Welin

Executive VP and Managing Director, Starcom USA, JA Chicago Board of
Directors, JA Alumnus, Sweden

> *JA gave me my first opportunity to be an entrepreneur
> and have the joy of creating an idea, executing that
> idea, and turning it into revenue and profit. That
> was a very powerful thing for me emotionally.*

My JA Experience:

"I grew up and went to school on Gotland, an island off the coast of Sweden. I
was fortunate because my teacher was one of the pioneers doing JA. So we all
participated in the JA Company Program. We were very inspired by the idea of
having our own company. We created three companies, and I was voted the
managing director of one. They all had different products, and my company
made T-shirts. The idea was to make and sell T-shirts with the JA logo on them
to all 2,000 students in the school. All three companies were quite successful.

"I was nominated for an award and scholarship given by one of the most
famous entrepreneurs in Sweden. JA advisors recommended JA students for
the award. I was brought to Stockholm and interviewed by a panel of judges,
which for me at 18 years old was quite exciting. After all the interviews I was
selected. So I became Entrepreneur of the Year in JA Sweden for 1987.

"JA gave me my first opportunity to be an entrepreneur and have the joy
of creating an idea, executing that idea, and turning it into revenue and profit.
That was a very powerful thing for me emotionally. In fact, I made a goal for
myself at 18. I would become an entrepreneur, have my own company, and
somehow I would become a Swedish millionaire by my thirtieth birthday. Of
course, it was not really about the money—it was only about US$100,000—it
was about the achievement. That was just the way I described my goal at 18
years old. So yes, JA had a big impact on my life."

My Career / Business:

"With my scholarship money I was able to go to college one year in the U.S. at
LaGrange College in Georgia. After I came back to the University of Stockholm,
I continued studying marketing communication. After university, in 1993, I
started working for one of Sweden's first commercial TV stations. Advertising

wasn't allowed at first on TV in Sweden, and it still wasn't very popular, so it was a great job for me to work in that pioneering landscape, talking to advertising agencies and convincing them to give TV a try. I even began thinking about starting my own media agency. As it happened, one of the famous advertising people in Sweden, Ulf Sandberg, was also starting his own agency, and he asked me to join him. So together we started up Sandberg Media in 1995. I was young but became the CEO and a 10 percent shareholder. We were quite successful in building Sandberg Media across Sweden. We grew to about 160 professional staff.

"Then in 2001 we sold the company to Starcom, the global media company based in Chicago, and a subsidiary of Publicis in Paris, the world's third-largest communications group. Going back to the goal I set after the JA program, that I wanted to be a Swedish millionaire by 30, again not so much money in dollars, I achieved the goal plus a bit more. Anyway, I stayed on with Starcom and ran their entire Nordic operation, which we grew to become one of the top five agencies across the Nordic countries. In 2014 Starcom brought me to the Chicago headquarters, where today I am executive vice president and managing director of Starcom USA.

"I had always stayed close to JA Sweden, speaking for them, being a juror in competitions, anything to help them. So when I moved to Chicago, the CEO of JA Sweden introduced me to the president of JA Chicago, and I was invited to be on the JA board in Chicago. When JA Chicago turned 75 in 2015, my agency joined with Leo Burnett, another subsidiary of Publicis, to provide a campaign for JA Chicago's celebration. It was a $2 million pro bono gift and made them even more famous in Chicago. Of course, JA Chicago is already the largest JA office in the world, with an amazing 575,000 students last year. Anyway, I continue to contribute to JA in any way I can."

My Advice to Young People:

- "First, get serious about doing something you like and getting really good at it. I spent about 30,000 hours on basketball and became one of the top players in Sweden. I've spent about 40,000 hours on the media business, and I've had a very successful career. This is what young people should do to become successful at anything.

- "Second is to dream big. Visualize where you want to be in the future. When you do that you can start working toward that dream.

- "The third point is, getting and giving feedback is a gift. There is no such thing as being the best with nothing else to improve. And you can only get better if you continuously get and give feedback."

CHAPTER 7

Leadership and Responsibility

Taking Ownership of a Project, Group, or Task

Mark Hamister

Founder, Hamister Group, LLC, JA Alumnus, New York, USA

> *I can honestly say, the JA program got me more excited, and more motivated, and more driven, than anything I had done in my life up to that point.*

My JA Experience:

"I'd like to say that I joined JA as a 14-year-old because I had the wisdom, the courage, and the foresight to know it would be the way to launch my entrepreneurial spirit. But I can't say any of that, because it was my parents' foresight. I had no clue at that age and usually felt bored and unchallenged at school. But my father saw something in me that suggested I needed to try a bunch of different things—so he had me go through scouting, and sports, and then he suggested JA. When I got into JA, however, it only took two or three meetings of the group for me to understand this was going to be very exciting.

"I discovered very quickly that I was challenged by JA and it really grabbed my attention. Our adult sponsors were two executives from the famous Ocelo sponge company. In our first meeting we were supposed to elect officers and decide on our product. We didn't do either. We couldn't agree on a product or who the officers should be. None of us liked each other's ideas. Later at home I spent some time debating this with my dad, and he said one thing to me which was very meaningful. That was I should pick a product that frustrated me, or didn't work right, and figure out how to fix it. Well, at that time my family didn't have a dishwasher, and every fourth night it was my turn to wash the dishes after dinner. One of the things that always frustrated me was I could never find the Brillo pad. I liked washing with the steel wool Brillo pad, it took less scrubbing than the sponge or washcloth. But I could never find the stupid thing. I always found the sponge in the sink, but I could never find where my mom put the Brillo pads.

"So, at our second JA company meeting I suggested that we take a steel wool pad and a sponge and glue them together and cut them into one piece. The two-sided product would be easy to find in the sink and would actually make washing dishes a lot easier. Remember, the Ocelo sponge company was our JA company sponsor—and of course they loved this product idea also. They even helped us manufacture it in their plant. Well, our JA company did very well with that product. We sold out all we could produce. I think what really turned us on was that we were filling a real need in the marketplace with our product. Later on the Ocelo company adopted it as a product, and they're still selling it today. Obviously, it's become a well-known product around the world.

"I was elected president of the JA company, and we actually won the national sales award that year. We were number one in sales for all JA companies across the United States. As a result, I was sent to Indiana to the 1964 NAJAC conference, which was great. What JA did for me, personally, was to really turn on my creative juices and my entrepreneurial spirit. I can honestly say, the JA program got me more excited, and more motivated, and more driven than anything I had done in my life up to that point. What JA really did for me was to demonstrate how much fun entrepreneurship is.

"And then, about 20 years ago, JA of Western New York State inducted me into their Hall of Fame. And believe it or not, Ocelo, which by then was owned by the 3M company, was the sponsor of the awards dinner—and they had placed an Ocelo sponge/scouring pad package, which our JA company came up with in 1964, on every seat in the room. Even though I never got a royalty check from Ocelo for the product we invented in high school, I guess that awards dinner was some payback!"

My Career / Business:

Author's note: Mark Hamister is a recognized leader in both the healthcare and hotel management industries. The Hamister Group, which he founded 40 years ago, has a remarkable record of business success. He revolutionized the assisted care industry by transforming his properties from a hospital-based model to an upscale hotel model—with unparalleled customer care. It was this process of creating hotel style environments for assisted care and nursing facilities, that inspired him to expand his business beyond healthcare to hotel management also. Because Mark's career is well documented, and his comments on his JA experience and his advice to young people are so powerful, I'm using our limited space here to fully record those thoughts.

My Advice to Young People:

- "First, figure out your passion. It's very easy to have fun when you're pursuing your passion. You shouldn't pursue something because your siblings did it, your parents did it, or your classmates did it. You should pursue your individual passion, first and foremost.
- "Second, I believe every young person should decide, do they want to be an entrepreneur and lead the pack, or do they want to be an intrapreneur and work for somebody else but exercise an entrepreneurial spirit inside that company. Of course, the majority of kids will be intrapreneurs, and that's fine. I certainly want intrapreneur type people working for me.
- "Third, be 'the best of the best.' Being average is not fun, but being the best of the best is exciting no matter what your role in life. There are lots of ways to be the best of the best, but it's never easy. It's hard. It's challenging. But when you are consciously going the extra mile, to learn more, to do more, to deliver more, you will be the best of the best.
- "Finally, there's one additional point. Always listen to your customer. No matter how much experience you have, your customer's needs, wants, desires, and demands can change day-to-day in our fast-moving society. If you're not persistently asking your customers what they need and want, if you're not carefully listening to them, the competition is going to leave you in the dust."

Daneil Cheung

Social Enterpriser and Activist, JA Alumnus, Hong Kong

> *JA inspired me to be an advocate for youth development and look beyond my own borders to be a social enterpriser.*

My JA Experience:

"I first joined the JA Company Program in Hong Kong in 2007 when I was a secondary school student. I then entered into the JA International Trade Challenge in 2008 and got the chance to participate in the final competition in Malaysia. This was my first opportunity to travel outside of Hong Kong and was a truly eye-opening experience for me. My JA experience stimulated my interest in international travel and inspired me to begin my career as a travel journalist.

"I've also been invited to be a guest speaker at JA Leadership Seminars in 2014 and 2015. Over a thousand JA students attend these events, and I was honored to be asked to share my thoughts with so many fellow JA students and alumni. JA inspired me to be an advocate for youth development and look beyond my own borders to be a social enterpriser."

My Career / Business:

"I started my career as a travel journalist, and after that I developed myself as a content marketer, public relations advisor, and project manager for a number of large events and platforms. They include DCFever.com, one of the largest online lifestyle portals in Hong Kong; Wheel Power Challenge, where I am a cofounder of a series of experimental programs to empower wheelchair users to have fuller and more physical lives; TEDxChaterRoad, where I am the license holder for Hong Kong–based events, and Asia Pacific Youth Club, which advocates the idea that travel is not only for fun but should also provide educational exchanges and networks.

"I am also passionate about youth development. I've held various positions and advisory roles in different youth development projects. In this capacity, I've delivered career development speeches and leadership seminars in Hong Kong, Singapore, Malaysia, Korea, India, and as far away as Estonia."

My Advice to Young People:

- "Most importantly, you must build up your own credibility in your field. This includes building up your own personal integrity—so that everyone respects and trusts you. These are the most valuable things you can do to further your career.

- "Secondly, expand your network to not only receive the advice or help of others, but also be ready to give advice and help to others. Find mentors for yourself, and be a mentor to others."

Leen Abu Baker

Vice President, INJAZ Al-Arab Alumni Board, JA Alumna, Palestine

Do what you love—the only thing that will keep you going is your passion.

My JA Experience:

"It all started way back in my primary school days, where I began to learn about business through different JA programs. But the most significant turning point was when I became part of the JA Company Program and discovered the leader in me—and that I could actually do something of value. School programs, the Company Program, camps, being on the regional competition jury, and participating in the INJAZ Al-Arab Alumni Network summarizes my experience with JA so far. It's obvious that as I grew up, INJAZ Palestine was there each step of the way; it helped me discover and acquire new skills, influenced my personality, and let me experience magnificent opportunities. I had the chance to meet outstanding colleagues, like-minded people, who I now consider to be as friends and family. I have learned a lot through their inspirational stories, great experiences, and hard work. All this gave me the courage to pursue my dreams, to work harder, and to help my society. I'm glad to be part of this amazing family. I believe we will achieve great goals and continue our INJAZ journey, but now as INJAZ Al-Arab alumni ambassadors."

My Career / Business:

"I just graduated a month ago from An-Najah National University in Nablus, Palestine—with a bachelor's degree in computer engineering. I have now started a full-time job as technical procurement officer at the biggest tele-communication company here in Palestine. I've chosen a job where I can practice computer engineering and business development—as my journey with INJAZ made me realize that business and management are the main pillars of any career. I took this step to get some experience and prepare myself for the master's degree I'm aiming to get in business intelligence. I believe that all of this will help me in the upcoming few years to start my own initiative or company."

My Advice to Young People:

- "Do what you love—the only thing that will keep you going is your passion.
- "Start searching for your interests at a young age, and don't be afraid to share them with the surrounding community.
- "Always believe in yourself and spread positive energy around you. And always remember that failures are just the beginning of success!"

Nyi Mas Gianti Bingah Erbiana

Chief Legal Counsel, Mitsubishi Indonesia, JA Alumna, Indonesia

If you have integrity, people will trust you, they will follow you, you can be a leader.

My JA Experience:

"First my friends call me Ghea. The JA program was in my school in my home-town of Bogor, Indonesia—which is near Jakarta. The first year I was finance manager of the company, and the second year I became the president. The products in the first year were cookies, chocolates, and sweets. We really wanted to earn money, and we made these products because they were so easy to sell to the children in the high school. The second year we held special events for mothers and children, which we call a "kebun" in Indonesia. At these festivals or bazaars, we sold food and other locally made products. The main thing I took away from my JA experience was learning about leadership and teamwork.

"I just want to thank JA. The JA program was one of the greatest experiences I've ever had. It opened my eyes to the world. I saw I could become anything I wanted. When I joined they told me about the possibility of developing myself. Well, the mentors in the JA program were so nice and helpful. They don't treat you like a child. They treated you as a partner. It made me feel comfortable. I learned so many things from them—and the entire JA staff in Indonesia, including Mr. Gardiner, the head of JA Indonesia."

My Career / Business:

"Currently I am the chief legal counsel of Mitsubishi Company, a joint venture with PT Krama Yudha Ratu Motor, in Indonesia. I've been here for six years. I got my LLB law degree at the University of Indonesia. And just last year I took a one-year study-leave to get my LLM master's of law degree at the University of California, Davis. I also worked in New York for Mitsubishi International before coming back to Indonesia. Going back to my JA company experience, I've always seen a strong connection between business and law. Without good laws, you can't really have a stable business environment. How the law is applied in operating the company is critical. In my thinking, a company is not just about earning a profit, but a company should also be an agent of change that creates ethical behavior in its stakeholders and promotes social awareness in the community and nation through its social activities. In pursuing both the profit and social goals of a company, the law provides tools in the form of rules and regulations which have to be respected by the business players.

"At UC Davis I studied business law so if I ever start my own business I will have a good background in both the law and in business. Of course, working for the Mitsubishi joint venture in Indonesia is my full-time job, but I am thinking about having my own business someday. I haven't done it yet, but my dream is to start an educational company for children. Going to the JA program was probably the main reason why I got my scholarship to law school, and I would like to give back to other young Indonesian people some of the opportunities I've had."

My Advice to Young People:

- "The first point is that young people should be persistent and have a strong will. No matter what obstacles you face, if you are persistent, and you don't give up, you can achieve what you want.
- "The second one is to be flexible. It doesn't mean that you become a follower or you don't have your own identity. But you have to be a person who can adapt to changes in the world and be able to compromise with other people.
- "The last one is to have integrity. I think it's really important today. Sometimes in business and society it's hard to be someone who sticks to their values. You can find smart people everywhere, but finding honest people with integrity is so hard. If you have integrity, people will trust you, they will follow you, you can be a leader."

Tunji Eleso

Cofounder, Growth Capital, JA Alumnus, Nigeria

> *To entrepreneurs I say just start up! You can't know the end from just seeing the beginning, so there's no point being overly cautious.*

My JA Experience:

"I graduated from Obafemi Awolowo University in Nigeria in 2001, where for three years I was also involved in AIESEC, the worldwide student exchange organization. At that time, I wanted to pursue a career as a management consultant in a big prestigious firm. It was clear that having other notable activities on your CV could give you an edge during interviews. Then I heard about JA and the wonderful opportunities it offered to someone like me. I could contribute to society through the JA Elementary School Program (ESP) by teaching primary school kids about businesses and watch them grow as they played out roles.

"Shortly after my first JA volunteer program in the summer of 2001, I was selected to attend, as one of 40 young professionals, JA's Venture into Management Program (ViMP) in Lagos. That experience totally blew my mind. It was a one-week mini-MBA course with top faculty of the Lagos Business School (now Pan Atlantic University.) It was a one-of-a-kind program that was the envy of young university graduates in Nigeria. It was a live-in program, which made the experience even more exciting, as course work was discussed late into the night. Many of the attendees have become close colleagues and good friends.

"Going through the ViMP program helped answer a question that had always bothered me. Was I cut out to be an entrepreneur, or was I just a traditional nine-to-five person? Getting the answer to that question, early in my career, set me up very well for the rest of my career. I left ViMP in 2001 believing that I could make it as an entrepreneur. A decade later, I started my entrepreneurial journey at Co-Creation Hub Nigeria—with the JA experience having prepared me well for this phase of my career."

My Career / Business:

"I started out in a professional services firm with the aim of becoming a management consultant. While there, I was part of a team which led some of the most successful enterprise transformation projects in the Nigerian banking industry. My work experience involved helping companies develop and execute strategies to improve their growth. Clients included bank and nonbank financial institutions and small businesses. After nine years of being a management consultant, I decided to join a nonprofit focused on financial inclusion in Nigeria. There I had the opportunity to work on a nationwide survey on Nigerians' use of, and demand for, financial services. It was a rich experience that helped me see the whole country and have perspectives that I wouldn't have as a predominantly Lagos-based professional.

"Then in 2011, Bosun Tijani, the cofounder and CEO of Co-Creation Hub (CcHUB), which provides venture capital and business advice to social enterprises, asked me to join his team. I jumped at the chance, especially since it involved working with people who were turning social business ideas into viable projects. From the onset, I was treated as a partner and was involved in critical decision making of the organization. Two years later, I legally became a part owner of CcHUB. And last year, five years into this journey, Bosun and I cofounded a new CcHUB company, Growth Capital, which focuses on seed funding for technology companies looking to grow and scale up in Nigeria. I'm the managing partner of this business."

My Advice to Young People:

- "It's great to be young and have the world at your fingertips, thanks to the Internet, but it's still important to have a mission or plan and pursue it from an early age. Create goals, tweak them as required, understand market trends, and most importantly stay ahead of the curve by being dedicated to your craft.
- "To entrepreneurs, I say just start up! You can't know the end from just seeing the beginning, so there's no point being overly cautious. The key is to position your business to get immediate feedback from your customers to improve your products.
- "Technology has made it possible for any business to be national, regional, or global. Take full advantage of this technology, but start with inexpensive prototypes to test the markets.
- "Creativity, persistence, knowledge, and having good mentors can all guide you on your journey."

Creativity

Engaging Imagination to Create and Innovate

Bonnie Chiu

Founder, Lensational, JA Alumna, Hong Kong

> *Always start with the "why." It's the most important question to ask in building your life and your career: Why am I doing this? Why do I care about this? Why is it important to me?*

My JA Experience:

"I was 16 years old when I joined the JA program in Hong Kong. To be honest I never thought about myself as a businessperson. I was quite set on studying law. But I thought, OK, it will be an interesting thing to join even if it's not necessarily for my future career. So I started the program, and there were 16 of us with two advisors. We came up with the idea to make a cup which we called the iCup. It was a mug like you get at Starbucks, but you could take out the tumbler and change the paper around it so you could personalize it. We called the company iLove because we wanted to show love for the product, the customers, and ourselves as employees. We made over 200 percent profit on our investment, and we gave about 40 percent of those earnings to Make-A-Wish Foundation. We won the JA Hong Kong Market Potential Award, which we were really excited about. Later, we also won the JA Hong Kong Corporate Social Responsibility award, which to me was the most important award to win. I think even then there was a desire deep inside of me to make some difference in society.

"The big takeaway for me from the JA experience was understanding that anyone can be an entrepreneur. As a 16-year-old girl, I didn't know that was even possible as a career path. So it was a very valuable experience, and it definitely shifted my thinking about my career. In fact, I dropped my plans to study law at university and I studied international business instead. So JA had quite an impact on me. I really think without the JA experience I wouldn't be running my own social enterprise company today."

My Career / Business:

"I was born and raised in Hong Kong. I moved to London in 2013 to complete a masters in international relations at the London School of Economics. While completing the final year of my university degree, with zero funds and a dream to create a system that connects marginalized women across the globe, I founded Lensational. It's a social enterprise organization which seeks to fight gender inequality by providing women with a means of expression and also the option to create an independent source of income. If participants so choose, they may continue their photography work after the conclusion of our free workshop, and Lensational will sell their work in exhibitions and on our e-commerce platform, with the majority of the revenue going back to the women photographers.

"As the CEO, I've led Lensational to grow to a team of 100 volunteers across the globe, and we've trained over 600 marginalized women across 15 countries. Their creative work and stories have reached millions and been featured by media outlets including *Huffington Post*, TEDx, and the *Guardian*. We've also secured partnerships with major corporates including Standard Chartered, Getty Images, and WPP. I've also been asked to present the Lensational story at prestigious venues such as the Clinton Global Initiative, and I was honored to be named a Forbes Europe 30 Under 30 Social Entrepreneur in 2017.

"My passion and hope is that Lensational will grow as a worldwide social enterprise and continue focusing on helping women through the medium of photography—through telling their stories and also providing a livelihood by selling their photography via our platforms. This is what we are working toward today."

My Advice to Young People:

- "My first advice is actually what I wrote in the JA Company annual report eight years ago. It has always stayed with me. It said to be successful you have to have your heart in your business and your business in your heart. I think the emotion of 'love' is an underestimated force in business, and realizing how you channel it into your business career is very important.
- "Next, is to always start with the 'why.' It's the most important question to ask in building your life and your career: Why am I doing this? Why do I care about this? Why is it important to me?"

Christophe Robilliard

Founder, Easy Taxi Peru, JA Alumnus, Peru

> *You can imagine how much "fun" it was to announce to my mother that I was leaving McKinsey & Company, the world's top consulting firm, to open a taxi company.*

My JA Experience:

"I joined the JA program because I had always been trying to make business out of everything. For example, starting at the age of 10, I would perform as a comedian during school recesses and charge people who wanted to listen. I admired entrepreneurship, and I wanted to also learn how to manage a company. I was made responsible for the JA company's finances, which helped me understand how costs and taxes impact business and how to make the best financial result out of it. The program convinced me of the potential of entrepreneurship, and has guided my professional decisions from that time on."

My Career / Business:

"While studying industrial engineering I realized there weren't many quality celebration events for people at my university throughout the year. So I started a nightlife entertainment business organizing parties to celebrate the end of exams, Halloween, New Year's Eve, and so on. The 20 events we organized produced revenue of over US$700,000 with more than 16,000 attendees.

"I left the entertainment industry when I finished college to join McKinsey & Company, the world's leading business consulting firm. At McKinsey I learned a lot about strategy, processes, and corporate finance, but I also learned that I wasn't born to be a consultant. My real passion is to see things getting done, and I was getting frustrated in the theoretical world of management consulting.

"Before I completed my second year at McKinsey I was contacted by a venture capitalist who was searching for a young consultant who might just be bored by the corporate lifestyle and be ready to launch Easy Taxi in Peru. Easy Taxi was a start-up that was created in Rio de Janeiro to solve public transportation problems by hailing public taxi drivers. At the time, it operated only from Brazil, and the team wanted some new cofounders to join and expand across Latin America. I took the opportunity and jumped into the pool without really knowing if it was full or empty. You can imagine how much 'fun' it was to announce to my mother that I was leaving McKinsey & Company, the world's top consulting firm, to open a taxi company.

"After four years at Easy Taxi, leading a team of 100-plus people in Peru, the company is the biggest Latin American urban transportation technology company. Easy Taxi's growth allowed us to join a regional group which just surpassed US$1 billion in valuation, and we are fighting at the same level with Uber—the giant U.S.-based competitor valued at over US$60 billion globally."

My Advice to Young People:

- "Find new problems you can love solving every day, but never get in love with your current solutions. If you are doing things right, your solutions to problems will pivot indefinitely.
- "Seek complementary, brilliant, and loyal partners.
- "Learn from every experience, no matter how unrelated it might seem to be with your entrepreneurial activity, because everything you learn adds to your capabilities and your knowledge which you can use in the future."

Alan Tsui

Founder, Kites, JA Alumnus, Hong Kong

> *In the media, they say to do what you love and follow your passion. I would argue that if you want to be successful you should be doing what you're good at first.*

My JA Experience:

"I grew up in Australia, and then my family returned to Hong Kong. I was always interested in trying out small ventures, whether it was a garage sale, or a Pokémon club competition, or being an online trader for electronics going from Hong Kong to the U.S. So when JA popped up in school it was quite natural that I joined the program. I learned two big things from JA. First was focus. We learned firsthand about the 80/20 rule with our products and that having focus was so important for the company. The second thing was how hard it is to be a leader and manage other people. I went to a private school in Hong Kong where there were a lot of 'type A' personalities. Everyone in the program wanted to be the leader, choose the product, and make all the decisions. I was elected the CEO of the JA company, and it was very difficult to manage all those 'type A' personalities."

My Career / Business:

"I went to the University of Chicago in the U.S. After college, back in Hong Kong, I started a data company focusing on location data, or points of interest, such as looking for a restaurant or whatever on Google maps. This had been a problem in Asia, and my company was trying to solve the problem. We raised some money and organized a team of 12 people. I figured even if we failed, it would be a great learning experience. What ended up happening was our technology and the expertise of the team was more valuable than the revenue stream our customers brought in, and one of our biggest customers said why don't we just acquire your whole company? It wasn't a huge acquisition, but we were acquired by Cathay Pacific Airways, the Hong Kong flag carrier. I thought we would collect a payout and I would be done with it, but in an interesting twist the airline wanted to retain me and my team to build up an analytics business inside Cathay Pacific. It's been like a start-up inside a bigger company. So today I'm the head of audience analytics at Cathay Pacific, and I'm still doing what I started doing in my own business, but under the umbrella of a large company. I now have a good taste of being an entrepreneur and being entrepreneurial in a big corporate environment."

My Advice to Young People:

- "The first thing is perhaps a contrarian view. In the media, they say to do what you love and follow your passion. I would argue that if you want to be successful you should be doing what you're good at first. Even if you don't or can't love what you're good at, you can still become successful at it—and that will allow you later on to do something you may find more meaningful.
- "Another thing I've learned during my last two years in the corporate world—there is more to life than career success. I've enjoyed more personal time and have managed to use the airline benefits to do a lot of traveling. So I would say, especially to all the 'type A' people, think beyond just being successful in your career. There is your family, your health, your hobbies, etc. These things are very important to keep in mind.
- "Finally, when you're young, and you're a smart guy, and you've graduated from a top school, you think you know it all. However, it's still important to find mentors who are straight up with you. Not mentors to cheer you up, but mentors who sit you down and tell you you're an idiot and you're too arrogant. Somebody who will tell you the truth. I actually found this with the CEO of JA Hong Kong. Her name is Vivian Lau, and she was very straight up with me. Meeting her was actually the best thing I got from JA."

Raymon Setiadi

Cofounder and CEO, Aitindo, JA Alumnus, Indonesia

Set your dreams as high as you can imagine, but also be realistic. Find the balance between dreaming and executing.

My JA Experience:

"I joined the JA program in Indonesia when it was offered by my university. I was interested to know more about entrepreneurship and leadership. I heard about the JA Company Program. They told me it was about starting a real company, and I was really interested to be part of it—so I joined. I believed that having some real organizational experience would be a good way for me to learn. It gave me a boost of confidence as I got a glimpse of what it was like to run a real company. It taught me to see the multidimensional perspective of managing a business—from running meetings to boosting teamwork to resolving conflicts. I think all of those experiences, early in my university career, helped shape my mindset and my understanding of entrepreneurship. I continue to support JA Indonesia in various ways to pay back for the wonderful learning and mentoring I received early on."

My Career / Business:

"At the time I was studying computer science in the university, and my business today is in digital marketing—so it's really in the same field. I started my IT company, Aitindo, right after graduating. I am only one of the company founders, so I have partners from the university. The company is 10 years old, and we have about 60 employees today. We started as an IT company but over time evolved into a digital marketing company. We've basically learned everything by doing it ourselves. We were all computer science graduates at the beginning, so we had to learn things like sales, project management, finance, legal, and HR. We are a creative technology company, and we have two business focuses today; the first is around our agency services, and the second is based on our platform products. The service side is our digital agency, where we work with brand owners on their digital marketing strategies for branding, user acquisition, or sales conversion. We provide services from consultancy, execution, and monitoring for their websites, mobile apps, and social media presence through various channels like Google, YouTube, and Instagram. On the product side, we partner with subject experts to produce online platforms in various fields such as fashion, lifestyle, and healthcare, where we connect patients and doctors online. Our latest service is an online wedding directory across the Asia Pacific market.

"The digital marketing industry is growing very fast due to all the technology advances. It's also a 'people industry' as it relies heavily on employee talents to produce good strategies, designs, and content. This is a good combination for me; I like interacting with people, as well as taking part in the evolving technology. I believe all this can lead to many new opportunities for our company in the future."

My Advice to Young People

- "Set your dreams as high as you can imagine, but also be realistic. Find the balance between dreaming and executing. A lot of people know how to execute, but they forget to dream. On the other hand, some people just keep on dreaming and are afraid to make a move or execute.
- "Never think that you know everything, and never feel too comfortable. Because when you think and feel that way, you are not giving yourself any room for improvement.
- "Lastly, I always remind myself and my team to keep learning and stay humble."

Jerome Cowans

Jamaica House Fellow, Office of the Prime Minister, JA Alumnus, Jamaica

> *I traveled to New York and received an entrepreneurship award from the United Nations—which was all due to my exposure to JA in Jamaica.*

My JA Experience:

"I'm very passionate about JA. I joined many years ago, when I was just 16 years old, because there was something very different about the program. First, I would be part of an inner-city community group. JA would come into our community to expose us to business and financial management. It all seemed very practical. After the first meeting, I was completely sold on the idea and signed up. We started our own JA company. We came up with "Glow In The Dark" pottery as our product line. We made the pottery and then used glow paint to make Jamaican designs on the pieces. We started shipping out the product as we learned more and more about the market. Well, the customers just loved our product. We were just teenagers, but we even sold the pottery pieces to companies and banks to go into their lobbies and offices. I was the PR manager of the JA company.

"I learned so many things from JA. The most important was not just getting business knowledge, but actually putting it into practice. That was my biggest takeaway. It's fine to learn things in class about balancing the books and marketing, but when you actually do it, especially as a teenager, it gives you an understanding that is unparalleled. It helped me in school as well when, for example, we discussed business and economics. In JA I was literally doing the things we were talking about in class. We continued our company after the JA program ended because it was such a success. A group of six of us decided to just continue making the pottery, selling it, and pocketing the money. And I ended up receiving an award from the UN. I traveled to New York and received an entrepreneurship award from the United Nations—which was all due to my exposure to JA in Jamaica.

"After I did the JA Company Program, I became a JA instructor for other programs for younger students. And now, 10 years later, I'm still involved. If the president of JA Jamaica calls and asks me to do something, I just do it!"

My Career / Business:

"This year I am a Jamaica House Fellow, in the office of the Jamaican prime minister. It's a special program similar to being a White House Fellow in the U.S. I'm an economic analyst in the program, and I consult on various projects across the country. I started the fellowship only four months ago, as I just completed my master's degree in management at the University of Birmingham in the UK. I also have a bachelor's degree in economics from the University of the West Indies here in Jamaica."

My Advice to Young People:

- "Number one would be to pay equal attention to practical knowledge and academic knowledge. This is the same point I learned in JA, but it's important for all young people. All through your life it will be important for you to understand the practical side of what you're doing as well as the theoretical.
- "Second, is to work really hard. This may be a cliché, but I think younger people have started to drift a bit to getting things done too easily with technology. It's important to balance that with hard work as well.
- "Finally, try to find something that you are really interested in. I would also encourage young people to think about the medium to long-term

perspective for their careers. You could do something now as a career that will be obsolete in 5 or 10 years. So do something that you love to do, but also be prepared for changing it in the future."

Claudio Rossi

Cofounder, polarlab ag, JA Alumnus, Switzerland

> *Well, maybe Roger Federer is more famous today—but at that time Heidi was still the most famous Swiss in history!*

My JA Experience:

"It was back in 1999 when I read a newspaper article about the new JA program in Switzerland. It sounded interesting, so I went to the school to learn about the project—and decided I wanted to try it. We were 18 or 19, and we started with really basic business ideas. But I think our product idea was unique and pretty cool. Just as JA's one hundredth anniversary is next year, the year after our JA company project would be the one hundredth anniversary of the death of Johanna Spyri, the author of *Heidi*, the most famous Swiss character ever. Well, maybe Roger Federer is more famous today—but at that time *Heidi* was still the most famous Swiss in history! Anyway, building on that, we were thinking about doing something about *Heidi* and her creator Johanna Spyri.

"We decided to publish a new book highlighting all the parallels between the life stories of author Johanna Spyri and her famous character, *Heidi*. And as we discovered in our research, there were many. So our JA company product would be a new book about *Heidi* and her creator, Johanna Spyri. We called it a cultural touristic guide. We also learned the Japanese are crazy about the book *Heidi*. So along with the German edition, we also translated and printed a Japanese version since there would be a good market there also. There were a lot of challenges, of course, but we had turnover of about 20,000 Swiss Francs with the first printings. That may seem a small amount today, but it was amazing to us that we could achieve anything like that, and it made us feel very proud. We could say this is our baby and we worked very hard at it night and day because we loved it. The progress we made by having small steps of success, with all the setbacks of course, was so inspirational and it incited curiosity in us to try new things.

"And remember, the JA program in those days did not come to us through our school. It came through the ad in the paper. We saw the article, and I said to my colleagues, 'let's try this,' and we all said, 'OK let's go do this!' So we really owned the project and the success."

My Career / Business:

"We are not really a financial institution, but a service company. After the JA Company Program, I was always interested to try starting a business for myself. But after finishing university in Switzerland, you get very spoiled because even your first job gives you an amazing salary. And really that's very comfortable. So I started working in investment banking. It was the heyday of investment banking, but with all of the industry consolidation going on, it was not the place I wanted to be forever, so I said to myself, I'm still young, so I'll try something else, and I moved to a small financing company for real estate. After a while I thought this is still not the place I want to be—and I decided I really wanted to do my own thing. I talked with some colleagues and we thought we could get a few clients who would trust us, or at least give us a chance.

"So we started up. Today we are actually three companies, all finance related. One is a software services for finance, one is an advisory brokerage service, and the third has to do with traditional debt financing. We very much want our specialty in all three sectors to be working in the entrepreneurial financial space, and I think it helps that we are entrepreneurs ourselves—and understand the financial needs of other entrepreneurs. We started with one good client earning money from the beginning, which was really important in our start-up phase. We're still a young company, but we are four partners across the three companies who all have experience, knowledge, and contacts in the finance industry—so we are excited with our possibilities.

"Everyone asks about our name, polarlab. Names are sometimes just a random exercise, but we chose ours because its reminds you of the North Star—something that shows you the way, that shines at night. Some people make fun of it, but they also remember it—and that's the point.

"Today I'm pleased to be on the board of JA Switzerland. And this year I'm also the president of the jury for the JA Student Company National

Competition in Switzerland. I've always stayed close to JA. Shortly after finishing my own student project years ago, I actually joined the staff of JA and have been working with them ever since—in one capacity or another."

My Advice to Young People:

"JA is amazing because it inspires young people and exposes them to ideas they would never ever have in such a protected environment as Switzerland. JA teaches what entrepreneurs actually have to do: you have to get the start-up money, you have to create a product, you have to find clients. It's not learning by theory, it's learning by doing in JA. In summary, JA is one of the best experiences I ever had in my life—and here are a few key pieces of advice:

- "At the end of the day, I think it's all about inspiration. You have to find the business or career that interests and inspires you.
- "My best advice really is to participate in a JA program. You know the education system in Switzerland is quite traditional. Very little really is taught about business or even economics to young schoolchildren. So that is the place for JA to come in and help the students."

CHAPTER 9

Teamwork

Cooperating and Working with Others to Achieve a Common Goal

Bill Covaleski

Cofounder, Victory Brewing, JA Alumnus, Pennsylvania, USA

> *If we didn't have our restaurants as a gathering place to tell our story and get feedback from our customers, I don't think we would've made it.*

My JA Experience:

"My JA experience is linked to my business partner, Ron Barchet. It was his father's suggestion that the two of us devote some of our 'idle time' to the JA program. We began in 1978 when we were 15, and living in Collegeville, Pennsylvania. Ron and I did pretty much everything together, so we joined JA together. We had two products in our time in JA. First, was a roadside emergency lighting tool. If you were on the side of the road and needed to do repairs at night, you could plug the light into your car lighter and safely fix the problem. It was a nice product, actually. The other one was a wooden, sculpted desk pen holder.

"My key takeaway was collaboration—among ourselves and with the JA advisors. We were young, and our only experience in collaborating with others was playing on the school grounds and being on a sports team. What was fascinating about the JA experience was that while our teachers at school were trying to teach us and get academic results from us, the instructors from JA, advisors with real business experience, were helping us achieve *our own* practical results. It was a different dynamic. It wasn't us trying to succeed for a grade, it was having advocates who helped us bring our ideas to fruition by working within a collaborative team environment."

My Business / Career:

"My father grew up just after the Great Depression in the coal region of Pennsylvania, and was a very resourceful guy. He was an avid gardener who would can vegetables and grow other food for the family. He also had a taste for European style lagers, but didn't have the budget for them. Then, President Carter's administration in 1979 made home brewing legal in the United States. It was one of the things that had been overlooked in the Twenty-first Amendment abolishing prohibition. So it became legal to start making beer at home, and my dad embraced the opportunity. And after many years of being his assistant, making beer in our basement, I began to play around with it for myself.

"By 1985 when I graduated college, I had become thoroughly enthralled with home brewing. In fact, I gave Ron a home brewing kit as a Christmas gift that year. He had graduated from UCLA and was working in Washington, DC, as a financial analyst, and I had graduated from Temple University and was working as an art director and designer in the Philadelphia area. But bit by bit our mutual passion for brewing started overtaking our careers. In 1989 Ron made the career jump, and I followed suit a year later. We first started working for breweries here and then both went to study brewing in Germany. The opportunities within the industry were expanding at a fast rate, and we started planning and raising money in the mid-nineties. We started up Victory Brewing Company in February of 1996. We did some interesting things like opening a restaurant in our first brewery to use as our advertising tool and educate the public about the taste and quality of European style, but locally produced, beer. We were lucky getting in at the earlier stages of the craft brewery boom in the U.S.

"We're now up to three brewery locations, all with restaurants, in Pennsylvania. Our brands are distributed to 37 states in the U.S. and nine countries around the world. When we were writing the first business plan there were 1,100 craft breweries in the U.S., and today there are 5,300. Our first brewery cost $1.3 million, which included a $650,000 SBA loan, and the most recent brewery we built cost $39 million. So you can see how the industry is growing."

My Advice to Young People:

- "First, do your research and solicit input from others. Get to know people in your industry whose ideas may have succeeded or failed. It's really the failures you need to pay attention to, because they can recur if you are unaware of them.

- "Second, be open-minded. If your vision isn't understood or appreciated by detractors, don't dismiss them. Learn from them. Learning from people who say your idea is no good can be really valuable.

- "The final thing is to be aware of the community you serve. For example, if we didn't have our restaurants as a gathering place to tell our story and get feedback from our customers, I don't think we would've made it. Having real engagement with your market, and getting their feedback early on, is so valuable."

Gcina Dlamini

Cofounder, Smiling Through Investments, JA Alumnus, Swaziland

Consider that entrepreneurship is a career that not only provides the owner with income—it also provides employment to others to support their families, and finally it contributes to the entire country's economic prosperity.

My JA Experience:

"When I first joined the JA Company Program, I was faced with several choices of doing extracurricular activities, such as sports and other cultural activities in my school. I considered all the choices and discovered that I was very interested in the science of business. I wanted to learn how people made money through business. As I listened to what JA Swaziland was offering, I learned that participants would go further than just knowing about business—we would also be exposed to the practical aspects of actually running a business. That motivated me to choose investing my time and energy in learning how I could become my own boss in the future, while also getting practical hands-on business experience. While I was enrolled in the program, I began to experience a love and passion for entrepreneurship, which impacted me so greatly that I decided to study business management at university and eventually choose a career in business. The program influenced me to view my capabilities in a whole new direction; no longer seeing myself as an employee, but becoming an entrepreneur and creating employment for other young people in my country."

My Career / Business:

"At university, I chose to do a degree in business management, specifically agribusiness. I chose agribusiness because food is the major problem facing the African continent. The world population is increasing at an alarming rate, but agricultural resources across Africa remain static. It was very important to me to know the strategies we can adopt to ensure we can feed Africa and the whole world. It also seemed to be a career opportunity—to join forces with the government in identifying the agricultural needs across our country and hopefully providing a profitable solution for those needs.

"So during my second year at the University of Swaziland, I teamed up with other JA alumni and we founded Smiling Through Investments (STIN). STIN is a 100 percent youth-owned business, specializing in green mealies production, bean seed production, and organizing agribusiness fairs. Our projects during the years at the university were the first of their kind: We hosted a Farmers Field Day on the university farm where we showcased our bean seed to more than 100 community farmers. The reason we've ventured into bean seed production is because food security is dependent on seed security, and beans are the major source of protein for most families. Next, we hosted farmers' seminars to unlock new agribusiness opportunities for them and help ensure that Swaziland becomes food secure. We also held award ceremonies to honor new agribusiness companies. Finally, we hosted the first national Agribusiness

Fair in 2015. That was a three-day event which started with a school festival for high school students to expose them to agribusiness opportunities. They visited agribusiness companies and heard testimonies from other young agribusiness entrepreneurial start-ups like STIN. The University of Swaziland recently adopted our Agribusiness Fair, and it is now an annual event, celebrated nationwide, to revolutionize the agriculture sector of Swaziland.

"The projects and enterprises we started at the university have also received some recognition in other African countries. I've been invited to present our ideas in South Africa, Kenya, and other countries. Our theme at these conferences is: Fighting Youth Unemployment Through Entrepreneurial Agribusiness Projects."

My Advice to Young People:

- "My advice to young people is that they need to follow their entrepreneurial passion no matter what—and their attitude will determine whether they will succeed or not.
- "Consider that entrepreneurship is a career that not only provides the owner with income—it also provides employment to others to support their families, and finally it contributes to the entire country's economic prosperity.
- "Some of the enterprises young people start will fail, but they need to keep on trying until they succeed. As young people we need to be ready to pay the price of being entrepreneurs. The rewards are worth it.
- "Lastly, God bless all the young people as they set up their new business, and follow their entrepreneurial passion, regardless of the challenges they encounter."

Chris Slater

Cofounder, Simply Business, JA Alumnus, United Kingdom

So my advice is to pick an industry where the bar is rather low . . .

My JA Experience:

"I've got really fond words to say about Young Enterprise—or as you call it, Junior Achievement. I do a lot of work with them in the UK. I'll be getting involved with them in the U.S. as I'm moving to Boston shortly. My early experience with them was the catalyst for the entrepreneurial skill and appetite I have today. I was a very studious student in school, head in the books sort. I was introduced to Young Enterprise at age 15 and saw it as an interesting opportunity. I always wanted to get into commerce, the legal side or corporate finance side, and I was fortunate enough to not land there. Actually I was the finance director of my team's Young Enterprise company. We raised the capital, we built three different types of first-aid kits as our products, and we were able to flog them. And then, believe it or not we even got taxed by the authorities.

"The key things I took away from it were being forced into a team with people I hadn't worked with before, taking an idea from concept to getting it in front of customers, and the very rudimentary basics of building a business. I've started companies twice in the UK and will be doing it for a third time in the U.S., and those foundational learnings from the YE program still hold true today. It's finding quality people you can trust, focusing on solving the really near-term problems, and solving the customers' problems by getting a product in their hands as quickly as possible."

My Career / Business:

"I was frustrated working for large insurance organizations. So I cofounded Simply Business following the concepts I'd seen in the small business and start-up space. Insurance is a product I feel passionate about—but it has a huge perception problem. The industry doesn't do a good job of simplifying or making it easy for customers to understand what they're buying. So using good technology, producing good user experiences, using data to solve customers' problems, is really what we've been trying to do at Simply Business. We created this marketplace, or platform, to give customers a better experience, on their time, with transparency around what they're buying. And then for the insurance carriers, it gives them distribution channels at a lower cost, better data, and better insight around the customers' problems. And we sit neatly in between serving those two parts of the insurance value chain. We had first-mover advantage and spent 13 years continuing to invest in our technology, our data, and most importantly our people. In both 2015 and 2016 we made the *London Times* list of 100 best companies to work for in the UK. So that's the story of our business, We're now the largest online insurance broker in the UK with 420,000 customers, and we're just starting our international expansion in the U.S., as a brand-new acquisition of the giant carrier The Travelers.* So I'm moving to Boston!"

My Advice to Young People:

- "My advice has changed over time. The opportunities that are open to young people today to start their career are boundless. Years ago the idea of starting your own business was out of the question, whereas now you can spin a website, build a social media campaign, get a product in front of customers in days rather than years, all from your bedroom. My key bit of advice is if you've got an idea, just go out and test it, even if you fail. Many of the best entrepreneurs will fail once or twice or three times. What's the worst that can happen? It fails and you end up going to work for a big company anyway.

- "The second bit of advice, which I'm passionate about, is recognizing that you can't do it all on your own. I see a lot of young people with very grand ideas, with a sense of arrogance really, say that they can do this all on their own. I think one of the reasons for my own success is I've been humble in my approach. I've absolutely loved working in teams. As your career develops you need networks of people at different points along the way—so be humble and ask for help.

- "The third one is very real for me. I've been successful in insurance because you don't need to be that great, frankly, and you can put that in your book, I don't mind. So my advice is to pick an industry where the bar is rather low, an industry that is perceived as dull, overly complex, overly burdensome. Those are great industries to have a go at, because if you get it right you can really make a huge change, a huge impact. And there are loads of these industries that are still back in the 1950s."

---

* *Author's note:* Chris was too modest to mention it, but the press reported in March 2017, the month before I interviewed him, that Traveler's Insurance in the United States had acquired Simply Business for a whopping $490 million! Chris will be the CEO of the new U.S.-based operation.

Max Tang

Real Estate Developer, JA Alumnus, China

It takes time to become an expert—but it's exactly that experience that makes you valuable.

My JA Experience:

"I joined the JA program in 2002. I was introduced to it in my university. I also became a JA volunteer after graduation. The JA program gave me a different perspective on education from our contemporary system in several ways: First you learn and understand there isn't just a single right answer. Second, you learn to be a team player. Third, you learn from the real business world, not solely from teachers. And finally you learn the value of volunteerism.

"JA helped me to be better equipped before starting my career. The program taught me how decision variables can affect business results. It provided business logic for nonbusiness students and real business cases as shared by JA volunteers. The team spirit taught in the program has helped me build more trust in teams. The entire experience has helped me understand my employer's business model and decision-making process, which has helped me to grow very quickly in my organization. And finally the volunteerism displayed in JA has encouraged me to help others by sharing my own knowledge and experience."

My Career / Business:

"I have been in the real estate industry since finishing my undergraduate education. I spent six years as an investment associate in residential development and then three years in commercial real estate. I went to an MBA program in 2009 before my thirtieth birthday and then started to do industrial real estate investment for five years. Currently, I am working in a real estate private equity firm and starting a new division.

"Honestly, I entered the real estate world by accident. At the time I was trying to sell an IT solution to a real estate company. I was actually thinking I might become an IT guy for a career since the Internet was booming. But when I got more understanding about real estate, I started to really like it. Anyway my experience has covered marketing to investment management to project positioning and initial design management. I also experienced the bad financial period and decided that real estate finance might be the next step for me to learn. So thanks really to my JA activity, I started my MBA program after the financial crisis.

"My current work is like an internal start-up. We decided to step more into early stage real estate companies. So, I've started this business as a quite new idea and it will fit into the booming trend of small business start-ups, and will be quite an innovative activity."

My Advice to Young People:

- "You need to discover what you are passionate about before you plan out your entire career. It must be in your area of interest, so that even if you have some difficulties, you can still carry on. Try different kinds of work before you make your final career decision.
- "Don't change your career once you've decided on what you want to be. You can change your specific path but not your career itself. It takes time to become an expert—but it's exactly that experience that makes you valuable.
- "Keep an eye on what your peers are doing and see how their experiences can be applied to your business. This would be a way to be more innovative.
- "Don't lose passion for your business—everything depends on it."

Richard Chang

Venture Capitalist—U.S. and China, JA Alumnus, Canada

> *The combination of enjoying what you do and being good at it is the holy grail of career development.*

My JA Experience:

"I did the JA Company Program for two years—'87 to '89—my junior and senior years in high school in Toronto. We got together with a group of other students, from all over Toronto. Each JA company had a sponsor. Ours was General Mills, who provided volunteers to be our mentors. For me, it was a chance to expand beyond my limited area and the neighborhood where I grew up—to be with other students from across Toronto and collaborate with them to do something exciting like starting a company. I was always interested in business, and the idea of starting a company was exciting. JA provided the platform and blueprint to do that. I had a very positive experience.

"The program was well structured, and we had adult supervision from industry. We had to think about everything from incorporating the company, to holding officer elections, to creating the product idea, and then developing a marketing plan. It was well set up and really exposed me to business. I eventually went to the JA national conference with other high school students from around Canada, and that exposed me to kids outside of Toronto. I thought the whole experience was great, and the JA program had a big impact on my life.

"I went on to college, a BS in economics from Wharton, an MA in politics, philosophy and economics from Oxford, all of which was partly influenced by my early exposure to JA. While I was in college I wanted to give something back, so I became a volunteer instructor for the JA Company Program. I ended up doing another JA program to teach simple economics to grade 6 students in public schools. So overall I had a very positive experience with JA—and now that I'm more settled in my career, I hope to get involved again somewhere in the San Francisco area where we live."

My Career / Business:

"I started off with a relatively traditional career; working on Wall Street and working in large companies like Sony in Asia. To be frank, Wall Street was very attractive and popular at the time. Most of my classmates ended up going to large consulting firms or banks. However, I eventually ended up coming to Silicon Valley to work in venture capital. That really was the beginning of my entrepreneurial life. I was working with a lot of start-ups, and what I enjoyed most was being hands-on with the companies we invested in. I've sort of evolved into a mixture of being a venture capitalist for company start-ups and at the same time working closely with the entrepreneur and the management team at the early stage. Also the time I've spent in Asia has been instrumental in attracting companies to work with us in Asia and particularly in China. Silicon Valley is still an incredible place, of course, but with the rise of China and Asia, you see a lot of the companies in the Valley thinking more about China and the companies in China thinking more about Silicon Valley and the U.S. So today I consider myself a Silicon Valley venture capitalist with a special knowledge and interest in Asia and specifically in China. That is kind of my niche."

My Advice to Young People:

- "First, young people should not be afraid to take risks, especially early in their careers. There's very little downside to trying different things, things that don't seem to be standard, perhaps a bit contrarian, like dropping out of school to pursue an interesting idea.
- "Second, the combination of enjoying what you do and being good at it is the holy grail of career development. It's become the holy grail because it's so true!
- "Third, having great mentors can obviously give you a leg up. It can save you a lot of time and provide you with a lot of good advice. So find them early on in your career."

CHAPTER 10

Perseverance

Completing Tasks and Goals Despite Difficulties or Delays

Yesenia Cardenas

Attorney and Partner, Bowman and Brooks, JA Alumna, Texas, USA

> *One of the JA volunteers was a female lawyer, who had also been a Rhodes scholar. That was very inspiring to me as a young girl from one of the poorest districts in the state of Texas.*

My JA Experience:

"I first experienced JA in the eighth grade. It was part of an honors program at my school. The JA volunteers were from the USAA insurance company. My school was selected for this program because it was in a very poor community. It was a financial literacy program, how to do taxes, how to open a checking account, and I really enjoyed it. We even got checks from the bank with our names on them—and most of our parents didn't even have bank accounts, so it was exciting for us. We also got to interact with and learn from professional people, who were nicely dressed and worked in an office. My mom worked in a factory, so for me to be with people who worked in an office, it was like, wow! It's one thing to have a schoolteacher teaching you in the classroom, but it was another thing to have businesspeople, who you didn't know, take time out of their life to come and talk to us about finance, business, and things like that.

"The second time I was in JA was in high school. I was taking an advanced class in economics and was selected to participate in the JA program. At that point I was already thinking about college and my future career. Again the mentors came from USAA. One of the JA volunteers was a female lawyer, who had also been a Rhodes scholar. That was very inspiring to me as a young girl from one of the poorest districts in the state of Texas, where a lot of people don't graduate from high school and even fewer go to college. I came from a single mom family, and our future ambitions were rarely talked about. But these JA volunteers were very encouraging and talked to us about our future goals and desires. I still remember saying I wanted to study in England one day, and my classmates made fun of me, saying, 'She's just a dreamer, she can't afford to do that,' but the JA volunteers weren't laughing at me. They took it seriously and said, 'That's great Yesenia, go for it!' That was so impactful to me.

"I know most young people say JA helped them become an entrepreneur or a successful businessperson. But for me, and the students in my group, JA was more about having role models that we could look up to—that we didn't see in our everyday lives. I think it was also the aim of the volunteers to do more than just teach us the JA curriculum. It was to open up the future possibilities for us. So my main takeaway from JA was that the volunteers were role models and showed me what could be possible in my life. It was all so inspiring to me."

My Career / Business:

"After graduating from high school I went to Southern Methodist University in Dallas and obtained a bachelor's degree in finance/accounting and a second bachelor's degree in foreign languages—French and Spanish. After that I thought about what I wanted to do and decided law school would be the right fit for me. I always considered myself an advocate, so to speak. I graduated with honors from SMU's law school. Since then I've been working for a national law firm, Bowman and Brooks, and I represent mostly vehicle manufacturers like Toyota, General Motors, and Honda in their product liability cases. Two years ago I became a partner in the firm, an entrepreneurial role I suppose, as we are the owners of the firm. I'm happy with my career. I work in a wonderful firm and we have amazing clients.

"I was the first person in my family to go to college and certainly the first to go to law school. And in fact I actually did get to go study in England. I studied for one year as an undergraduate at University College London, and later I studied at Oxford University while I was in law school. So my girlhood dream actually came true."

My Advice to Young People:

- "First is perseverance. If you have a goal or dream you want to accomplish, whether it's being a lawyer, owning a business, or having a family and raising great kids, there are going to be obstacles or people who question your dream. It's so very important to stay true to your goals and your dreams and work hard to persevere. That has worked well for me, and I encourage all young people to do that.

- "The second piece of advice is to give back. Sometimes our lives are shaped by volunteers or other individuals who have come into our life and influenced or encouraged us. For example, the volunteers who drove down to my community every Friday afternoon, and stood in front of the classroom and talked to us, made a world of difference to me as a young girl. It's important to give back what you've received. I try to do that myself. I volunteer with JA. I work in a program for socially disadvantaged youth. I still go back to my community and try to be a role model for the kids there today.

- "Finally, one thing I would say to young women—there's no such thing as a male centric career or a female centric career. Today you can do anything that any other person can do. I see it in the legal profession, you can see it everywhere. So my message to young women is, you can do whatever you want in any profession and any career."

Bob Coughlin

Founder and CEO, Paycor, JA Alumnus, Ohio, USA

Today people ask me: "How did you start your company?" I always tell them that it actually reminded me of starting the JA company back in the 1970s.

My JA Experience:

"I joined JA my sophomore year in high school, about 1975. I didn't excel in anything in particular in high school, but then one day somebody came into the classroom and started talking about setting up a JA company after school. I can't tell you what compelled me exactly, but I joined the group along with sophomores, juniors, and seniors all mixed together from multiple schools. We had business mentors. We sold $1 shares of stock in the company. We had to make a product. We had quality control. We actually had to sell the product. We had to keep records and figure out the costs. And if any profit was left over we had to pay it back to the investors. We were sponsored by Formica Corporation, and we made plexiglass planters as our product. I was the quality control manager. I really enjoyed the experience that first year, so I joined again in my junior and senior years. I also went to NAJAC, the national JA conference. I got exposed to a lot of things, a lot of people, a lot of know-how about the inner workings of a basic business. I really had fun, and I developed a lot of confidence from the experience. JA definitely planted the entrepreneurial seed in me."

My Career / Business:

"Today people ask me: 'How did you start your company?' I always tell them that it actually reminded me of starting the JA company back in the 1970s. I sold shares of stock to friends and family for the start-up money, I needed to create a service that the market needed, I put a lot of sweat equity into the business, and we knew we had to create enough revenue to overcome our expenses to give my shareholders a good return. So I felt like I had been through this once before as a youngster with JA. It certainly gave me the confidence to go ahead and say, 'OK, this is not rocket science, I can figure it out . . .' I really don't think I would've started Paycor if I hadn't been in JA. I tell people that all the time—and that's why we've made *youth development* our company's mission. We're very involved in the community, not just with JA, but in many other ways, adopting classes at schools, community activities, and really helping kids. I believe that the mentors I had in JA were businesspeople volunteering their time, who gave me something that allowed me to ultimately start my own business, so I want to pay that back and help young people today in the same way. Of course my company and I are very involved with JA here in Cincinnati. We provide a lot of mentors, we support all their programs, and I, along with my former CFO, who was actually in the same JA program with me all those years ago, are I think the two biggest individual sponsors of JA here locally.

"It's hard to put 27 years of Paycor's history in one paragraph, but our business essentially helps take the burden off our clients of handling their human capital automation needs—which used to be called HR services—covering everything from recruiting employees, to paying them, to managing their benefits, and everything in between, so the client can focus on their own real business. As you know, our founding competitive advantage was to provide our clients with the highest level of service in our industry—and that still holds, but I think today our 'secret sauce' is we provide better human capital software technology, and still delivered with a higher level of personal service than any of our competitors. Today Paycor is a human capital technology company with a high-level mission of providing great customer service."

My Advice to Young People:

- "Consider your first job, and then every job you ever have, to be your most important job. Every job is a building block for gaining experience, developing good habits, and establishing credibility. Your entire career will be a series of these building blocks.
- "Raise your hand and get involved. Don't just do the minimum. Look for opportunities to volunteer. Take advantage of as much training as you can. Do whatever you can to improve yourself.
- "Know thyself. Don't try to be what you're not. Understand your strengths, use your strengths, and surround yourself with people who can help you overcome your weaknesses.
- "If you really want to be an entrepreneur, you cannot put any boundaries on your effort. It's not a nine-to-five day or a five-day week. There will be more to get done than there are hours in the day—you can't just hire people or outsource the work when you're starting up.
- "And finally, when you're starting a business, it's all about your personal credibility with the investors you attract, the employees you hire, the customers you sell. They will all look at you and say why should I believe you?"

Georgi Kadrev

Founder and CEO, IMAGGA, JA Alumnus, Bulgaria

> *I think people need to have life goals that are really huge and ambitious, because then they will put in a really huge and ambitious effort to achieve them.*

My JA Experience:

"Starting when I was 16, I was always working on some kind of software project on the side, beyond the regular syllabus of my school. I worked with my high school math teacher on some projects about image recognition, and image analysis, and stuff like that. I entered some national competitions and won awards for student computer projects. One of my projects was on digital morphing. You know, like the Michael Jackson video *Black and White*, where they were changing faces and morphing from one image to another. So, this kind of technology gave me a very strong technical background. I was always building software and trying to commercialize the technology. But I was young, naïve, and inexperienced back then.

"I finished my bachelor's degree in computer science and hoped to start on my master's degree. I was fortunate because the year I got my bachelor's degree, a master's program in technology and entrepreneurship was starting up. It was a collaboration between Intel education and UC Berkeley in the U.S. and a professor here in Bulgaria at Sophia University. They started the master's program in technology and entrepreneurship, and one of the classes there was actually a JA program for the university level. I had the chance to meet with Milena Stoycheva, the head of JA Bulgaria, and got very inspired. That was 2007.

"I joined the program. We formed a team to participate in the student competition at the University. We were still quite young, and in Bulgaria it was not typical for people to start a product or technology business. If you said you were an entrepreneur in Bulgaria 10 years ago, it was like, 'Oh, he must be building a building somewhere or doing real estate.' That was our idea of the entrepreneur in those days. But, I was very excited, and I made a lot of new friends from the JA experience. We formed a company with a new and different idea—to modify the look of phones, by attaching a sticker with a custom-made image. It could be you and your wife, or your dog, or your favorite movie or cartoon character, or whatever image you wanted covering the face of your phone. We named the product Sticker Art.

"I had several takeaways out of the whole JA experience. One thing was the 'soft skills': to be able to communicate with other people, to be able to defend your ideas, to be able to listen to other people's ideas. Next, as we finished the website, created the products, and started to sell, we began to build some resilience. Even with our successful JA company, we had some downfalls and expectations that were not met—and I believe we developed the kind of resilience that's really important for entrepreneurship. And last but not least, the experience led to us having a chance to pay back to the community in a way. Because we were successful on the local level, and we won second place in the national JA competition in Bulgaria, we were invited to mentor other students. JA in Bulgaria asked us to go back to the school, mentor younger people, and from that I learned a certain level of responsibility.

"So the JA Company Program was a very important experience for me. Today when all of us from the team think back about our JA company, everybody still talks very positively about it. I'm not just saying this out of courtesy. JA is really something that ignites your entrepreneurship. Maybe you have some doubts, maybe you don't know much about business, but for young people especially—JA gives you a safe environment to start. But it's also competitive and ambitious—they are not babysitting you in the JA Company Program."

My Career / Business:

"As I mentioned earlier, all my life I've been interested in computer programming. And for 16 years, in one way or another, I've been involved in the image recognition field. Even back when we were starting our JA company, I was already working on the image recognition ideas that I use in my company today. IMAGGA is a company that consolidates different types of services for image recognition. I haven't started other companies in other fields. This is it for me. This is my life.

"Originally my company started as a visual search engine for stock photography and stock imagery. We built a technology where you provide an image and you can search out any other images that are visually similar. This was back before Google and Microsoft were even in this business. The typical user is anyone, or any company, who needs to find just the right photo to provide a visual reference instantly. For example, an advertising agency, or a news organization, or of course individuals. In 2013 we introduced an advanced model of our technology. Google and Microsoft followed us again, two years later. It's not very humble, but I can say we have been quite visionary in expanding the number of images that people can search, and we know that this trend is exploding, especially with smartphones. People and organizations are going to take more and more photos. The problem with photos is, they're so much easier to take than to catalog or explain. But we can greatly optimize this process, and functionalize it, for news organizations, advertisers, researchers, and individuals.

"Currently we have more than 200 customers around the world, spread out across 35 different countries. We have a presence in Europe, Asia, and the U.S. Our big competitors are Google, Microsoft, and IBM Watson. I'm proud to say that when we go up against them for commercial customers, we usually win the contract. Last year we were selected as one of the three most innovative companies in this space worldwide. The other two were in San Francisco and New York. And we sit here in Sophia, Bulgaria, where we've had only a half million dollars of outside funding and the rest we have bootstrapped ourselves—while the two other companies in the U.S. have had venture capital funding in the tens of millions of dollars. So we're very proud of what we've achieved."

My Advice to Young People:
- "I just have one general piece of advice that I always share with young people. It's that the higher your ambition, the better your chance of achieving it. I think people need to have life goals that are really huge and ambitious, because then they will put in a really huge and ambitious effort to achieve them."

David Meltzer

Cofounder and CEO, Sports 1 Marketing, JA Alumnus, California, USA

We're winning honors and living by our motto of creating abundance—making a lot of money, helping a lot of people, and having a lot of fun.

My JA Experience:

"I grew up with a single mom, with six kids in my family. I had one big objective as a young man. I grew up in a very happy household, but I wanted to be rich—because the only time there was any sadness or disappointment in my home was when mom couldn't afford to fix the dishwasher, or she couldn't send me to summer camp, or one of my siblings needed something costly. So, when I was very young I equated making money and being rich to happiness. Therefore, the opportunity to be a young entrepreneur and understand how you could generate wealth, through the JA program, was extremely exciting to me. I went to this camp in San Diego and participated with other kids, had my first JA mentors, and the program really inspired me.

"I came from a conservative family where my siblings all went to Ivy League schools. We were driven to be professionals like doctors and rabbis and lawyers—the professions which give you a very stable income. My mom was a teacher, for example. But at JA I felt good about having a great vision for myself, and that I wasn't going to be limited by a job that just paid by the hour. I remember my mom telling me: 'Oh, you could make $500 an hour being a lawyer,' and I thought to myself, I'm worth more than that! I can only work so many hours, and I want to make $5 million, not $500. So why limit myself? For me, these ideas were not only validated, but encouraged, by the JA program.

"JA empowered me to believe that I could do whatever I wanted—but even more importantly, it could have a social purpose. Anyway, at a very young age I learned to shift the paradigm. JA challenged me to not just create wealth but to look at things that needed to change for the social good. I wanted to figure out how I could not only make money from business but more importantly how I could affect change in society. That's what the JA program really gave me as a youngster. Later I even wrote a bestselling book, *Compassionate Capitalism*, on that theme."

My Career / Business:

"As I said I grew up wanting to be rich. I thought I had only two choices: I could either be a professional football player or a lawyer. But I also had this huge entrepreneurial spirit inside me. Well, I finally went to college, and played football, and soon realized I wasn't going to be a professional football player. So I threw myself into being a lawyer and discovered I had two choices again. I went to Tulane University Law School, which was well known for its maritime oil and gas specialty. There were also legal opportunities in this new thing called the Internet. I went to my mom for advice and asked her, should

I be a real lawyer, an oil and gas litigator, or should I take this job selling legal research online on the Internet? My mom actually said to me: 'Be a real lawyer because this Internet thing is a fad.' It was beautiful because for the first time in my life I realized that just because somebody loves you, doesn't mean they always give you good advice. Anyway, I sensed the Internet would be more than a fad, so I went to work for Westlaw legal publishing. Well, I became a millionaire in nine months when Westlaw was acquired by Thomson Reuters for $3.5 billion in 1995! I parlayed that into an executive position with Every-path, a wireless proxy server start-up in Silicon Valley. From there I became CEO of PC-E Phone, which was the world's first smartphone. At 32 I had become a multimillionaire.

"I used to tell people that I retired at 32, but the truth was our business under Samsung grew so big that I was "in front of my skis" and they forced me out with a lot of money, which was fine with me. I then became a true entre-preneur: an angel investor and advisor/consultant with multiple interests. But unfortunately, I broke a golden rule that I had learned early on in JA. The idea that you surround yourself with the right people and the right ideas. And here I was, a very empowered young man, who had lived his dream coming from nothing to everything I desired—but for the first time I wasn't happy—because I had entitled myself, and surrounded myself, with the wrong people and the wrong ideas. It's a long story, but suffice to say I managed to lose everything. Everything, except for my values, and my wife, and my three beau-tiful daughters.

"At that low point I decided to rebuild my career and my life. I met Leigh Steinberg, the founder of the most famous sports agency in the world—the firm that the Tom Cruise movie *Jerry Maguire* was based on. I became the chief executive officer of Steinberg Sports & Entertainment where Warren Moon, the Hall of Fame quarterback, and I were partners with Leigh in the firm. In rebuilding my career, I started surrounding myself with the most exceptional people on earth. Warren and I then spun off a sports and entertainment mar-keting venture seven years ago that has done extremely well. We are working with the biggest sports and entertainment events in the world such as the Super Bowl, the Pro Football Hall of Fame, the Masters Golf Tournament, the Kentucky Derby, the ESPYs, the Emmys, the Oscars, the Grammys, Cannes Film Festival in France, and Tribeca Film Festival in New York. We're winning honors and living by our motto of creating abundance—making a lot of money, help-ing a lot of people, and having a lot of fun."

My Advice to Young People:

- "First, figure out what makes you happy, and then enjoy the pursuit of your potential within your career or business. Detach yourself from the outcome, or end result, and really enjoy the pursuit of your potential.

- "Understand that being an entrepreneur is believing in yourself and surrounding yourself with the right people and the right ideas. As I said earlier, a true entrepreneur is someone who creates more value than he takes. But, with all these different lessons, you also have to understand that your goal as an entrepreneur is to stay in business. If I'm really going to enjoy the pursuit of my potential, I do need to stay in business.

- "Finally, there are four things you should look at for your career, whether you want to be an entrepreneur or not. The first is what are your personal values—like family, health, character, integrity. The second are the experiential values—what experiences I've had that are aligned with my pursuit of happiness. The third thing is your giving values. Throughout my career how do I want to help others? What legacy do I want to leave? And finally, look at your receiving or your financial values. What career path should I take according to the financial rewards or receiving values that I have? When you clarify these four values and get focused on them, it will give you the confidence to know you're pursuing the right career."

CHAPTER 11

Resourcefulness

Observing Situations and Skillfully Addressing Difficulties

Camilla Ljunggren

Founder, Pluring, JA Alumna, Sweden

> *I continued to run the company after the JA program ended because I couldn't say no to my customers who just kept calling to say they wanted to order more of the product.*

My JA Experience:

"I joined the JA program at 16 and soon realized it would be more fun if I had an idea of my own for a product to sell. I started to think about products I could make and realized it wasn't so easy to find an idea. One day I was in my kitchen taking a glass of water and noticed the dirty dishcloth on the tap. It hit me right then, why are we hanging dirty dishcloths over the water tap? Next, my small, young cousins were visiting at our summer home by the sea, and they couldn't reach the hook to bring down the towels in the bath. So they pulled really hard and the hook broke. So I started thinking about why we hang dirty washcloths over clean water taps, and why we hang towels through a hoop too high on the wall for children—and through those questions I started to discover a new product idea for my JA company.

"I designed a completely new kind of washcloth and towel hanger, one where you pushed the towel through the center of a ring and it stuck there, and you could attach the ring hanger on any wall. A manufacturer helped us do the prototype, and we started up. It was so much fun to sell the product, meet customers, and hear their feedback. It wasn't the kind of feedback you get in school. There you get a grade on a paper, but I was getting people telling me this new hanger is so smart and useful. I found that amazing. I did JA that first year and had so much fun I decided to do it another year. In the second year my product was importing leather sandals made by a youth group in Kenya. And I had a new goal: to reach the JA Europe championships, which were going to be in Paris. We won the JA Sweden competition, so we made it to Paris and were the first runner-up there.

"I'm turning 34 years old on Sunday, and I've been in business 16 years already. It was not my plan at the beginning. I was supposed to be a lawyer. So it was really JA that changed my mind. I learned how much fun it was to run my own company!"

My Career / Business:

"I continued to run the company after the JA program ended because I couldn't say no to my customers who just kept calling to say they wanted to order more of the product. So I decided I had to continue, and I started my own company. I also decided that everything I earned in the company would be reinvested in the business to make it grow organically. When I started the JA company, I put in 10 Swedish kronor, about one dollar, and I've never had to put any more money in since.

"Early on we began doing our own manufacturing. It's mostly by robotics, so we have a very lean manufacturing setup. We also decided to go into the big retail stores with the product, which we branded Pluring. The first store in Stockholm that took the product was a very large store in the middle of the city. The sales went very well. We've been on their top 10 sales list every week for almost 15 years now. Of course we have many other retailers who carry the product and it has become quite well known in Sweden and the Nordic countries. We also export all over the world. I want to continue growing this way: manufacturing the products ourselves in Sweden and shipping them around the world.

"I've had offers from large corporations to sell, but I decided not to because for me, it has never been about the money. I run the business because I like it, I think it's fun, I meet interesting people, and I'm not in it just for the money."

My Advice to Young People:

- "Whatever you choose to do, you must know that it takes time. I can tell you in 10 minutes how I built our factory and it sounds so easy. But it's not easy. It takes time. It's taken me 16 or 17 years to do this.
- "I will also say that it's important to surround yourself with great people. I have a network of about 400 top leaders in the world who I can ask for advice, in different areas. I really think it's important to work with other people and learn from their experiences and listen to their advice.
- "The last piece of advice is to have fun in whatever you do. That's the most important thing in life—have fun and be happy."

Daniel Antwi

Founder, People Initiative Foundation, JA Alumnus, Ghana

Passion, time, and skills, not cash, are your biggest assets in the early stages of your journey.

My JA Experience:

"The best decision I ever made was to join the JA Club in high school, at St. Augustine's College, in 2003. As a student who studied business in high school, I had an inquiring mind on business-related issues. Upon hearing there was a business club on campus that ran a lot of entrepreneurial programs, I became interested and quickly joined. One other convincing factor was that the patron of the club happened to also be my business management studies teacher. Hence I was very convinced that the JA Club was the right place for me.

"2004, I was elected marketing executive of the JA Club. When we started up, there was no cash in our coffers, so we had to think of ways to raise money.

As a team, we came up with something that I think had never been done by any high school club in Africa. We floated shares in the school for students to buy with their pocket money.

"We needed to raise the cash in order to produce our school's banners and other paraphernalia which most of the students wanted to wear during the sports competitions. In the central region of Ghana where our school was located, sports competitions were very competitive, and strong rivalries existed between the various schools. Our strategy, which I led as the marketing executive, was to go to classrooms and talk about our upcoming share offering and what the students stood to gain as shareholders. We also went to the dining halls and made announcements, and posted flyers on school notice boards. Our shares were oversubscribed, and we raised a lot of money. We immediately used half of the cash to buy shares in the Ghana Oil Company, as a reserve, and used the rest to produce our sports paraphernalia, which was in high demand. We made a lot of revenue with good profit margins.

"Today I am a social entrepreneur, and looking back I can say that joining the JA Club in high school was my magic step. My public speaking skills, business acumen, marketing skills, and people skills were all unleashed as a result of my association with JA."

My Career / Business:

"I developed a passion for entrepreneurship at an early stage as a result of my association with the JA Club in high school. However, my early professional career, spanning seven years, was spent with two great companies, Hewlett-Packard and Guinness Ghana Breweries, where I learned a lot of leadership and management skills. After that corporate experience, my partner and I established People Initiative Foundation, which creates programs to promote cultural diversity while nurturing and mentoring the vision, talents, and ideas of young people who are making positive change across Africa. Our foundation's initiatives include TEDxAccra, Africa Internship Academy, and Africa Dialogues. We also have a Social Impact Consultancy which has done extensive work for organizations such as Reach for Change Africa and Smart Africa."

My Advice to Young People:

"I started early as a young entrepreneur and made a lot of mistakes. They all turned out to be blessings in disguise for my journey. So as a lifelong *JA-preneur* myself, here are 10 nuggets from my own experience that I want to share with future social entrepreneurs."

- "Have an idea with social impact value—that addresses a social issue.
- "Know the UN's Sustainable Development Goals (SDGs) to solving the world's pressing issues, and align your social innovation with any of the SDGs to contribute to global change.
- "Begin small, with your current resources, but have a big picture in mind.
- "Remain focused on your target and stay within your track to ensure impact.
- "Connect with other impact hubs and innovation labs to gain new knowledge and ideas.
- "Take a chance and work with all social innovations that come your way.
- "Volunteering can be a game changer in the ecosystem of creating social impact.
- "Passion, time, and skills, not cash, are your biggest assets in the early stages of your journey.
- "Financial viability, in the early stages of your journey, may not be clearly defined.
- "Believe in *yourself* and discover your *strengths*."

Boris Kolev

Cofounder, DigiMark, JA Alumnus, Bulgaria

We were one of the poorest nations in the competition in 2005, so it was very motivating to beat the big countries like Germany, France, and the UK. We felt very patriotic.

My JA Experience:

"I was first introduced to the JA program when I was just 12 years old. I think it was the seventh grade. We had some extracurricular activities, and we had to choose from three. One of them was the student company. A few friends from my class and I signed up. The first day the teacher came and said the students were going to make a business, and we asked are we going to earn money, and he said yes. So that was interesting. He brought us the JA books and we started the class. So we had our first company—and went to the national competition. We were the youngest team there. We didn't get any awards that year, but we were very motivated. The second year we were very motivated again, and we wanted to get the prize. We didn't win the best company award, but we did win four prizes: best marketing plan, etc. The third year we were even more motivated. We did the Company Program again and had a very interesting product. We produced business cards made from CDs. We won the Bulgarian national competition with this, and went to the international competition in Brussels. There we won third place for all of Europe. It was one of the most motivating moments of my entire life. We were one of the poorest nations in the competition in 2005, so it was very motivating to beat the big countries like Germany, France, and the UK. We felt very patriotic.

"I personally won another JA competition in 2006. It was an essay competition, and they sent me to the United States to the Junior Leadership Conference in Florida. More than 500 JA kids from all around the world were there, and it was very cool. I was 17, and I fell in love with the U.S. So, I came back and took all the English classes, the SAT exams, all the exams needed to go to the states to study. I was accepted at a few good schools, but a few months before I was to go we had an accident in my family and I lost my father. It was a few weeks before I turned 18, and all my plans just disappeared. I was left with my mom and my little sister who was eight, and I had to find a job very quickly to help my family. I was an 18-year-old kid with no diploma, and it was difficult to find a good job. The first person to give me a hand was Milena Stoycheva, who as you know is the CEO of JA Bulgaria. She asked me to help them with the computers in the JA office. So my first job was actually in the JA office in Sofia. She couldn't give me a big salary, but it was enough so I could help my family. And then Sasha, who as you also know was the board chair for JA Bulgaria, and the CEO at Hewlett-Packard, called me to say there was an internship available at HP. She was a very important person in Bulgaria, and I didn't know her, but she just called and said: "I'm Sasha from HP, and I know what's happening in your family and I want to help you. We have an internship position at HP which you can have." So I got into HP with the internship, which was very helpful. So JA Bulgaria and HP Bulgaria gave me so much help."

My Career / Business:

"I told my classmates, we've been doing this JA Company Program for many years, so let's continue it as a real company. I put the word *international* in the name and registered my first company as JT International. I was just 18 years old. We started off just doing more website work. But I soon realized the market needed something more innovative than just website design, so we searched for other technologies and services to get into. I looked around Europe and discovered Bluetooth marketing, which led to the creation of our second company, BlueMark.

"We've been in business 10 years now, working under the group name DigiMark. We also have investments in other tech companies. I spend a lot of time in that investment company trying to find new companies to help. Our CEO is my original partner, and he is managing all the teams so I'm able to travel overseas to find new business. Today DigiMark has 30 employees, and we've opened offices in Portugal and the U.S.

"Finally, I am in the JA Europe Alumni Club. I stay very involved with JA in Bulgaria and the rest of Europe because I owe a lot to JA and it provides a valuable network. For example, we currently have three good clients from the JA Alumni Club in Europe. It's also happening here in Bulgaria. The alumni are young, but they are all in good positions: in companies, in government, and in politics. We all work together because we know and trust each other. So JA has provided this amazing network of alumni."

My Advice to Young People:

- "One very important thing I learned from my JA experience—set up big goals, and even if you don't reach them you'll be far ahead. It's very motivating to know that if you work hard, success will come.
- "From my experience, I will offer one final piece of advice to young people everywhere: Join JA as a student, or even as an advisor. Believe me, it will be one of the most important and rewarding activities you will ever undertake."

Alex Kyalo

Founder, Tapifare Kenya, JA Alumnus, Kenya

This was an entrepreneurial gamble that has truly paid off!

My JA Experience:

"Ten years ago when I went through the JA Company Program, I had little knowledge of what impact it would have on my life. My experience in the Company Program was the real start of my career. JA was my first 'teacher' in what the global market really is.

"Starting with the setup of the company structure and the division of responsibilities, I remember with pride becoming the corporate secretary and human resources vice president. It was exciting to have such a key role in my first-ever company engagement. Next came product development involving the packaging, branding, and sales of our products, with the flagship being honey from our beehives. The entire 19-month life cycle of the company was fun, but it also included very important business lessons that are still relevant in my day-to-day operations today."

My Career/ Business:

"My career took a nonconventional path due to my experience at JA. Having undertaken a technical degree program at university, I never expected to start off as an executive assistant to the managing director of Kenya's largest motor dealership. However, as a career launching pad, nothing could have been better for a 22-year-old. My experience there led directly to my taking the helm of Tapifare Kenya in 2014. My new company has the mandate to develop a distribution network across Kenya, Tanzania, Ethiopia, Burundi, and Rwanda for Ctrack-Inseego, the worldwide fleet management and tracking service.

"I took the path of doing a start-up business because I saw this as a once-in-a-lifetime opportunity to successfully build and run a business—with the support of a global leader in the field. Creating a company from the ground up, and becoming profitable within 12 months, was a tall order. At six months I already had an active team of well-trained technicians, a branded vehicle carrying out demos with potential clients, and a market research department that could identify worthy customers for our products. Fast-forward to 2017, and Tapifare Kenya is a fully operational and profitable business. This was an entrepreneurial gamble that has truly paid off!"

My Advice to Young People:

- "To be young, at this time in Africa, may be the greatest gift you could ever have. Nearly half of the top 10 fastest-growing economies worldwide are in Africa, making it fertile ground for budding entrepreneurs.

- "Don't be afraid to fail, and when you do fail, simply 'fail better' next time. Young people should recognize that entrepreneurship often comes with a lot of stumbling blocks along the way. It's all about how we learn to do better next time, without giving up.
- "Go the extra mile with undivided focus. Young people must seek to be 'extra' if they want to be successful. You cannot be average in your decision making, or in your level of focus, and expect to reap maximum benefits from your endeavors.
- "As an entrepreneur be ready to solve a real problem, build a global product, and hit the road running without looking back. Accept counsel from industry experts and mentors, don't be afraid of criticism, and don't accept conventional wisdom.
- "Most importantly, volunteer as a mentor to JA (or similar organization) to give back to your younger brothers and sisters by sharing your experience. It costs nothing to impart your knowledge and experiences to others—and you have everything to gain by giving back what was received completely free from JA."

Benjamin Kainz

Founder, Young Care, JA Alumnus, Sweden

> *But I quickly became a university dropout as I was too interested in my project—my new business.*

My JA Experience:

"In the beginning, I didn't think about having my own company. I saw myself studying and then working for a big company. That was my plan, but then we were invited to join the JA program. It sounded interesting, so I, with three other friends, started the program. We put a lot of effort into the program. We started with an idea that one of my friends had—bricks that looked like Legos toys, but much bigger so you could build real walls with them. They worked just like bricks, but you didn't need any mortar. It seemed like a good idea, but it was more difficult than we imagined. We created the whole concept and then saw that the investment to bring it to market was too big for the first year. Anyway I think that experience gave us the most practical education we got that school year because it was the first time we had to do something ourselves, without anyone saying how or what to do. In JA you see the results of what you do. You put effort into something, and you quickly see what you get back. You also make contact with new people outside of the school. I think the whole process provided the most benefit we got from the school year. It was fun, and there was a bit of a competition with other teams. We thought the competitions were quite fun, and we did quite well. We only brought the product to the prototype stage—but we actually won the JA Company of the Year award in Sweden. At the end of the year we even had a meeting with the founder of IKEA, and he really liked the product also. So it was great fun and a great learning experience."

My Business / Career:

"We really liked the way the JA program worked, and we had one year left in school, so we decided to start a real company for our last year. The business idea was inspired by a personal situation. My grandmother was living a few hours from my home, and my grandfather was retired and living in Germany, quite far away. I saw them only a couple of times a year, and I saw that many other students had the same situation as my family. They also had elderly relatives living in another city or another country. At the same time, we knew it was quite hard for young people to find a part-time job. In the care sector, for example, there are a lot of legal requirements. So we thought about combining those two problems: care for the elderly and finding employment for young people. So we started our company, Ung Omsorg, or Young Care, just before we graduated from high school. It was to be a summer project at first, and I actually entered the university to study economics. But I quickly became a university dropout as I was too interested in my project—my new business.

"We saw this need all across the country. I'm not sure we really saw it as a market at first. It was just something that was needed, and we tried to do something about it in an organized way. The idea was quite simple: we wanted to hire young people to provide light care for elderly people, take a walk with them, talk to them, sit and read the newspaper out loud, just comfort them—an exchange experience between the generations.

"We went to the local government in our hometown and had a little luck. We found one politician who liked our plan, and he got the project approved.

The municipality paid for the service, and we got some sponsorships from local companies. We advertised the jobs for something like $7 an hour, we trained the teenagers in what to do, and had our first 20 employees in just a few weeks. So we started up our first pilot program in our hometown in Sweden.

"Today, 10 years later, we have over 900 employees with projects all over Sweden. In the beginning we didn't really see it as a business. We just thought it was a nice summer project, but it's turned out to be a strong and growing business. We could operate like a nonprofit, but early on we realized we didn't want to be dependent on charity or the funding of foundations. We thought if Young Care is going to survive in the long term, there must be someone willing to pay for the service—just like any for-profit business. So we operate as a legal for-profit business and promote Young Care as a private company trying to do good work for society."

My Advice to Young People:

- "Of course, start with an idea you believe in. Something you really feel strongly about. Otherwise after a few years you may get bored or discover there is something else you want to do more. In my case, for example, after 10 years in business I have more energy for my company than when I started.

- "If you want to get practical, I see a lot of young companies fail because they start selling too late. When you first come up with your idea, start talking to prospects or those who have a problem you hope to solve— because their early feedback may highlight some problems you can correct early on. Then you can focus on the right strategy for your business from the beginning. So start selling early.

- "Give yourself lots of opportunities to get lucky! I mean it's important to meet up with people who know a lot about your field or market sector. You never know who can open doors for you or teach you things. For example, we didn't really have any experience in the healthcare sector, and we had to learn fast from other people.

- "And finally, I would encourage young people everywhere to consider doing something in the healthcare sector. As the population ages, there's a big need for new people and new solutions. It's a huge problem in Sweden and most other countries too. But it's also a huge opportunity for young people to get inspired by working with the elderly—and become social enterprisers to find new solutions in this fast-growing market."

CHAPTER 12

Self-Efficacy

Having Belief or Confidence in Your Ability to Succeed

Wise Banda

Founder, Primelink, JA Alumnus, Zambia

> *Having an entrepreneurial attitude is the way you can add value to people's lives, contribute to your country's development, and ensure your own financial freedom.*

My JA Experience:

"I grew up as an enterprising child, selling a lot of items such as drinks and clothes and raising chickens and so on. I was therefore very excited when I learned that JA Zambia had introduced a program in schools to teach pupils business skills. I quickly enrolled in the program at my school, Matero Boys' Secondary School, in 2002. Through this experience, I learned how to raise money through issuing shares. It was my first time understanding how share-holding actually worked in real life. I also learned how to organize and run a business in a structured, formal way. I realized that when a business is formally registered, it can more easily access financing and take advantage of other opportunities such as tax exemptions, bidding for contracts, and so on.

"Since the JA training, my thinking has never been the same. I continued on with several entrepreneurial activities. After high school I opened an IT shop where we provided typing, printing, and photocopying as well as other secretarial services in my community of Mandau. This proved to be a very popular business as I was the only one providing these services. The market appreciated this, and I became well known throughout the entire community. Starting with just one computer and a printer, I managed to grow the business to three offices. The funds raised from this activity helped me fund my expenses at the University of Zambia. It also helped provide employment for my brothers and sisters. Later at the university, I established a microfinance company called Junior Entrepreneurs Company. I also ran other businesses including transport, agriculture marketing, and real estate."

My Career / Business:

"I am now a trained economist and international development graduate holding a bachelor's degree in economics and a master's degree in development finance. However, my professional career has been in the field of banking.

"As mentioned earlier, I formed a student microfinance association called Junior Entrepreneurs Company. The name was inspired by my experience in the JA program. The aim of the association was to provide loans to the student community on soft terms as a way of bridging the financial gap before their government stipends came. I also saw this as a way of sharing my entrepreneurship knowledge with university students so that they too could learn to set up small businesses of their own. Although we began small, our clientele grew rapidly as many students appreciated our work. We provided funding for books and other school requirements as well as for other minor personal issues.

"More recently I founded Primelink Agency—a general trading business with special interests in agricultural marketing and processing, real estate development, and microfinance. Now, having acquired knowledge and experience in the financial sector, I am planning to launch several new businesses in agriculture and SME financing, energy, and real estate development."

My Advice to Young People:

- "My advice to young people is that they should take entrepreneurship very seriously as a career option.

- "One major challenge, especially in Africa, can be raising funds for start-ups. From my experience, banks are reluctant to finance a start-up. One way of raising funds would be selling shares to friends and family. Another would be to partner with institutions which may have particular interest in the sectors you choose to work in.

- "Another vital aspect of entrepreneurship is to network with people who share your entrepreneurial drive. Using mentors, joining training programs, and general networking are all useful in this regard. Through such activities, you may also find investors or partners.

- "Finally, there are a lot of entrepreneurial opportunities out there which young people can take advantage of. Having an entrepreneurial attitude is the way you can add value to people's lives, contribute to your country's development, and ensure your own financial freedom."

Jim Hemak

Founder, Webincs, Inc., JA Alumnus, Minnesota, USA

For a kid like me, it was the biggest thrill of my life!

My JA Experience:

"I was a sophomore in high school in Minneapolis, Minnesota. I was an awfully shy and reserved kid, and wasn't involved in a whole lot of things—and then I got invited to participate in the JA Company Program. My job in the company was to set up the production line for the precut parts for the birdhouses we were assembling and selling. We were having a quality problem with staining them, and it occurred to me that we should stain and paint them before we assembled them. It solved the problem—and lo and behold, everyone thought I was an engineering guru! At the end of the year, we got the Rags to Riches award and I was asked to go up on stage in front of a thousand people and receive the award. For a kid like me, it was the biggest thrill of my life. I still get goosebumps thinking about it.

"The most important thing I learned from JA was that I could make a difference. That putting energy and effort into a project or goal was worthwhile and I would be rewarded for my success and achievement. Second, I learned that inspiration is not only important, it's vital. Without inspiration, which I got out of JA, you just don't have much to work with. So it was important for me to learn the importance of being inspired and that I could actually make a difference. Those lessons from JA have remained with me for my entire business career."

My Career / Business:

"I went to the University of Minnesota and studied business. After college I joined the Army and served in Vietnam. (*Editor's note:* Jim was awarded the Bronze Star.) After my military service I actually went to work for JA in Richmond, Indiana. Then I worked for the national organization a couple years, and next I became the president of JA in Seattle, Washington, a large operation. I was only 27 years old but still got that terrific opportunity in JA. From there I went back to the national organization with service responsibility for JA operations in the western U.S.

"With a growing family, and moving every couple of years in JA, I started thinking about what might be an alternative life. Going back to my JA experience, I thought there's got to be some business opportunities out there. I went to a business seminar and learned that four out of five start-up businesses are out of business in five years, but over 90 percent of franchises are still in business—so I began looking at franchise opportunities. Then one day, out of the blue, I received a promotion from a company called Great Clips. By coincidence I had just read a story about the hair salon industry in the *Wall Street Journal*, so I was interested. I called them up, met with them, and learned they only had 15 franchisees at that time. I was impressed with the people and I was impressed with the concept, so I started up with them in 1984. They still refer to me as their first franchisee who wasn't a friend or relative. Today with more than 4,000 franchised salons throughout the United States and Canada, Great Clips is the world's largest hair salon brand—and I became their largest single franchisee, with the most locations.

"I've learned over the course of my career that education and inspiration go hand in hand in terms of being successful. When I hire people now I look for both their level of motivation and their level and type of education. On motivation, I go back to my JA experience in high school and the need for inspiration in whatever you. And on education, so many things that are significant in terms of being successful are not taught in business school. They're learned through personal experience or perhaps from a mentor such as JA provided."

My Advice to Young People:

- "Take advantage of opportunities to get involved in organizations as you go through school and life. These can be great learning experiences for any kind of career or business. Certainly, being involved in JA has been a lifelong benefit to me. I'm still involved today in two or three capacities and support JA financially. So, be a joiner.
- "For anyone thinking about franchising or starting a business, my advice is do your homework. People are always saying, find the next big idea. That's the wrong approach. What's more important is to ask what you can become inspired about. Find something you are personally interested in and passionate about, not just the next franchised Hulu-Hoop or whatever."

David Mata

Founder, Pynk Systems (Ergon Desk), JA Alumnus, Spain

While you should always be creative and innovative, it's even more important to simplify and focus on the key points—and keep your feet on the ground.

My JA Experience:

"There were two forces working on me. One was my architecture and design education. I studied that for years, and I was already working at it when I decided to go to the university management program to also learn about business. It was at the management school where I took the JA program— and that made me think more about starting my own business, but using my architecture and design education. In the JA program, my team and I started a project we called Pynk Systems, where we focused on the ergonomic design of office furniture. That was the company project we took to the

JA competitions. After winning the various JA competitions and honors (the Youth Entrepreneurship Award and the Brilliant Young Entrepreneur prize), we became quite excited and confident, and decided to officially start up the company, naming our product line the Ergon Desk. And of course we had the prize money to help us start the business. So yes, it was because of the JA program that I started my first business."

My Career / Business:

"After winning the JA award in 2014 we decided to go to Silicon Valley to develop the first product concepts because of what the United States could provide. We were actually six people there developing the product concept and designs. We spent three months in the U.S., so perhaps we could say we were a "Silicon Valley start-up," but of course reality set in when our visas expired and we had to return to Spain! Anyway that was the start of Pynk Systems, my business today. Our customers are large businesses who buy our computerized ergonomic desks and chairs for their offices, and we provide between 4 and 40 desks per sale—so each sale can be large, and they take some time to close. The two main benefits we offer customers are higher office collaboration and productivity plus employee comfort and health. We're still a young company marketing primarily in Europe but also looking to the U.S. where the opportunity for our products is very large—and also in the Africa and Middle East markets.

"I must say that JA gave me a big opportunity, connecting my project to real life and giving me the needed push for starting up the company. To give something back, I am still connected with JA as a member of the JA Alumni Association in Spain, where I work with other students and young entrepreneurs to help them with their projects. I believe that JA alumni, who have experienced business reality and have made many teachable mistakes, can provide hands-on help to bring more JA student projects to reality. This is our goal at the JA Spain Alumni association."

My Advice to Young People:

- "My first piece of advice is to dream big about those things that motivate you and make you happy, and don't waste your time thinking about things that don't interest you.
- "Second would be to never give up. This advice has helped me a lot. Young people need to believe that while things can be difficult sometimes, you can always find a way to overcome the obstacles.

- "Third is that while you should always be creative and innovative, it's even more important to simplify and focus on the key points—and keep your feet on the ground."

Mario A. Escutia

Founder, The Barber's Spa, JA Alumnus, Mexico

When I was eight years old, I started my career in sales. I saved the candies and toys that I received from birthday party piñatas and sold them to my friends.

My JA Experience:

"When I was a kid, I always thought that I would be a doctor. Taking care of patients and saving lives seemed amazing, but I also felt a passion for sales and business. When I was eight years old, I started my career in sales. I saved the candies or toys that I received from birthday party piñatas and sold them to my friends. I even sold my own toys, but this was not a great idea because my parents needed to talk to our neighbors and friends to get the toys back and had to return the money. When I was around 9 or 10 years old I had my own puppet show and provided entertainment at kids' parties. This is when I had my first employee: my brother was the one carrying the little theater. After that I always had a summer job.

"I was in high school when JA came into my life. My friends and I decided to create our first JA company, and at the beginning it was more an excuse to get together outside of school than to prepare us for the business world. My first position was marketing director, as they said I was a good speaker and very creative.

"It was an enriching experience and a place where I could develop my entrepreneurial spirit. So I continued the adventure for another year, but as the CEO. We were very successful, so much so that one of the department store chains wanted to carry our product. However, the demand on our time would have required us to quit high school and dedicate ourselves exclusively to the company. We decided not to pursue this any further and focused on finishing school.

"In the same year our company represented Mexico as part of the JA delegations in El Salvador and Puerto Rico. From that moment on I understood the value of overseas travel, and international business travel became a big part of my professional life. After these two years in JA I decided to change my career path to marketing in order to focus on satisfying the needs of business clients and their customers."

My Career / Business:

"My professional career started at the age of 20 in JA, when I was hired as operations manager for JA Mexico City. The spirit and lessons I learned from the JA team led me to reach out to hundreds of students to participate, and more than 900 young people joined, which was a record at that time. One of the most satisfying experiences was visiting CEOs. I had the opportunity to meet and talk with the leaders of important companies such as IBM, Bimbo, Bacardi and Co., P&G, Kodak, Colgate, Avon, and many more. From those experiences I had a new dream: becoming the future leader of a major international company.

"I pursued that dream for more than 23 years. I was an executive in multinational companies, with positions in sales and marketing. I was a fundamental part of the development of new products, expansion strategies, company mergers, and led sales forces of more than 1,000 employees. I was locally and internationally recognized with awards such as Executive of the Year, and developed marketing campaigns that became icons in the world of advertising in Mexico. I lived in countries as diverse as Poland and Costa Rica, and after 19 years of effort I obtained the position of general manager of one of the most important pharmaceutical companies in the world.

"In 2014, with the advice of the entrepreneur I admire the most, my dad, I decided to embark on a new professional life as an entrepreneur. I developed a barbershop franchise in Mexico City. Just three years after starting operations, we have more than 25 locations, 150 employees, and serve more than 10,000 customers per month. But the most important thing is that we brought back the status of barbers by adding a newfound prestige to the profession, which was disappearing in Mexico. With such incredible demand, we have created our own barber school and are awaiting the official certification from the Ministry of Education. This will be the first barber school in the country to achieve this designation. We also have plans for international expansion."

My Advice to Young People:

- "My advice to young people is that no matter where you come from, whatever your social class, your ideology, or the school where you studied, your dreams can come true. Hard work and honesty is always rewarded.
- "Second, trust your instincts, surround yourself with experts, develop your intelligence, and give everything you have to achieve your goals.
- "Third, when you start a business, look for ways to differentiate yourself from others in the market and communicate this. Nowadays, customers want life experiences, so you have to create them.
- "Finally, above all else, enjoy the process of creating and generating jobs, because where there is work there is less crime and no violence in society."

Joseph Fortuno

Internship Director, Gladeo, and University Student, JA Alumnus, California, USA

> *Sometimes in life you have to take some risks—to become a better person.*

My JA Experience:

"I'm Philippine American, and grew up in Hercules, California, a small town near San Francisco. I was a free-spirited kid who had a lot of ambition but didn't know which way to go. In high school I was just one of those kids around; I didn't join gangs, I wasn't involved in clubs, and I didn't really have a lot of friends. Also I had bouts of depression and anxiety and a lot of people didn't seem to understand me. Going into my junior year, my mom got together with a new man, and they told me they were going to move far away from Hercules, which I really didn't want to do. Things went from bad to worse at home, I had a major falling out with my family, and my mother told me to pack my bags and move out. So at 17, I found myself living on the streets and virtually homeless.

"I thought, this is really hard: living on my own, going to high school, working part-time, and living off the mercy of a few friends who took me in.

I thought every day, how do I go about finding a better way for my future, my life? How do I find that one thing in life that really inspires me to achieve? And then it happened. I remember it well. It was my eighteenth birthday when I first heard about JA. I was in class when the instructors told us they were going to start the JA Company Program. They asked if I would like to join, and I said 'sure,' not knowing exactly what it was. I guess they saw some potential in me because they later asked if I would like to be a candidate for the CEO position. I said, 'OK, why not? I'll be the CEO and we'll all find out what you see in me.' So there I was, just a regular kid, who could hardly afford to feed himself, but I became the CEO of the JA student company—and my life began to change right then and there.

"First, our company, Herban Movement, which published a top-selling healthful cookbook and produced an eco-friendly bag that replaced plastic grocery bags, took top honors for Best Business Plan and Best Commercial at the JA Northern California Company of the Year Competition. Following our awards in the California competition, my team and I went on to the JA National Student Leadership Summit in Washington, DC, where we took top honors for social entrepreneurship and won the Microsoft Social Innovation Award for the year. Next, I was honored and interviewed on national TV at the annual American Graduate Day ceremony, broadcast from Lincoln Center in New York City. The show is sponsored each year by the Public Broadcasting System. On the show I was interviewed by ABC's *Nightline* anchor, Juju Chang, who is herself a JA Alumna.

"And finally, in late 2015, I was invited to the White House in Washington, DC, to meet President Barack Obama in the Oval Office—as part of the National Entrepreneurship Month celebrations. I had been selected, along with five other young people, as a good example of youth entrepreneurship across the USA. Just being in the White House was so surreal for me, the whole thing was like a dream. I met the president and told him about how I developed my JA company, and he gave me wonderful advice in return. That was the moment when I realized my journey had come full circle—and I felt so good about it. I was only in Washington, DC, for 24 hours, but it was an amazing experience.

"Through JA I've been able to find that passionate meaning in life which helped me get to where I wanted to go. As a small thank you, I still work with JA as an alumni ambassador for entrepreneurship, attend JA events to talk about my experience, and mentor young JA students, So I'm very heavily involved in JA still."

My Career / Business:

"Today I attend Cogswell College in San Jose, California. I'm majoring in business administration and digital media management. But I still have to work. For the past two years I've been the internship program and creative director for a nonprofit called Gladeo, which is dedicated to helping young people find and pursue their dream career in the media world. I'm a full-time student and work part-time to help put myself through college. And I should add, I've mended my relationship with my family . . ."

My Advice to Young People:

- "I only have one piece of advice—never be afraid to try and even fail! If that 17-year-old Joseph had been too afraid to go out on his own, and become homeless really, I would never have gotten to where I am today. I would never have found JA. I would never have met President Obama. I would probably have not even gone to college. And I would not be here today being interviewed by you, Larry. Sometimes in life you have to take some risks—to become a better person."

Youmn Mahzoul

INJAZ Alumni Ambassador, JA Alumna, Morocco

The result of the JA experience is not always the creation of a start-up business. It can also be a shift in the students' mindsets—from being comfortable with the status quo to focusing on personal growth and achievement.

My JA Experience:

"I joined JA at 16 when the program was launched for the first time in my high school. That's when my life literally changed for the better. Over the five months, I learned that launching a business, and actually making it work, is not a luxury reserved to people of privilege, rather it is a challenge that anyone can undertake. Even high-schoolers with zero knowledge of business!

For many of us, it was the first contact we'd ever had with a company, private institutions, and managers from big corporations. Hearing their encouraging words and their interest in our work was mind-boggling for our teen-age minds!

"I can still remember the look of the jury members during the competition: with serious faces they treated us like adults, CEOs, managers, and most importantly, as the leaders we were aspiring to become. It was a real eye-opener and a foretaste of what was awaiting us in the future.

"After the JA Company Program experience, I decided to switch my career plan from engineering to business and management. Having just graduated from university this year, I've now started my career as a digital marketer in Morocco.

"I have truly grown with INJAZ. From participating in the JA Company Program, to becoming an INJAZ alumni ambassador, to launching the Morocco and Arab region alumni network, I have forged ties with many entrepreneurs, entrepreneur 'wannabes,' and consultants. I also got to take part in many JA events: representing the Arab Alumni Initiative in the JA Europe Alumni Conference in Copenhagen, being a mentor for the Arab Company Program Competition in Oman, and representing Arab alumni as a juror in the JA Europe Company Program competition in Brussels. I can now proudly say that the INJAZ / JA Worldwide organization is my entrepreneurial support network."

My Career / Business:

"I'm now concentrating on the professional career I've just started as a digital marketer. I want to master the field and learn as much as possible while preparing for my entrepreneurial journey. In the future, I would like to launch an initiative where art and education will be combined to facilitate learning and personal development.

"As a side note, one aspect of the INJAZ experience that often comes up in discussions with Moroccan and other alumni is that the result of the JA experience is not always the creation of a start-up business. It can also be a shift in the students' mindsets—from being comfortable with the status quo to focusing on personal growth and achievement. Making that shift is something I'm personally proud of achieving."

My Advice to Young People:

- "First is about how we perceive success in society. The metrics we use to gauge success are often biased, relating mostly to financial success. While being financially stable is important, having a meaningful life is what humanity should strive for the most. Success could mean working in a non-profit for low wages but saving lives, as well as launching your own 'unicorn start-up' and succeeding at it.

- "Second, if you have a business/initiative/project idea you really want to make a reality, don't wait for the perfect moment to do it. Just go for it as soon as you can. Perfection is the enemy of developing good ideas, and overplanning is the enemy of execution.
- "So let us all do our best to succeed, each in our own way, and make our dreams a reality!"

The Entrepreneurial Attitude

Doing Something Great with Your Life!

> *The inclination of my life has been to do things and make things which will give pleasure to people in new and amazing ways. By doing that I please and satisfy myself.*
>
> **WALT DISNEY,** Founder, The Walt Disney Company

The goal of *The Entrepreneurial Attitude* is to help you do something great in your career and in your life. And one more time, what exactly does that mean? Well, the best summary description I've ever seen of having an entrepreneurial attitude in business and in life comes from that master of creating dreams for young people everywhere, Walt Disney. He described the four fundamental practices of entrepreneurs perfectly: "Inclination" as mission, "making things and giving pleasure to people" is all about customer/product vision, "new and exciting ways" is a perfect description of innovation, and finally, "by doing that I please and satisfy myself" says I am self-inspired by my work. In this book we shorthanded those entrepreneurial basics as follows:

THE FOUR ENTREPRENEURIAL BASICS

■ Sense of Mission
   Creating an Entrepreneurial Strategy and Culture
■ Customer/Product Vision
   My Customer, My Product, My Self-Respect
■ High-Speed Innovation
   The Necessity to Invent, the Freedom to Act
■ Self-Inspired Behavior
   Love What You Do and Get Very Good at Doing It

Getting and using an entrepreneurial attitude is the best way ever invented to create prosperity for you, your family, and even your country. Indeed, the world's fast-changing economy, combined with the growing entrepreneur-friendly environment around the world, makes today the best time in all history for young people to take advantage of the amazing power of the entrepreneurial spirit. Millions of new, young people, from every corner of the globe, are starting new businesses, new social enterprises, and new entrepreneurial style careers every year. So why not give it a go yourself? All you really need is to get an entrepreneurial attitude.

JA ALUMNI INTERVIEW

David Lammy

Member of Parliament, United Kingdom, JA Alumnus, United Kingdom

> *I wanted to change the world, and that's what led me from law to politics.*

My JA Experience:

"My name is David Lammy, and I'm the Member of Parliament from Tottenham. My background was really one of poverty. My father arrived in Britain in 1956. He came here from Guyana in South

America. He came with big dreams. He wanted to be a pharmacist. Things didn't quite work out, but he met my mother and they settled in a small flat in North London. Actually, where they settled is the area I now represent as the local member of Parliament. Things weren't easy—in fact my father's business didn't go so well and he left us when I was young. It was a difficult time for us in Britain at that point.

"Well, I got my big break when I was given a choral scholarship in music to go to a Cathedral school in Peterborough. That was my opportunity, and that's where I came across JA. I did not come from an entrepreneurial background. My only experience at business was watching my father's small business fail. JA, or Young Enterprise as we call it in the UK, gave me a kind of confidence. It gave me the sense that I *can*. We were a team, across all ages in our school, working together for the first time and producing things and selling things. It created quite a buzz. I remember it with lots of joy."

My Career / Business:

"Eventually I became a lawyer, a barrister, in the UK. After studying law at University of London, I was able to go to Harvard Law School* as well. You know, lawyers deal with one problem at a time, case by case, but I was wanting to change the world. I would wonder, why is this guy in jail? Why is this business bankrupt and everyone lost their money? I wanted to change the world, and that's what led me from law to politics. But you know both of those things, being a lawyer and being a politician, require a kind of self-belief and confidence. And there's no doubt about it—JA was part of that confidence building. I came from a poor background, and it was tough, and part of the self-belief and confidence that I got from JA was the idea that different things are possible in life—and the joy really of JA was the thought of, 'My goodness, what about owning a business, or running a business, or having an enterprise or a big idea.' That's really what led me personally to the belief that I could be a lawyer and that I could one day be a member of the Parliament. And you know, as a member of Parliament, where you have to be independent-minded, where you have to make judgments, where sometimes you have to sell in the sense of persuading people to follow you—I think a lot of those skills I use today came from that JA period."

* *Editor's note:* David Lammy is the first black Briton to ever attend Harvard Law School!

My Advice to Young People:

- "The first thing is, I'm a great believer in the work ethic, learning by experience, and getting on with it. I worked all through my early years. I delivered newspapers, I worked in the local public library, I worked at Kentucky Fried Chicken, I worked at McDonalds, I worked in a warehouse, I worked as a security guard at the university, and I worked in Harrods, the London department store. I think it's really important for young people to work out early what they like to do and then get on with it.

- "The second thing I would say is that some people know exactly what they want to do. I was a bit like that. I was pretty clear in my mind that I was driven to help others through public service, and that's why I became a politician. But if you aren't driven, if you don't know what you want to do, I think it's quite important to know what you *don't* like, what you're *not* good at. So I think it's good for your readers who are not so clear what they want to do, to at least be able to articulate that—and then make a decision and give something else a go.

- "Third, we're all living longer, but there is no such thing as a job for life. You know that 40 percent of the jobs that kids entering elementary school today will take have not even been invented yet. So we have to keep on learning and acquiring knowledge—as what we thought we knew might change as the decades and generations pass. I'm a great believer in lifelong learning for everyone.

- "In the end, education is the passport to success. The wonderful thing about education in developed countries, in most countries in the world in fact, is that it's free. All you've got to do is take what's in your teacher's brain for free. Steal it all! Particularly if you're from a poor background, that's what you have to do. Just get to school, take what's in the teacher's brain, put it on the page, pass your exams, and off you go. So that's my advice."

JA ALUMNI INTERVIEW

Feyzi Fatehi

Founder and CEO, Corent Technology, JA Volunteer, California, USA

> *I do believe my JA volunteer experience probably had more impact on me than I had on the students I was mentoring.*

Author's note: This ultra-successful Iranian/American entrepreneur wasn't involved with JA as a student, but rather as a volunteer instructor. I've included Feyzi's story here because of his unique perspective on the personal value of being a JA volunteer.

My JA Experience:

"I was born in Iran and came to the U.S. in 1976 as a teenager. I went to school in Princeton, New Jersey, and then Norman, Oklahoma, and finally the University of Texas, where I got my degree in solar engineering, my master's in software architecture—and finally my MBA at Santa Clara in California. After school I was hired by Hewlett-Packard, and that's how I became involved with JA.

"HP was supporting JA, and they asked employees to volunteer to become JA mentors. I volunteered and was appointed to the Mountain View, California, high school to help the JA students. The goal was to help them actually create and run a company. There were five of us from HP, as mentors to the students, and it was a phenomenal experience. We helped the students build a company from scratch, and we mentored each of them in their respective roles.

"Years later I met a woman at a business conference who recognized my name and asked if I was the same Feyzi Fatehi who had mentored JA programs at Mountain View high school which her son attended. I said yes, and she went on to tell me how the program had so inspired her son that he decided to major in business at college and had recently started his own company—and that he claimed the JA program and his JA mentors, specifically me, had been the most impactful experience of his high school life!

"That was great feedback to me because I realized that what we mentors had considered a fun activity and an act of good citizenship actually made a huge difference in the lives of the JA students. Perhaps even more dramatic, and what we didn't realize at the time, was that our JA mentoring experience may have helped us even more than we helped the students themselves. Being a JA volunteer and mentor was a phenomenal opportunity for me and has greatly impacted my own career. For starters, it introduced me to the whole notion of building a company from scratch. That experience indirectly made me think, 'Hey—I could do this for myself versus just helping others do it.' After the JA experience, I became an intrapreneur at HP, which ultimately led to my becoming a real entrepreneur and creating my own start-ups. I'm thinking, honestly, the root cause of my whole entrepreneurial experience was my involvement with JA helping those students build a company from scratch.

"Another important thing I got from my JA exposure was the value and the joy of coaching others. JA was my first formal mentoring experience. Of course, mentoring others is a side interest of mine compared to running my company—but again, it all started with my being a mentor in the JA program years ago. Considering my career as an entrepreneur and my interest in coaching—I do believe my JA volunteer experience probably had more impact on me than I had on the students I was mentoring. *I highly recommend the JA volunteer role to all businesspeople.*"

My Career / Business:

Author's Note: Feyzi's business career and his founding of Corent Technology are well documented elsewhere, so I've concentrated here on his unique JA role.

My Advice to Young People:

- "The best advice, which I would have given myself when I was younger, is to get to know yourself better. That will allow you to understand what you want to do in life, based on your own values. Ask yourself, what are the essential things I value, and then build your life around the things you value, you enjoy, and are enthusiastic about.

- "Second, get to know the person you want to become. Find the perfect role model, perhaps 20 or 30 years older than you, who you want to become. That becomes a fantastic target for the rest of your life. Do whatever you can to be aligned to become that person.

- "Third, and my favorite definition of success: you are successful if you like who you are, you like what you do, and you like how you do it. That says it all!"

JA ALUMNI INTERVIEW

Leo Martellotto
President, JA Americas Region, JA Alumnus, Argentina

But when the priests saw 800 kids coming from all the surrounding areas to learn about the Internet, they said: "You have turned the house of God into hell, but it seems for a good purpose."

My JA Experience:

"In my last year of high school in Cordoba, Argentina, we had a visit from a very well-dressed person. It was the first time that someone wearing a suit showed up in my classroom. He was there to invite us to become entrepreneurs, and I didn't even know what that meant, but it sounded very exciting. He said that he would help us come up with a project, but we would be the ones running the company. I thought that sounded really challenging. He also mentioned that JA had a global network, which was also exciting because I was interested in traveling and meeting people from other countries.

"In those days, what we usually heard from adults, our teachers and our parents, was that we youth were kind of lost, going to drugs, causing troubles in the neighborhood—so the message to us was usually pretty negative and dark. So for me JA was a way to prove that young people could make good things happen. Well, our JA company was very successful. We had an 800 percent return in just three months. Our 'product' was really an event. The Internet was new, so we ran a conference for all of the schools in the area about using the

Internet. We sold a lot of sponsorships and had 800 people showing up for the event from all around the city. We were in a religious
school, so we converted the church into a conference hall for the
event. When the church leaders first came and saw all our banners
and promotions in the church, they didn't like it. But when the priests
saw 800 kids coming from all the surrounding areas to learn about the
Internet, they said: 'You have turned the house of God into hell, but it
seems for a good purpose.' The best part was telling the shareholders,
the same adults who viewed us as 'lost youth,' that we were giving
them back 800 percent more than they invested. They were very surprised, and we were very proud.

"At 18, I didn't fully appreciate the value of what I did. Today I do.
When that volunteer invited us to join JA, my simple *yes* answer is why
I'm here today being interviewed by you."

My Career / Business:

"Because I was so successful in selling sponsorships, the executive
director of JA Cordoba invited me to join his team as a volunteer to
bring in new partners to JA. It was my first job, and it was during the
summer before college. Then I made a decision, which my parents
supported, that I would go to university at night, and work during the
day. It took me eight years to get my degree, but I continued working
at JA as an assistant—and I've been working there ever since.

"When I was 22 I became the development director for JA Cordoba. Shortly thereafter, the founder of JA Cordoba left, and he
convinced the board that I was the right person to replace him. We
had 25,000 students a year, 200 partners, and a staff of 14, when I
became the executive director of JA Cordoba at 24 years of age. By
the time I reached 28, I felt the cycle was completed for me in Cordoba; I was getting more than I was giving back, and I needed a fresh
challenge. I informed the board I was going to leave and do something else. I didn't really have a plan, however, even though I was
getting married soon—and my wife told me: 'Are you crazy? We're
getting married and you're going to quit your job!' Then, surprisingly
just at the same time, Linda Reimer, the president of JA Latin America
and Asia, called me and said: 'Leo I have a new job for you—you're
starting in one month as my director of operations for all of Latin

America, the Caribbean, and Canada. This was a dream job for me, so naturally I stayed.

"The final step was that several years later, Linda decided to retire and yet again she said: 'Leo, you're the right person to take my job.' So again I went through the process with the board. I was 32 and the board said: 'We don't think you're ready yet because you don't have a PhD, you don't have an MBA, you're only 32, but we will give the opportunity for one year while we search for a permanent president.' So I took it for one year and told the board to let me know when they found the new president. Right after that year they told me they had stopped the search for a new president, and I assumed they had found someone—but then they said: 'Leo, we want you to become the permanent president of the JA Americas region.' I thought they were going to kick me out after one year, but they gave me the job permanently. I was so happy. So in 2014 I became president of the JA Americas region, where I am today."

My Goals for JA Americas:

"For the first time ever, we have a regional strategy for JA Americas. First, we will become totally involved and relevant as a solution to the number one social issue that is concerning everyone—which is youth employment. How can we help our youth who are in vulnerable situations due to factors like gender inequality, the skills gap, drug abuse, gangs, and youth organized crime? The facts are, 20 percent of the youth population across our region is neither studying nor looking for a job. They are totally excluded from the system and the economy. And if we don't bring them back, it's not just that we will have lost them, but they will eventually show up as criminals, drug addicts, and of course become a huge social cost.

"For all of the social problems in the various countries in our region, whether in the rural areas or urban areas, the common denominator is youth employment. It's *the* social issue of our time. JA is not trying to be everything for everybody, but we are proposing practical actions and programs to help solve this huge social and economic issue. Our member nations are now aligned and focused on how to address this problem, and how we can convince governments that we are the right partner to help them.

"We currently reach over one million kids across 31 countries. Our three biggest economies, Mexico, Brazil, and Canada, represent 75 percent of our operations today. Our strategic plan says we will grow to reach 2 million kids by 2022—in just five years. We are confident we can achieve our goal because we already have countries like JA Argentina and JA Peru who are about to sign big, new, agreements with their Ministries of Education. Peru, for example, will be training up to half a million kids for the Ministry, all in the mission to help solve the youth employment issue.

"In summary, while the JA Americas region is growing rapidly, we are also in the process of adjusting our goals and tactics. Yes, we have to be consistent with JA Worldwide's mission and our three pillars—work readiness, financial literacy, and entrepreneurship. But today we also have to be very specific about JA's solutions to our number one social issue—which is youth employment. And this is exactly what we are doing across the region."

JA ALUMNI INTERVIEW

Jeff Hansberry

President, Advantage Solution / JA USA Board of Directors, JA Alumnus, Pennsylvania, USA

> *The value of JA isn't so much the specific programs on Work Readiness or Entrepreneurship or Financial Literacy—but what JA really stands for is helping young people have hope through understanding the possibilities for themselves.*

My JA Experience:

"I grew up in Pittsburgh, Pennsylvania. We were a blue-collar family, my dad was a carpenter—and when I was very young he became disabled, so I actually grew up in a family of really modest means—to the extent that we received government aid with school lunch programs and all that good stuff. I first came across JA in the eighth or ninth grade. I went to a presentation on the JA Company Program, and it was fantastic. I met a bunch of enthusiastic kids, an older gentleman who was our sponsor, and they formed us into company groups. At that point business was so foreign to me. I had no idea what any of the stuff was, but even so I still put my name in the hat to be the president and my student peers voted me in to be the president of our company.

"It was really fascinating; we learned all about how businesses run at a very basic level. We bought materials, we were making cookie sheets and hangers and bookends, and then sold the products to our friends and relatives. At the end we actually made some money, which was really cool. That was my first business experience, and it was just terrific. What I took away from that experience has helped shape who I am today. There are really two things: One was just a sense of how business works, which I had never ever seen in my life. Second I learned there are good people out there, beyond the world that I knew, who actually had an interest in my future. So JA was an experience from my early life that really helped shape who I am today. It was a most profound experience—and I had a lot of fun, too.

"The value of JA isn't so much the specific programs on work readiness or entrepreneurship or financial literacy—but what JA really stands for is helping young people have hope through understanding the possibilities for themselves."

My Career / Business:

"I was the first member of my family to go to college. I went to the University of Pittsburgh, with lots of student loans, and got my degree in economics. I returned to Pitt later to also get my MBA. I was lucky to land my first job with Procter & Gamble in New York and spent 17 good years with P&G in a variety of sales, marketing, and general management assignments in the U.S. and Asia. Next I joined E. & J. Gallo, the great winemaking family company, to help them launch their brands in China and Southeast Asia—based in Tokyo. I had a great assignment, loved what I was doing, and worked closely with the Gallo family. Then I got a call from Starbucks to work for Howard Schultz, the founder and CEO. How do you say no to that? They were launching their global packaged goods business and asked me to lead that for the company. So I joined and did that launch for three years, and then Howard asked me to go to Asia to run Starbucks retail stores across 15 markets—everything from India to China to Japan, based in Hong Kong. Finally I came back to the U.S. with Starbucks and led the integration of their health and wellness business, called Evolution Fresh, into their retail business. So I had worked for three great companies and spent a lot of time in Asia with each.

"In 2016 I joined Advantage Solutions, the huge sales and marketing agency, as president of the company. We provide sales, marketing, and technology services to over 1,200 consumer packaged goods companies. We now have 50,000 associates serving clients in 36 countries around the world. Our core focus is consumer packaged goods across the world, and we're headquartered in Irvine, California. It's obviously a tremendous opportunity for me. I feel I've been blessed in my business career.

"Over my career I've always tried to give back and stay in touch with JA. When I returned to Pittsburgh to get my MBA, I helped sponsor a JA company as part of their evening program, and that was great. Then when I joined Starbucks and got settled in Seattle, I joined the JA Board for the State of Washington. And finally, in 2014, I joined the JA USA Board of Directors where I still serve today."

My Advice to Young People:

- "You absolutely have to believe there can be a different life for you beyond the three- or four-block radius you live in, or beyond the people you know, or beyond the experiences you have now. There is something better for you beyond the world you live in today.
- "Next, even though sometimes you may not even see your final destination, if you keep doing the right things, and do them the right way, and stay positive, wonderful things will happen in your life. I promise you that!
- "Everyone needs role models and mentors. They may be your parents, your guidance counselor at school, or for sure you can find great mentors in the JA programs.
- "Finally, I'm a huge believer in education as a liberator. It is a life changer for people. So get all the education you can, in any form you can. It's all about creating hope through understanding your possibilities."

JA ALUMNI INTERVIEW

Cecilia Nykvist

CEO, JA Sweden, JA Alumna, Sweden

> *Then finally, I found my dream job, which was to become the CEO of JA Sweden!*

My JA Experience:

"It's been a while, but I remember those days well. I was in the Company Program at JA in 1991 and 1992. When I tell this to our students today, they say 'Oh, she's that old!' JA Sweden started in 1980, and in 1991 it was still quite small as an organization. There were about 4,000 students a year. Anyway, my five classmates and I grew up in a small town outside of Stockholm, and we decided to do the JA program. We thought it sounded so great. We decided to make boxer shorts. We made them ourselves, so it was not a very high-tech idea. But at the time there was a big discussion in Sweden whether we should join the European Union or not. So we made boxer shorts with the blue and yellow EU flag on them. We had our production of the boxer shorts in my parents' basement.

"Those were bad times in Sweden. There was a recession and a lot of unemployment. Anyway, we made our EU boxer shorts and got a lot of publicity. We were in the papers, and everyone was writing about it. We were even on national TV with our product. So it was a big item at the time, and we managed to insert the political discussion into our product marketing. Those shorts are actually still used as examples by JA. When our people are visiting schools, they hold them up and ask: 'Do you think this is a successful product?' Everyone says no because they're ugly. We then say: 'Well then, you need to get the context of that time in 1991. Our prime minister wanted several pairs. Even some Swedish royalty wanted to have them as giveaways! So we had a really great year, and it's a lesson about marketing.'

"We actually got the award for the best JA company in Sweden in 1992, and we went to Malta for the European championships. There, we won the entire European competition for JA Company of the Year for 1992—with our EU boxer shorts! We learned so much during that year, and that is what JA is all about. You can learn about all the other subjects in school, but in JA you learn how to put them into action. That's what we did. We had a lot of success, some failures of course, but you learn from all of it."

My Career / Business:

"That year with the JA program really caused me to think about what kind of education I would go for afterwards. So, I started in business and textile sciences at the University of Sweden—all because of the boxer shorts. I was going to choose just straight economics or something like that, but I was so inspired by my JA company experience that I became interested in entrepreneurship. After university, I actually worked for a couple of years at the JA regional office in my hometown. I was visiting schools and working with the JA students in the schools. Next I went to work for the employers' organization in Sweden, The Confederation of Swedish Enterprise, where I worked with entrepreneurship issues as well. I stayed involved with JA Sweden, and I was eventually elected to the Board of JA Sweden. Then I turned 30 and decided I wanted to do something else in my life, so I started my own business that year. We started an interior design shop and worked with a lot of different property agencies. We were also representing a few brands in Sweden from British and Spanish companies. I worked with that for seven or eight years, and I sold the business. I then started another business—a small communication business in Stockholm helping other companies to communicate better and so on. Then finally, I found my dream job, which was to become the CEO of JA Sweden. So that is my career story. I've been the CEO of JA Sweden for three and a half years now, and it's the best job I've ever had!"

My Goals for JA Sweden:

"Of course, there are a lot of challenges, being an NGO, but its's a brilliant job. Today we have in JA Sweden almost 28,000 students participating in the Company Program and around 60,000 students in all of our lower grades programs. For example, we use the JA It's My Business program for middle school, which I believe, Larry, you created for JA. So we currently have a total of 88,000 students going

> through the programs. This makes us one of the biggest JA countries in Europe, especially when it comes to the Company Program itself.
>
> "Our penetration rate in the secondary schools is 28 percent, as Sweden has about 100,000 secondary school students across the country. We are working to get the same good rate in the lower grades. That's what we are focusing on now. Our turnover is €10 million per year, and we have about 115 staff and 24 regional offices—so JA is quite a large operation across Sweden. We are all proud of what JA Sweden has accomplished over the years."

As a closing thought—I said at the beginning of this book that JA is just too good an idea to die. Very few organizations in history, let alone one approaching its centennial celebration, have perfected the "what" and the "how" of their worldwide "sense of mission" as effectively as JA Worldwide. And Jack Kosakowski's story (see the following interview), covering nearly half of JA's life span, illustrates why that's true. Jack has become "Mr. JA" to me and other observers. He was a JA student during high school in Toledo, Ohio. He then won a full JA scholarship to college, becoming the first person in his family to obtain a university degree. During college, he worked as a program manager for the JA office in Toledo, and upon graduation took a full-time job there. He's never worked anywhere else, and today, 43 years later, is the CEO of JA USA, reaching about 4.8 million students a year—putting him in charge of almost half of all JA Worldwide activity. So he's been involved with JA as a student and an employee for 48 years, nearly half of its entire 100-year history. His "sense of mission" is clear—a testimonial really to the power of JA's strategy and culture (its "what" and its "how"), and his story is a wonderful way to conclude the book.

Thanks for joining us, and we hope *The Entrepreneurial Attitude* will indeed help you do something great with your life.

JA ALUMNI INTERVIEW

Jack Kosakowski
President and CEO, JA USA, JA Alumnus, Ohio, USA

> *I immediately noticed this really cute blonde sitting in front of me. She was listening, and I'm watching her, and she signed up, so I signed up too—thinking, oh, this is a great opportunity!*

My JA Experience:
"I got involved in JA when I was in high school in Toledo, Ohio, back in 1970. I was one of those kids who got involved for all the wrong reasons. I was going to a Catholic high school, and they would recruit students for the program by bringing you into the gymnasium and the guy from JA would come out and talk. I was one of those kids who was an OK student, but terrible athlete, terrible at music, and so on. But my grades were OK, so I went to the presentation. I immediately noticed this really cute blonde sitting in front of me. She was listening, and I'm watching her, and she signed up, so I signed up too—thinking, oh, this is a great opportunity!

"Anyway, I showed up at the JA facility the first night of the old JA Company Program. We had a team of advisors from the DeVilbiss Company, a Fortune 500 company at the time. One of the advisors was Mr. Gimpel. I still remember him. Jim Gimpel was a salesman, and for whatever reason he saw something in me that my teachers hadn't seen and the coaches hadn't seen. I got very involved that first year in JA and became vice president of sales. And I was a kid who was afraid to talk to anybody. So I had fun for the three years I stayed in the program. One year I was president of my company, and my senior year I won the JA Treasurer of the Year award and went to NAJAC, the national JA conference, and participated there. So I was very active in JA.

"When I started it was only the JA Company Program. We were moving drill presses and band saws around, all the products that reflected that economy of manufacturing products. There were not any female staff members in the organization when I got involved. Most of the JA staff were like my eventual mentor, Tom Rutter, who was an old industrial arts teacher and knew about making those products. At that time it was normal to stay in the program for two or three years, as an extracurricular activity, in a different company every year—and you learned a lot. In those days the program started in October and ran through May, so it was a 28-week experience. It wasn't one of these 'wham-bam' experiences. You actually experienced the trials and tribulations of running a production line, and selling, and we often had to change products in the course of the year, so it was a very entrepreneurial activity.

"And remember, Larry, I came out of a household where my mom had a high school education and my dad dropped out of high school to join the Marine Corps during World War II, so there was no real focus in my house on education. But I got a full scholarship to college, to the University of Toledo, of all places, because of my involvement with JA. I received a four-year degree all paid for—books, tuition, and everything. It was because of JA that I was the first in my family to get a four-year university degree. So it did a lot for me. Of course it taught me about business, all the fundamentals, but I got more than that out of it. Coming out of my background, I had always thought things happen to you, and not that *you could make* things happen. For example, after my dad got out of the Marine Corps, he went to work in an automobile manufacturing facility and he hated what he did. He hated the union, he hated management, and I thought, 'God, for the rest of my life this is what I'm going to do?' That was really the spark that JA gave me at the time. From JA, I learned about self-efficacy. As much good as JA does in teaching about business, the bigger lesson for me was the self-efficacy part. The confidence in one's ability to make things happen, to change the world, and so on."

My Career / Business:
Author's note: Jack's career accomplishments, summarized above, are well known throughout JA. So for this interview we have concentrated on his early recollections as a JA student and his future goals for JA USA.

My Goals for JA USA:

"I think it's a fair statement that we're the largest nongovernmental educational organization in the U.S., and the entire world for that matter. And with our footprint, we really need to stay focused on our mission. Think about it. We operate in 109 markets in the U.S. alone. We've got 1,600 staff people around the country. We've got 237,000 business volunteers in the schools teaching for us—no other education organization even comes close to that number. And, of course, we're now teaching about 4.8 million kids per year in the U.S. So we've got both the curriculum and the distribution system like no other—and at least once a week I'll get the latest, greatest idea from somewhere, that somebody has written a book, or somebody has a new game, and they want us to deliver it out through this vast JA network.

"So we really have to stay focused on what our core competency is—and what our *mission* is. As I said earlier, *what* we focus on: financial literacy, workforce readiness, and entrepreneurship for young people—has never been more critical at any time in history. And there's something very special about *how* we do it—the connection we make between the business community volunteers, the teachers and the schools, and the kids who we teach. That's really our secret sauce!"

Applications

My Entrepreneurial Start-Up Action Plan

APPLICATION 1

YOU'RE AN ENTREPRENEUR! WHAT NEXT?

Imagine you've just started your own business. It's the first day in your new role as an entrepreneur. You want to be successful and grow. You sure don't want to go bankrupt. You've mortgaged your family house to raise the money to get started. Everything you have is on the line, including the welfare of your children.

You have an idea of a product and market that excites you. You think it has potential. But with your limited financial resources, you have to get started fast! What will you concentrate on? How should you spend your time? What will your priorities be as an entrepreneur?

There are no "right" or "wrong" answers for this first Application. It's simply intended to get your "entrepreneurial juices" flowing—by seriously thinking through what you would really have to focus on as a start-up entrepreneur. When you finish Part 1 of the book, you should return to this page to see how your initial answers stack up against what you've been reading. You may be surprised!

MY ENTREPRENEURIAL PRIORITIES

1. _____

    _____

2. _____

    _____

3. _____

    _____

4. _____

    _____

5. _____

    _____

2

CREATING ENTREPRENEURIAL BUSINESS PLANS

What do you love to do, and what are you good at doing? What needs do you see that are going unmet, or not being met adequately? Within these questions you will find the market/product business(es) that will carry the highest chance of success for you as an entrepreneur. Obviously, starting a business in something you hate doing, and are no good at, and for which there is no market need, is a recipe for disaster. Completing this four-part application won't guarantee your entrepreneurial success, but it will ensure that you have asked the right questions, which is the starting point for every successful entrepreneur. Review the "Creating Entrepreneurial Business Plans" section in Chapter 1 for more background.

Finish the first column and then translate your answers into a potential business activity in the second. "I like computers" could become "computer repair," or "I'm good at gardening" could become "landscaping service." Some of your interests and skills may require creative thinking to redefine them as a business. A few might not work at all. Just set those aside and move on.

WHAT DO I REALLY LIKE TO DO?	MARKET/PRODUCT WINNERS

WHAT AM I REALLY GOOD AT DOING?	MARKET/PRODUCT WINNERS

WHAT MARKET NEED DO I SEE?	MARKET/PRODUCT WINNERS

PICKING MARKET/PRODUCT WINNERS

List your market/product winners (potential businesses) from Application 2. For each of your market/product winners, rate both the market need and your likely competitive position, using a scale of 10 to 1. Use your best estimates and your common sense to answer these questions. Be as objective as possible. The generic questions for each rating are:

- **Market Need.** How big is the market in number of customers and in sales volume? Is it growing, declining, or staying the same? How critical is this need to the market? Is it a necessity, a luxury, or a passing fad?

- **Competitive Position.** How much better, cheaper, and faster could you provide this product/service compared to how it's currently being offered by others?

MARKET/PRODUCT WINNERS	RATINGS (10 HIGH / 1 LOW)	
From Application 2	Market Need*	Competitive Position*
1. _____	_____	_____
_____		
2. _____	_____	_____
_____		
3. _____	_____	_____
_____		
4. _____	_____	_____
_____		
5. _____	_____	_____
_____		

* Note any critical information you will need to verify later.

(continued on next page)

PICKING MARKET/PRODUCT WINNERS, *continued*

Plot the ratings of your market/product winners from the prior page of Application 3 on the matrix in Figure A.1. For example a "9 market need" with a "9 competitive position" rating would be very near the upper right-hand corner. A "3/7" would be near the center of the upper left-hand quadrant, and so on. This matrix will give you a visual overview of the combined market need and competitive position for each of your possible market/product ideas. This analysis will highlight your real "market/product winners."

1. **Small Market/High Competitive Position.** Good possibility of success in this Rolls-Royce type business. Work to find more markets for your excellent product.
2. **Big Market/High Competitive Position.** High possibility of success, but once successful, you will likely attract a high level of competition. Be prepared for strong competitors.
3. **Big Market/Low Competitive Position.** Good possibility of success, but you may have to compete on price at the low end of the market. Work to raise your competitive position.
4. **Small Market/Low Competitive Position.** Poor chance of success. Avoid this business like the plague.

Figure A.1

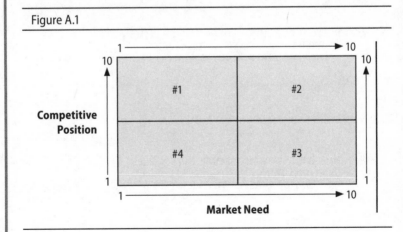

APPLICATION

4   IT'S START-UP TIME!

Application 3 identified your market/product winners with the best possibilities of success. Based on that, what are the most important actions you should take over the next 90 to 180 days to get started? Your actions should be focused on the fundamentals required to get any business up and running. Although described earlier, they are restated here as action questions.

ACTIONS TO IDENTIFY AND PROMOTE TO POTENTIAL CUSTOMERS/MARKETS?   **WHEN**

1. _____   _____

2. _____   _____

3. _____   _____

ACTIONS TO DESIGN AND MAKE THE FIRST VERSION OR PROTOTYPE OF THE PRODUCT/ SERVICE FOR TESTING BY A CUSTOMER?   **WHEN**

1. _____   _____

2. _____   _____

3. _____   _____

ACTIONS TO SET UP THE OPERATING CAPABILITIES REQUIRED TO "MAKE, SELL, AND SERVICE" THE PRODUCTS AND CUSTOMERS?   **WHEN**

1. _____   _____

2. _____   _____

3. _____   _____

ACTIONS TO IDENTIFY AND SECURE THE SOURCES OF CASH (INCLUDING CUSTOMERS) TO COVER THE START-UP PHASE OF THE BUSINESS?   **WHEN**

1. _____   _____

2. _____   _____

3. _____   _____

APPLICATION 5

CREATING ENTREPRENEURIAL BUSINESS VALUES

Values determine what you focus on, and become great at, operationally. Therefore, the values you select must be things that give you competitive advantage in products and markets and will have the commitment of the bulk of your employees. The other two columns in the following chart are checkpoints to reinforce the importance of competitive advantage and employee commitment. Identify below what specific actions you can take to implement your future business values. Review the "Creating Entrepreneurial Business Values" section in Chapter 1 for more information and examples.

WHAT VALUES DO WE NEED TO ACHIEVE THE PLAN?	WHAT'S THE COMPETITIVE ADVANTAGE?	HOW WILL I GET EVERYONE COMMITTED?
1.		
2.		
3.		
4.		

WHAT ACTIONS CAN I TAKE TO IMPLEMENT THESE VALUES?	WHEN
1.	
2.	
3.	

6   KEEPING THEM ALIVE

What can you do to ensure that you focus on and maintain your selected values? The three greatest influences on keeping them alive are shown below. For each, jot down one or two ways in which that particular factor could have the greatest impact on supporting each value. Then, identify below what specific actions you can take now, or in the future, to make that happen. Review the "Keeping Them Alive" section in Chapter 1 for more information and examples.

VALUES	MANAGEMENT BEHAVIOR	RITUALS & PRACTICES	EMPLOYEE REWARDS & PENALTIES
1. _____	_____	_____	_____
	_____	_____	_____
2. _____	_____	_____	_____
	_____	_____	_____
3. _____	_____	_____	_____
	_____	_____	_____
4. _____	_____	_____	_____
	_____	_____	_____

WHAT ACTIONS CAN I TAKE TO KEEP THESE VALUES ALIVE?	WHEN
1. _____	_____
_____	_____
2. _____	_____
_____	_____
3. _____	_____
_____	_____

"LOVING" CUSTOMERS AND PRODUCTS

As the leader of your company, creating a passion for customers and products may become the most important job you have. Application 7 is designed to give you a jump start on keeping customer/product vision alive in your entrepreneurial venture. As you tackle the questions, keep in mind the key practices described in the "Loving the Customer" and "Loving the Product" sections in Chapter 2. For the future, consider holding monthly brainstorming sessions using Application 7 as the format. This will be a simple way to maintain your customer/product passion and give you a constant source of great ideas.

GREAT IDEAS FOR "LOVING" THE CUSTOMER   **WHEN**

1. _____   _____

2. _____   _____

3. _____   _____

4. _____   _____

GREAT IDEAS FOR "LOVING" THE PRODUCT   **WHEN**

1. _____   _____

2. _____   _____

3. _____   _____

4. _____   _____

8
GROWING THE OLD-FASHIONED WAY

Application 8 may become the best growth-marketing tool you'll ever have. After all there are only four ways to grow any business—and they're all on the simple chart in Figure A.2. So focus on *what products to what markets*, identify the most promising areas, and plan the actions to get you there. You can use this "Growing the Old-Fashioned Way" application over and over again, every time you want to find new ways to grow your business.

Figure A.2

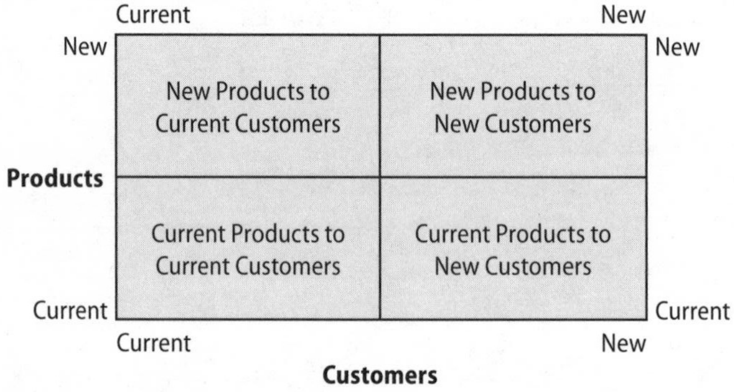

	Current	New
New	New Products to Current Customers	New Products to New Customers
Current	Current Products to Current Customers	Current Products to New Customers

Products

Customers — Current / New

	ACTIONS	WHEN
1.	_____	_____
	_____	_____
2.	_____	_____
	_____	_____
3.	_____	_____
	_____	_____
4.	_____	_____
	_____	_____

9 CREATING HIGH-SPEED INNOVATION

High-speed innovation is the fastest, cheapest, and surest way to gain competitive advantage in the marketplace. It truly is the entrepreneur's secret weapon. Now is the time to think through the actions you should take to make high-speed innovation a major thrust in your new business. As you tackle Application 9 , keep in mind the specific examples of the sections "The Necessity to Invent" and "The Freedom to Act" in Chapter 3. What are the most important actions you should take?

TO ENCOURAGE INNOVATION:
IMPROVE SOMETHING, ANYTHING, EVERY DAY. **WHEN**

1. _____ _____

2. _____ _____

3. _____ _____

4. _____ _____

TO SPEED UP ACTION:
CREATE A SENSE OF URGENCY. **WHEN**

1. _____ _____

2. _____ _____

3. _____ _____

4. _____ _____

TO WIPE OUT BUREAUCRACY:
GROWING BIG BY STAYING SMALL. **WHEN**

1. _____ _____

2. _____ _____

3. _____ _____

4. _____ _____

SELF-INSPIRED BEHAVIOR—RAISING COMMITMENT AND PERFORMANCE

Creating and maintaining a great company ultimately depends on two essential ingredients: the commitment and the performance of the managers and workers. From commitment flow pride, dedication to the mission, and plain old hard work. From performance flow expertise, innovation, and working smarter. If you're looking for competitive advantage, it's hard to beat people who love what they do and are good at doing it. You can start planning now how you're going to instill commitment and performance in yourself, your first few critical hires, and ultimately every employee in the company. What are the most important actions you can take now to create or raise employee commitment and performance in your new venture? Before you do Application 10 you might review the key practices in the "Creating Entrepreneurial Commitment" and "Creating Entrepreneurial Performance" sections in Chapter 4.

CREATING HIGH COMMITMENT   WHEN

1. _____   _____

2. _____   _____

3. _____   _____

4. _____   _____

5. _____   _____

CREATING HIGH PERFORMANCE   WHEN

1. _____   _____

2. _____   _____

3. _____   _____

4. _____   _____

5. _____   _____

11
THE ALMIGHTY POWER OF CONSEQUENCES

Use the "Entrepreneurial Performance System" troubleshooting guide in Figure A.3 to raise the commitment and performance of your employees. Before you try it the first time, review Chapter 4 for a more complete description of the EPS. By going through the following questions, you should discover which of the EPS components needs to be adjusted to change the behavior of the employee or employees. And remember the *power of consequences*! The easiest, cheapest, and surest way to change behavior is to make sure every employee feels positive and negative consequences from his or her performance. Based on your analysis, take the appropriate action to make the necessary changes. You should find this EPS guide a valuable, ongoing performance management tool.

Figure A.3

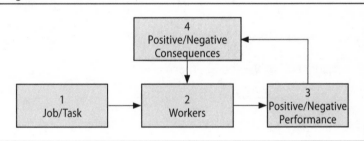

COMPONENT	QUESTION TO ASK	SOLUTION
1. Job/Task	Does the worker know *what* to do?	Set clear job standards.
2. Worker*	Does the worker know *how* to do the job?	Provide training.
3. Performance	Does the worker have the resources to do the job?	Provide tools, people, time to do the job.
4. Consequences	Are the positive and negative consequences to the workers in balance?	Rebalance positive & negative consequences.
	Is the worker aware of the consequence?	Give accurate, timely, and powerful feedback.

* Physical/mental disability, as a cause of poor performance, is rare and is not included here.

WHAT'S REALLY REQUIRED? THE THREE REQUIREMENTS

The three broad, but essential, requirements for getting your new venture off the drawing board and into the real world are: operating in as supportive an environment as you can, securing the necessary money for the start-up period, and arming yourself with great product and market knowledge. Application 12 will help you think through how you can manage to meet and surpass these requirements. For each one, what are the most important action steps you can take, and when will you take them?

SECURING THE NECESSARY BIT OF MONEY   **WHEN**

1. _____   _____
2. _____   _____
3. _____   _____
4. _____   _____
5. _____   _____

ACQUIRING THE NECESSARY BIT OF KNOWLEDGE   **WHEN**

1. _____   _____
2. _____   _____
3. _____   _____
4. _____   _____
5. _____   _____

ENSURING AN ENTREPRENEUR-FRIENDLY CULTURE   **WHEN**

1. _____   _____
2. _____   _____
3. _____   _____
4. _____   _____
5. _____   _____

13 MY "GETTING ENTREPRENEURIAL" START-UP ACTION PLAN

We started off, in Application 1, asking you to imagine the most important things you would have to do to get a new company up and running. Now that you've completed the book and all the other Applications, it's time to ask the same question again—for real. What are the most important actions to take, starting today, to *actually* get your entrepreneurial venture off the ground? And if you've already started your own business, which I suspect many of you have, what are the most important actions you can take now to keep it on a steady course of high growth? In the following spaces, write down the actions you commit to take over the next three to six months, to *really* start getting entrepreneurial.

WHAT ARE THE MOST IMPORTANT ACTIONS TO TAKE?   **WHEN**

1. _____   _____

_____   _____

2. _____   _____

_____   _____

3. _____   _____

_____   _____

4. _____   _____

_____   _____

5. _____   _____

_____   _____

6. _____   _____

_____   _____

7. _____   _____

_____   _____

Index

About the Author

Larry Farrell is the founder and chairman of The Farrell Company, the world's leading firm for researching and teaching entrepreneurship. He founded the firm in 1983 to do his groundbreaking research into the high-growth business practices of the world's great entrepreneurs. Today, with affiliates in North America, Asia, Europe, South America, and Africa, over six million people in forty countries across nine languages have attended the company's programs. Over the past three decades, Larry has personally taught entrepreneurship to more individuals, organizations, and governments than any person in the world.

His work has received praise from Peter Drucker, Tom Peters, *Fortune, BusinessWeek*, The Conference Board, and more. His first four books have received critical acclaim and have been translated into numerous languages from German to Spanish to Chinese. Larry has a diverse background: Peace Corps volunteer, Harvard Business School, University of California Law School, vice president of American Express in New York and president of Kepner-Tregoe in Princeton, NJ. He is a contributing editor for *The Conference Board Review* in New York, a columnist for *Entrepreneur* magazine in India, and an advisory board member to Cambridge University's Enterprise Solutions to Poverty project in the United Kingdom.

Hundreds of demanding clients around the world have used his "Entrepreneurial Age" keynote address, the company's "Entrepreneurial Organization" seminars, its "Getting Entrepreneurial!" seminars for students and aspiring entrepreneurs and its "Creating Entrepreneurial Economies" projects for governments. Clients range from blue-chip global companies to world-class universities to government agencies responsible for job creation and economic development.

Larry lives with his wife, Sylvia, in Virginia and Arizona. For more information on Larry Farrell and his company, please visit www.TheSpiritOfEnterprise.com.